Problem-based Learning into the Future

Megan Yih Chyn A. Kek • Henk Huijser

Problem-based Learning into the Future

Imagining an Agile PBL Ecology for Learning

🐎 Springer

Megan Yih Chyn A. Kek
University of Southern Queensland
Toowoomba, QLD, Australia

Henk Huijser
Xi'an Jiaotong-Liverpool University
Suzhou, Jiangsu, China

Batchelor Institute
Batchelor, NT, Australia

ISBN 978-981-10-2452-8   ISBN 978-981-10-2454-2   (eBook)
DOI 10.1007/978-981-10-2454-2

Library of Congress Control Number: 2016955960

Printed on acid-free paper

This Springer imprint is published by Springer Nature
The registered company is Springer Nature Singapore Pte Ltd.
The registered company address is: 152 Beach Road, #22-06/08 Gateway East, Singapore 189721, Singapore

In memory of Howard S. Barrows

Foreword

We live, so we are frequently told, in a liquid age, an age that is at once fluid and unpredictable but also potentially challenging and even destabilising. In this situation, the idea of ecology has much to offer. It points both to systems and forces that stand independently of human perceptions that have a real presence in the world. It hints at the interconnectedness of those systems – both internally and across them – but also at their frailty. But more still, it suggests that humanity in general, and human beings as individuals, have possibilities for responding to this set of circumstances so as to advance well-being in the world. All of this has application to the world of learning, for learning can be considered as a set of interconnected systems, both personal and institutional and both formal and informal. And these systems can be fragile and impaired – learning may not be being enhanced as it might – and yet they could be enhanced by human interventions.

If this book, *Problem-Based Learning into the Future*: *Imagining an Agile PBL Ecology for Learning*, had just spelt out this story of learning understood through an ecological gaze, it would have earned its spurs. Here, for instance, the narrative shares ideas about the interrelationships between formal and informal learning, as well as learning through the lifespan ('lifewide' as well as 'lifelong' learning); about authenticity, as learners rightly have an interest in attending to their own well-being; and about learning as situated within learning communities. This book, therefore, opens a wide vista presaged by the very idea of ecological learning. However, it does much more than this, having – as I judge it – four achievements, all of which are hinted at in the title.

First, this book brings out the dual aspect of the idea of ecology, in that it both points to intertwined systems in the world and to the possibilities for human action that might enhance those systems. *Second*, it brings the idea of agility into play, in thinking about learning as an ecological space. This is a brilliant ploy, for the notion of agility speaks of nimble-footedness but also of powers of the mind and of systems and institutions. Nimbleness can be seen both in individuals, in their own learning stances and in learning arrangements, which have the capacities to encourage or thwart individuals' efforts. It can also be seen in institutions – educational institutions, for instance: do they have the capacities to respond swiftly to difficult situations and the capacities to reflect on themselves as learning institutions? *Third*, the book places problem-based learning at its heart. This is surely an astute gambit, for problem-based learning conjures up fluidity and flexible responses that have to be characteristic of ecological learning at all of its levels.

Fourth, the argument nicely brings out the significance of the imagination in developing ecological learning. Ecological learning is not given. It is not just already in the world, simply to be discerned. Rather, it has to be imagined, if it is fully to be brought off. And, in that imagining, all manner of considerations and judgements will need to come into play. What might it be to orient a particular curriculum more in an ecological direction? What could it be to enhance the experiences of a group of students (on this course, on that course) so that they are ecological learners? What might it look like for a university to tilt more towards a concern with an ecological conception of learning?

But this imagination – this imagining of ecological learning – has to live in the real world. Learning is already ecological, whether that feature is recognised or not. More than ever before, as they struggle through life, individuals are learning in all manner of ways and in all manner of situations. Inescapably, they have their being in multiple learning spaces, and those learning moments stand in various relationships with each other.

To a large extent, those learning experiences may be deliberately taken up, as *learning ventures*, and so show something approaching a coherent pattern. An individual, having say taken early retirement, might opt to take up learning the piano and to sing in a choir and consciously form a pattern of learning challenges that hold together in a personal self-narrative. But in a complex world, with individuals characteristically having multiple experiences even in the course of a single day, learning is also bound to be somewhat haphazard. One never knows what the day will bring and what experiential challenges may unfold.

An individual's learning ecology takes on, in turn, a significant degree of *untowardness*. And some of those experiences will present ideas that clash. This is inevitably the case, for ideas spring out of frameworks that themselves stand in tension with each other. For example, frameworks of justice, equity, freedom, openness, security, integrity, understanding, reason, emotion, duty and authenticity all have their own trajectories, criss-crossing each other with different velocities.

An individual's learning ecology is, therefore, *given* to some extent. It has – to put the matter formally – an ontological robustness. It really exists – in the real world. It springs out of a complex world, and additionally it poses real dilemmas and awkwardnesses. These latter are features of *super*complexity, that phenomenon in which readings of a situation and ideas proliferate and frequently stand in indissoluble rivalry. And this world, replete with both its complexity and supercomplexity, is the world in which individuals, communities and societies have to navigate. No wonder that many crave for order and simplicity and, on occasions, turn to ready-made ideologies that appear to make sense of the world.

Learning ecologies, accordingly, not only are present in the world but they may be impaired. It is here that both challenges and responsibilities open up for those in educational settings, for learning ecologies – at all levels, of individuals, communities and society – can become a focus of educational attention. This is not just a matter of their 'sustainability' (a term beloved of the ecologists) or even of their repair but is rather a matter of their enhancement and, thereby, and as stated, of their being *imagined*. This is a very considerable educational challenge, to assist individuals and communities in thinking about their own learning, in equipping them with the resources to forge productive connections across learning experiences, in helping them to be more agile in responding effectively to the many learning challenges that will assuredly present and in aiding their own imaginative powers and qualities to live purposefully amid dynamic learning situations.

It is a measure of this book that it works in all of these ways, providing conceptual, theoretical and practical resources as it does so, and its authors, Megan Kek and Henk Huijser, are much to be applauded. They have given us a volume that can be and should be mined many times, with its pretty well inexhaustible seams, which only open to yet further issues and possibilities. Like all good learning ecologies – and this book is a learning ecology in itself – it has its own qualities of continuing emergence.

Institute of Education   Ronald Barnett
University College London
London, UK
June 2016

Preface

We originally started this book with a notion of 'revitalising' problem-based learning (PBL) in university classrooms by wanting to sustain the key essentials of effective PBL through the revitalisation or transformation of the curriculum, problems, teaching approach and assessment. Even though PBL is being used differently in different disciplines, different cohorts and different cultures, not all are successful or have their expectations met. So, we started this book project with the intention to remind – to revitalise – teachers and administrators about the key essentials or non-negotiables considered critical success drivers of PBL in their classrooms, courses, programs and institutions. But something else happened along the way!

There are many factors that may explain why different teachers and administrators experience different results from their PBL implementation. It is only when we reflected on our own PBL teaching and implementation days – some good and some bad – that we were reminded of Howard S. Barrows, one of the founding fathers of PBL, as to the true intention of PBL in education. We remembered that it is always about the students and their learning. To which many would say, 'Me too, so what?' For Howard and us, it is all about recognising and respecting our students, that is, as soon as they complete their education, they can seamlessly immerse themselves into society as active members of their professions and communities. We would hope that they go on to become producers, creators, leaders and contributors in and for society, as much as they would become consumers. A PBL teacher's role is to create the relevant and appropriate landscape with creativity and imagination during the time students are with us to give them ample opportunities to engage and to be rewarded and energised, rather than simply comply. What happened along the way was that we began to explore in earnest the actual learning environments and everything that contributes to that environment. Partly based on Megan's PhD research and partly on reviewers' feedback on an earlier draft of the manuscript, this idea began to morph into what we have ultimately called *an agile PBL ecology for learning*.

So what started as revitalising PBL, and as reminding teachers and administrators on how to revitalise their university landscape, ultimately became *an agile PBL ecology for learning*, a process of iterative and continuous renewal in our own teaching and learning practices and a recognition of the complexity of factors that feed into, and out of, the learning process. The concept of an agile PBL ecology for learning thus helped us to illuminate the true intentions and purpose of PBL in education and thereby imagine future applications. That is, PBL must perpetually stay responsive to the dynamics of society to carry out our responsibility as teachers in preparing our students for society, as well as recognise and draw on what they bring to the learning environment, for each student has a history and a set of skills; no one is an empty vessel. However, students' learning, growth and development cannot be assumed. Hence, by focusing on a continuously adaptive approach to education renewal, we believe that an agile PBL approach to curriculum design, teaching, assessment, student support, scholarship of teaching and research, sustainability and evaluation is innovative and *agile* enough to extend on and sustain the true intentions of PBL in universities: to contribute to society through preparing students to be agile, adaptive, innovative and creative global citizens.

We invite you to explore our ideas contained in this book. In 'walking our own talk', this book is necessarily agile and cross-disciplinary, connecting with knowledge from a variety of disciplinary fields, including (but not limited to) educational psychology, learning sciences, student approaches to learning, approaches to teaching, management, educational technology, organisational behaviour, leadership, assessment, evaluation, marketing, media and communications, innovation, educational environment, professional learning, academic development, student development, student experience, human development, counselling and quality. In the end, we hope you will be able to recognise and situate yourself within an agile PBL ecology for learning, be that as a reader, educator or learner.

P.S. Henk and Megan contributed equally to the book – it was truly a partnership!

Toowoomba, QLD, Australia	Megan Yih Chyn A. Kek
Suzhou, Jiangsu, China	Henk Huijser
May 2016	

Acknowledgements

Our ideas in *Problem-Based Learning into the Future* are in part borne out of the challenges and failures that we have experienced in the past. Of course, there were also successes. But the challenges and failures energised us along the path to sharing our ideas, our dreams of a better university, a better society. We don't believe we have reached the destination yet with this book, and indeed we never will – such is the fate of a lifelong learner! However, much of what is in these pages is an ideal and a dream of sorts and as such requires a level of belief, but it is certainly not a dream based on quicksand.

Writing this book has truly been a team effort and an authentic partnership and collaboration. We have shared ideas, enthusiasm, work, ideals and also discouragement and angst. But we came out more energised. We must acknowledge our former students who have taught us to be better teachers. We acknowledge every student who is aspiring to enter higher education. We acknowledge every academic teacher and professional staff member who authentically works to support them to be the best they can be.

Even though *Problem-Based Learning into the Future* is a book of our vision for a renewed approach to education, it contains voices from many wise men and women from different fields. We acknowledge the libraries at the University of Southern Queensland, Batchelor Institute of Indigenous Tertiary Education and Charles Darwin University. To all the document delivery and acquisition library personnel who helped to hunt for the materials – some out of print and some classic and seminal papers buried deep in other libraries – and delivered them so promptly, thank you!

We would also like to acknowledge our many colleagues who have supported us. It is difficult to make a list of acknowledgements, as the luck of an academic would have it that you are constantly talking through and testing ideas, as well as picking up new ideas from colleagues you've never met, as well as colleagues and friends you see on a daily basis. We especially like to acknowledge the anonymous peer reviewers who have provided us with invaluable and constructive feedback that has not only motivated but inspired us to further improve our writing. Thank you all – you know who you are – for the continuous intellectual stimulation!

A special mention to the University of Southern Queensland who supported Megan by giving her time and space from her university daily chores, through an approved sabbatical, to write and complete the first draft of the book. Megan would like to honour the late Professor Howard Barrows, a truly 'disruptive' teacher, mentor and friend. He is remembered as the one who not only planted the PBL seed more than a decade ago but who encouraged her to be courageous and to 'listen and march to the sounds of your drums!' She also would like to remember the late Professor Kevin Marjoribanks, her PhD supervisor, who showed her the 'human and social side to educational environment' that is enduring throughout a student's lifetime and her own academic journey.

As always, Henk would specifically like to thank Trish, for her patience and blind faith, as well as allowing 'book time' to encroach on our precious weekends; love you forever! Megan would like to thank God, Takashi, Pa and Mum, for being a significant part of her life. We both thank our families for their unconditional love, support, encouragement, space to dream and food of course! It is our families' boundless love that gives us the courage in our writing and in our continued pursuit to dream of and contribute to a better society.

Contents

Chapter 1
Introduction

In this book we respond to a higher education environment that is on the brink of profound changes and that consequently requires a continuous flexibility to education renewal at all levels. When we say it is on the brink, what we are really saying is that many of these changes are already underway. There are numerous other examples of industries that have been slow to adapt – slow to recognise, respect and respond (Chickering, 2006) – to fast-changing contexts, and they have been forced to face the consequences. One example in Australia is the demise of the national car manufacturing industry and the most recent example is the journalism profession. To some who have worked in the journalism profession for a long time, such as long-serving newspaper journalists at newspapers like *The Age* in Melbourne or *The Sydney Morning Herald*, it must have felt like the bottom fell out of their well-established world from one day to the next, and they were obviously ill-prepared for it. After all, these newspapers had been Australian institutions for more than a hundred years; surely would this not change from one day to the next? Think again.

There is no doubt that we are in the midst of profound disruptions to the way things have been done for a long time, not in the least due to fast-changing technologies and the possibilities they afford. The Internet and the World Wide Web have had huge impacts, which in turn have influenced the social fabric of our lives through the growing ubiquity of social media, networking and mobile media tools. In education in general, and in the universities in particular, these changes have ushered in an age characterised by a rapidly increasing evolution of online learning with integration of online, hybrid and collaborative learning and, most recently, phenomena such as massive open online courses (MOOCs), the rise of big data analytics driving learning and personalised learning and support for students. Each of these developments have the potential to cause major disruptions in the way we operate in the universities, and if we do not prepare to engage with these changes and indeed respond, we are in danger of facing a situation where one day the bottom will have fallen out, and we would never have seen it coming. We need to recognise that changes are inevitable and respect that these changes are here to stay, some evolu-

© Springer Science+Business Media Singapore 2017
M.Y.C.A. Kek, H. Huijser, *Problem-based Learning into the Future*,
DOI 10.1007/978-981-10-2454-2_1

tionary, some revolutionary, and we need to respond but respond in adaptive and agile ways and, importantly, with imagination and creativity.

You may think that we are suggesting there is a sense of inevitability about this, in a technological determinist sense. This would betray a kind of defeatist attitude whereby we lack a sense of agency to influence or take charge of any of it, or that it is trendy or educationally fashionable. In fact, we suggest the exact opposite. Rather than seeing change as something that is 'done to us' and that we cannot control, we are concerned with responding by taking charge of the changes, through using problem-based learning (PBL) as an adaptive approach to empower students and ourselves. In this way we could enable everyone – students, teachers, administrators and policy makers – to engage with technology and with broader changes in productive and enriching ways. Such an approach to university education would recognise 'the teleological character of higher education – the fact that education always raises the question of its purpose – and account for the fact that the question of educational purpose always poses itself in relation to three different domains' (Biesta, 2015, p. 84), which are 'qualification, socialisation and subjectification' (p. 77). Qualification refers to the transmission and acquisition of knowledge, skills and disposition; socialisation is about students being presented with ways of being and doing; and subjectification addresses the qualities of being a subject such as autonomy, independence, critical reasoning and so forth (Biesta, 2015). Central to these three domains is having the judgement 'to maintain an educationally meaningful balance between these domains' (Biesta, 2015, p. 84). As such, we recognise that we will always have to engage with knowledge, skills and dispositions and the mechanisms of achieving results in each of them, but we argue that it is crucial to also consider the *person* whom the university is targeting and developing in a more holistic sense. In other words, the *person* is about a lot more than discipline-specific knowledge and skills and includes a level of adaptability and an ability to cross boundaries that are increasingly required to function effectively in a contemporary society.

The way we define the purpose of university education here is towards building meaningful participation and contribution between students and ourselves – teachers, administrators and professional staff – and the 'world' and vice versa. No longer are we satisfied with just enabling students so to do specific things or to perform (qualification), but we also want to ensure that they are being socialised (socialisation), through PBL, into what becomes a 'way-of-being' (subjectification), which includes attributes such as willingness and comfort in taking risks, critical reasoning, reflection, resourcefulness and being functionally autonomous – all qualities of lifelong learners – that can be applied when they work and live in a world where the only certainty is uncertainty. In this vision, universities have a big role to play, but not in a 'business as usual' kind of way. In this book, we focus specifically on the potential of PBL as a broad-based approach to learning and teaching in the universities to connect students and the world, and vice versa, for learning. Here, we share Ito et al.'s (2013) connected learning model of education, which:

advocates for broader access to learning that is socially embedded, interest driven, and oriented toward educational, economical, or political opportunity. Connected learning is realised when a young person is able to pursue a personal interest or passion with the support of friends and caring adults, and is in turn able to link this learning to academic achievement, career success or civic engagement.

Even though Ito and her team's connected learning model is targeted at young children, we share a similar notion of connectivity where students are connected to learning beyond the garden walls of university, where the world beyond the university is also meaningfully participating and contributing to education, rather than separated out. In Barnett's (2013, p. 4) words, 'we are at a fork: we are faced with a self-imposed entrapment within some very narrow ideas of the university in one direction and, in the other, a glimpse of the *possibility of possibilities* is just beginning to open'.

Since PBL's conception in medical education nearly 50 years ago (Barrows & Tamblyn, 1980), it has been incorporated into many learning and teaching contexts with varying success. PBL is still being adopted and adapted in a wide range of educational fields and levels. The 'elastic' quality of PBL has allowed for different types and culturally variant versions of PBL with associated challenges and successes in implementation (see, e.g. Hmelo-Silver, 2012; Hung, 2011; Hung & Loyens, 2012), and PBL continues to evolve with new types or 'constellations' (Savin-Baden, 2014, p. 197) for the uncertain and yet unknown challenges of the twenty-first century. New PBL constellations must 'embrace "liquid learning" – the sense that learning and knowledge are always on the move … within and beyond disciplinary areas' (Savin-Baden, 2014, p. 210). Interestingly, herein lies both its strength and its potential weakness, for PBL is obviously seen as elastic enough to be 'stretched' into a wide variety of context-specific versions, or indeed constellations, but at the same time this creates a potential danger of 'anything goes'. In this book, we choose to engage with PBL for its potential, and so we are consciously positioning ourselves on the side of the fence where (with Barnett, 2013) imagination is allowed to think about future possibilities in an unrestricted manner. However, we are clearly not the only ones to think along these lines. So what are we adding to this already crowded space? We acknowledge that much has been written about the practical aspects of PBL in the form of guidelines, 'how to' guides and evaluations of small-scale practices and case studies as well as larger-scale practices in some cases (O'Grady, Yew, Goh, & Schmidt, 2012). Moreover, much has been written about the impact of PBL on university students' learning and on tertiary teaching practices. Thus, we will not reiterate this material.

Rather, we are interested in *imagining* the future of the universities, through *imagining* ways to leverage the elasticity of PBL and enable Savin-Baden's (2014) liquid learning. In this way, we can respond to future challenges and PBL may be incorporated into practices that could reshape that future. This is not a book about ready-made solutions nor is this about a toolbox of answers. After all, how can you design ready-made solutions for problems or issues that may not even exist yet? So we *imagine*, rather, the 'person' that we would like our students to become while studying at the university and upon graduation and how we would approach the education of students in a world that is growing ever fuzzier and more unpredictable with the advances of technology. We agree with Barnett (2013) that the broader contemporary debates about 'the university' are stunted by rigidified and narrow neoliberal thinking and that 'we require, therefore, in the first place, a *proliferation* of ideas of the university, if only to begin to demonstrate that things could be other than they are' (p. 5). This is not simply about 'dreaming' (Barnett, 2013, p. 6). He urges us instead to generate what he calls feasible utopias, which means simultaneously thinking outside the square and carefully considering practical implications and applications. Barnett's discussion concerns the university itself and its position in contemporary contexts, and it is thus rather ambitious. In this book, we take up his challenge to some extent, but we focus it more specifically on approaches to teaching and learning that might be imagined and that might be feasible in yet to be defined future university contexts. More specifically, we explore PBL as an approach to learning and teaching with sufficient potential to be adapted to such futures, and in this sense, our discussion is closely aligned to Savin-Baden's notion of the new constellations of PBL.

This book explores the idea of *imagining* PBL as the catalyst in enabling dispositions, knowledge and skills of students that become habitual, like second nature, to them when they live and work in a world characterised by uncertainties; in other words, an enabler of a *way-of-being* – through minds, hearts and actions, with reference to Barnett and Coate's concept of knowing, acting and being (Barnett & Coate, 2004) and the qualities of being a person (Biesta, 2015). These qualities are deemed important for universities so as to enable them to prosper in the 'age of supercomplexity' (Barnett, 1999), 'in which there are no stable descriptions of the world, no concepts that can be seized upon with any assuredness, and no value systems that can claim one's allegiance with any unrivalled authority' (Barnett, 2004, p. 252). It is a world where multiple paradigms coexist and are co-located, making for a radically interdisciplinary world, in which disciplinary boundaries are increasingly porous.

The idea of enabling a way-of-being aligns closely with the original PBL spirit or essence, which has not always been explicitly stated. Having the necessary knowledge (mind) and abilities to perform (actions) are *not* sufficient in a contemporary context. It is only when students are also equipped with a strong and confident conception of 'self' (heart – the being) that they can be active agents in their environments (Bronfenbrenner & Morris, 1998) without fear or anxiety and that they can prosper in any contexts in which they decide to live and work. This conceptualisation of 'being' includes qualities such as passion, resilience and emotional intelligence, which are the types of qualities that are often considered too intangible to explicitly address as part of tertiary education outcomes. Moreover, the ability to quickly get accustomed to change, as part of a 'way-of-being', might also be seen as adaptive expertise (Hatano & Inagaki, 1984). Adaptive expertise is a term coined by Hatano and Inagaki as a contrast to routine expertise. They posited that both types of expertise comprise knowledge of the subject matter and the ability to perform efficiently and effectively in familiar situations to the same extent. However, when an individual encounters a novel or unfamiliar situation, i.e. when the task, method or desired results are not known in advance to that individual, the person who can only draw on routine expertise will struggle. By contrast, the person who can access adaptive expertise, which allows for individuals to easily overcome novelty or unfamiliarity, affectively and cognitively, can respond to the situation quickly, effectively and with an appropriate level of flexibility (Schwartz, Bransford, & Sears, 2005). In short, adaptive expertise allows individuals to perform at a high level in the face of supercomplexity and provides them with the ability to adapt, as well as be flexible and agile in their thinking, feeling and doing.

Consistent with the *Gestalt* tradition, as part of which the human ecology development model was developed, the whole is larger than the sum of its parts. In other words, in the age of supercomplexity, human beings function in complex ecosystems that are characterised by various intersecting layers, which impact on each other. To function successfully in such ecosystems requires knowledges, skills, abilities and dispositions, and, as we will argue, a particular way-of-being that allows individuals to deal in productive and creative ways with uncertainty. PBL, in its various adapted forms, is ideally suited to enable and develop a way-of-being in students, partly because of its inherent focus on metacognition.

In this book we propose and outline a human ecology for learning model that we propose is well suited for a supercomplex world and that positions students at the very core. This 'agile PBL ecology for learning'[1] model, as we call it, is adapted from Bronfenbrenner's (1979) pioneering work on ecological systems theory, which has continued to evolve in the last 40 years. Today, though a posthumous publication, it is known as the ecological model of human development (Bronfenbrenner & Morris, 2006). The ecology for learning model places the student squarely at the centre of any university's multiple rings of environments, ranging from the immediate (micro-system) to the distal (macro-system) contexts (Bronfenbrenner, 1979, 2005; Bronfenbrenner & Morris, 2006). The ecological model also reminds us to engage with the university contexts (exo-systems) that are situated outside the students' formal learning and teaching contexts and to seize the opportunity to reposition such contexts as seamlessly connected to formal learning and teaching spaces in a way that would embrace the liquidity and porousness of learning that is characteristic of contemporary global environments (Savin-Baden, 2008, 2014). Furthermore, repositioning PBL within a human ecology for learning model creates affordances and spaces for students to learn to become active agents and creators of change during their university studies and to continue to be habitual agents and creators when they leave university to live and work in an uncertain, supercomplex world. Thus the distinction between formal and informal learning is effectively loosened and watered down to the point where the two flow into each other like a

---

[1] We are aware of the association of the term 'agile' with 'agile software development' (Dingsoyr, Dyba, & Brede Moe, 2010; Waters, 2012), and we are attracted to the term for similar reasons, i.e. its use as meaning 'the ability to create and respond to change in order to succeed in an uncertain and turbulent environment' (Agile Alliance, 2001). However, we believe that our use of the term as part of the broader concept of 'an agile PBL ecology for learning' distinguishes it sufficiently from agile software development to avoid any confusion.

river system in the wet season. We argue that PBL has the potential to play a central role in this process, and PBL thus has the potential to contribute to awakening some sections of the university and to jolt them into rethinking their role and the meaning of university education. Our imagination of the university is one that can improve 'the course of human life at the levels of both individual and their social world' (Lerner, 2005, p. xix), but to realise this potential requires a catalyst to allow this imagination to 'fly'. PBL can be this catalyst.

As Barnett (2013) argues, 'if the contemporary range of ideas in relation to the university is restricted, then ways should be found to allow as many ideas of the university to flourish. There might even be a kind of imaginative mayhem, in re-thinking the university' (p. 40). This works on different levels: on the one hand, it applies to an imaginary of where (and what) the university could (or should) be, while on the other hand it applies to enabling students in a way that recognises and makes full use of the imagination, as a tool for making the world a better place. This, as Barnett contends, 'is precisely the role of the imagination: to open up a gap, a gulf or even a chasm between what is and what might be' (p. 21). We believe that PBL, within an overall learning ecology, has the potential to help us imagine what a university might be in the future and in the process create spaces for 'imaginative mayhem' for students, teachers and administrators. This is an important shift in an age that clearly requires it, but can paradoxically and increasingly be characterised as an 'age of the practical, the calculative and the empirical' (Barnett, 2013, p. 20). This is not to suggest that there is no room for practical skills, but rather that the age of supercomplexity requires more than mere 'technicians of the academic market-place' (Barnett, 2013, p.37). Imagination and creativity are key to a better tomorrow, and we believe that PBL is ideally suited to help set them free.

This book is divided into three parts. Part I explores the macro-systems that sur-round universities and the role of PBL from the onset. Starting with Chap. 2, we revisit what PBL is really about. We then move on to imagining PBL as the engine of development by introducing the ecology model for learning and its various con-cepts. We reposition PBL as the curricular and pedagogical vehicle to qualify, socialise and subjectify students to learn the habits of mind, heart and actions, towards a way-of-being from the first day they arrive at the university. This way-of-being ultimately becomes second nature to them when they navigate, and progress to, a world of super-uncertainty, where the boundaries that would provide stability are arguably more porous than ever before. Chapter 3 looks at a new generation of students and the skills they need to navigate in and manage a supercomplex world. This chapter also suggests imagining the macro-system boundaries as permeable and to reposition the macro-system as not mere 'receivers' of universities in the form of prospective workers or employees, but as a system that is imagined as an interconnected space where all players are engaged as partners in learning and teaching – co-educators, coresearchers, co-entrepreneurs, co-employers and, above all, co-learners.

Part II explores the micro- and meso-systems – the spaces within a university where processes and mechanisms related to education and students (and learning) are commonly situated. Again, the boundaries between these spaces are imagined as porous, with the distinction between formal and informal learning spaces increasingly fuzzy and with many available opportunities to embrace liquid learning. Chapter 4 discusses the curriculum by repositioning learning outcomes and PBL problems and imagining the roles and the forms they may take. In this chapter, we also discuss the role of teaching and in the context of an interdisciplinary curriculum. In a similar vein, Chap. 5 discusses the rethinking of assessment from assessment of learning to assessment for learning while at the same time aligning assessments with students' future learning needs.

Part III, explores the exo-system in which students are not explicitly situated, but the processes and actions undertaken in these spaces would nevertheless jointly and/ or individually impact on their development. Chapter 6 examines the student support environment. It discusses the preparation of students for a curriculum that in many ways will radically depart from what they may currently imagine when they think about studying and learning at university. It thus functions as one step in unlocking their imagination. Chapter 7 examines the professional learning of academic staff and serves a similar function, this time in a staff-facing context. Chapter 8 discusses the concept of quality. It is about sustainability and continuous improvement, and it involves the development of a culture of continuous improvement that should apply to everyone involved in a university. However, improvement is here imagined as applying to all layers of the university, rather than merely to a narrowly defined notion of learning outcomes, because each layer is imagined as a crucial element of the overall ecosystem. Lastly, Chap. 9 deals with the future of PBL by developing a sustainable research and scholarship agenda. It explores the importance of research and scholarship, both as a way of rigorously and continuously questioning our practices in an immediate sense, but also as a way of making educated guesses about the future and developing a longitudinal evidence base. Inevitably, it also imagines the dissemination of research and scholarship and how this may be recast in the future.

This book is our attempt to bring to the surface our ideas and thoughts about the potential of PBL in an imagined 'feasible utopia' of the universities. From an institutional point of view, this may sound like utter madness, because it would require massive and fundamental changes in the way higher education institutions, and particularly universities, operate. However, this is precisely our point. This is our attempt to respond to Barnett's (2013) timely calls for an imaginative university that engages with a breadth and abundance of ideas and provides spaces for self-reflection (conceptual spaciousness) and self-criticality (institutional self-criticality), situated in and within a culture of trust (trust) and mutual respect and humility (conviviality), through open communication and transparency (communicative openness), and that engages with the wider society on mutual terms (societal transactionality). What we present here is our vision of such an imaginative university, and we see this serving as a starting point for dialogue. With Barnett we see this as an instance of "'responsible anarchism' which is a necessary step in unleashing the imagination and letting it soar, without ignoring its feasibility" (p. 43).

Throughout this book, we will take the idea of an agile PBL ecology for learning seriously. In other words, an agile PBL curriculum is not contained in a discipline or a course, but instead is influenced by and affects the wider society. This, in turn, means that it affects others in various environments of the university and therefore should be the concern of all parts and layers of the university and beyond. All four systems in the agile PBL ecology for learning we are presenting here affect each other, and so they should. Agile PBL then is about reinvigorating university education and blurring rigid siloed boundaries. Our central argument throughout this book is that there is no one person, nor the teacher, who is responsible for educating students. Rather, it is everyone's responsibility, including the students, employers and wider social networks inside and outside the university. Agile PBL is about welding together imagination and experience in potentially every layer of society; it is thus about making connections, rather than erecting barriers.

Overall then, an agile PBL ecology for learning is about recognising, respecting and responding to supercomplexity in a fast-changing environment. It deliberately blurs the boundaries between disciplines, between students and teachers, between students and employers, between employers and teachers, between academics and professional staff, between formal and informal learning and between teaching and researching. It is based on the recognition that all of these elements are interconnected, rather than exist in discrete units. This is not about maintaining comfort zones, but rather about becoming comfortable with discomfort. The actual implementation is of course beyond the scope of this book and we envisage that changing perceptions towards this vision will be a mammoth task. However, we believe that the alternative of leaving things as they are will one day have us look down to a bottom that has suddenly fallen out and, more distressingly, will leave a generation of students fearful to think, feel, act, generate and challenge in a twenty-first-century context.

References

Agile Alliance. (2001). *Manisfeto for agile software development*. Retrieved June 23, 2016, from https://www.agilealliance.org/agile101/the-agile-manifesto/

Barnett, R. (1999). *Realising the university in an age of supercomplexity*. Buckingham, UK: SRHE and Open University Press.

Barnett, R. (2004). Learning in an unknown future. *Higher Education Research and Development, 23*(3), 247–260.

Barnett, R. (2013). *Imagining the university*. Abingdon, UK: Routledge.

Barnett, R., & Coate, K. (2004). *Engaging the curriculum in higher education*. Berkshire, UK: Mc-Graw Hill Education.

Barrows, H. S., & Tamblyn, R. M. (1980). *Problem-based learning: An approach to medical education*. New York: Springer Publishing Company.

Biesta, G. (2015). What is education for? On good education, teacher judgment, and educational professionalism. *European Journal of Education, 50*(1), 75–87. doi:10.1111/ejed.12109.

Bronfenbrenner, U. (1979). *The ecology of human development*. Cambridge, MA: Harvard University Press.

Bronfenbrenner, U. (2005). Ecological systems theory. In U. Brofenbrenner (Ed.), *Making human beings human: Bioecological perspectives on human development* (pp. 106–173). Thousand Oaks, CA: Sage Publications.

Bronfenbrenner, U., & Morris, P. A. (1998). The ecology of developmental processes. In R. M. Lerner (Ed.), *Handbook of child psychology* (5th ed., Vol. 1, pp. 993–1028). New York: Wiley.

Bronfenbrenner, U., & Morris, P. A. (2006). The bioecological model of human development. In W. Damon & R. M. Lerner (Eds.), *Handbook of child psychology* (6th ed., pp. 793–828). Hoboken, NJ: Wiley.

Chickering, A. W. (2006). Every student can learn – If …. *About Campus, 11*(2), 9–15.

Dingsoyr, T., Dyba, T., & Brede Moe, N. (2010). *Agile software development: Current research and future directions*. Berlin, Germany: Springer.

Hatano, G., & Inagaki, K. (1984). Two courses of expertise. *Research and Clinical Center for Child Development Annual Report, 6*, 27–36.

Hmelo-Silver, C. E. (2012). International perspectives on problem-based learning: Contexts, cultures, challenges, and adaptations. *Interdisciplinary Journal of Problem-Based Learning, 6*(1), 10–15.

Hung, W. (2011). Theory to reality: A few issues in implementing problem-based learning. *Educational Technology Research & Development, 59*(4), 529–552. doi:10.1007/s11423-011-9198-1.

Hung, W., & Loyens, S. M. M. (2012). Global development of problem-based learning: Adoption, adaption, and advancement. *The Interdisciplinary Journal of Problem-Based Learning, 6*(1), 4–9.

Ito, M., Gutierrez, K., Livingstone, S., Penuel, B., Rhodes, J., Salen, K., Schor, J., Sefton-Green, J., & Watkins, S. C. (2013). *Connected learning: An agenda for research and design*. Irvine, CA: Digital Media and Learning Research Hub. Retrieved from http://www.dmlhub.net/publications

Lerner, R. M. (2005). Foreword: Urie. Bronfenbrenner: Career contributions of the consummate developmental scientist. In U. Bronfenbrenner (Ed.), *Making human beings human: Bioecological perspectives on human development* (Vol. ix–xxvi). Thousand Oaks, CA: Sage Publications.

O'Grady, G., Yew, E. H. J., Goh, K. P. L., & Schmidt, H. G. (Eds.). (2012). *One day, one problem: An approach to problem-based learning*. Singapore, Singapore: Springer.

Savin-Baden, M. (2008). *Learning spaces: Creating opportunities for knowledge creation in academic life*. Buckingham, UK: McGraw-Hill Education.

Savin-Baden, M. (2014). Using problem-based learning: New constellations for the 21st century. *Journal on Excellence in College Teaching, 25*(3&4), 197–219.

Schwartz, D. L., Bransford, J. D., & Sears, D. (2005). Efficiency and innovation in transfer. In J. Mestre (Ed.), *Transfer of learning: Research and perspectives* (pp. 1–52). Greenwich, CT: Information Age Publishing.

Waters, K. (2012). *All about agile*. Retrieved June 23, 2016, from http://lpgupdf.cago.us/all-about-agile-agile-kelly-waters-84110873.pdf

Part I
Imagining Agile PBL in a Changing World for Learning

Chapter 2
Towards an Ecology for Connected Learning

Introduction

This chapter revisits PBL and examines new types or 'constellations of PBL' (Savin-Baden, 2014) that are being proposed to meet yet unknown and uncertain challenges of the twenty-first century and to develop a mode of knowledge creation, application and management that is suited for an 'age of supercomplexity' (Barnett, 2004). It then introduces an ecology for learning model that is underpinned by a student development worldview. We have adapted Bronfenbrenner's ecology of human development (Bronfenbrenner, 1979, 2005b; Bronfenbrenner & Morris, 2006) to imagine agile PBL operating in an ecology that positions students at the centre of multiple, evolving and interconnected environments, ranging from the proximal (micro-system) and the intermediate (meso- and exo-systems) to the distal (macro-system) (Bronfenbrenner, 1979, 2005a; Bronfenbrenner & Morris, 2006), where liquid knowledges and learning can be activated. This model is interesting for our purposes here, because it allows us to reposition PBL-based learning as a 'holistic' approach to connected learning, in which boundaries between formal and informal learning environments, between work and study and between public and private spaces are continuously blurred, and they frequently morph into each other and impact on each other. Blurred boundaries increasingly characterise twenty-first-century learning and teaching environments and are therefore a central theme in this book. As Sharples et al. (2014), for example, note (albeit in reference to pre-tertiary education):

> When students bring their own smartphones and tablet computers into the classroom, this action changes their relationship with the school and with their teachers. They arrive equipped not only with individual technologies that they maintain and improve, but also with their own personal learning environments and social networks. This means that teachers become managers of technology-enabled networked learners, rather than providers of resources and knowledge. (p. 4)

Although we do not necessarily agree with the idea that teachers have become merely facilitators or 'managers' of learners, Sharples et al. (2014) do draw our attention to radically changing learning environments. In such fast-changing envi-

© Springer Science+Business Media Singapore 2017
M.Y.C.A. Kek, H. Huijser, *Problem-based Learning into the Future*,
DOI 10.1007/978-981-10-2454-2_2

ronments, teachers need to be flexible and adaptable, and moreover, they need approaches to teaching and learning that are agile enough to be both responsive and proactive. We will argue in this book that PBL is indeed such an agile approach to teaching and learning, malleable to changing contexts, knowledge and learning.

Up until this point, we have made a lot of reference to 'fast-changing environments'. In order to specifically show how and why we believe PBL is a suitable approach in this context, it is important to be able to map the different elements of such fast-changing learning environments, or what we will call henceforth a learning ecology, with concepts borrowed from an ecology systems model pioneered by Bronfenbrenner (1979). A key focus in Bronfenbrenner's model is on the proximal processes or 'the engines of development' (Bronfenbrenner & Morris, 2006, p. 825) between the students and their immediate learning and teaching environments, which affect the desired developmental changes in students. What is appealing here is that the developmental change is posited to be enduring rather than restricted to a specific learning and teaching 'event', from the present moment in time to a future time. In practice, this refers to time that universities have a potential impact on students' learning journeys, which is from the moment students first step into their university environments until the moment they leave that part of their learning environment behind upon graduation. In other words, during their university studies, students would have acquired a particular way-of-being of a lifelong learner, characterised by a particular disposition and qualities such as critical curiosity, design thinking, creativity, entrepreneurial thinking and imagination (among others). This is about making a way-of-being dimension last throughout students' lives after they graduate from university studies. We propose repositioning PBL towards what we call 'agile PBL', as the engine of development that propels an enduring way-of-being, integrated in both curriculum and pedagogy (Barnett & Coate, 2004).

The ecology for learning model also reminds us to be aware of the interactions between the student and the multiple contexts that constitute the university, which includes spaces that the students do not necessarily encounter or interact with directly, and it includes spaces that are external to formal university spaces. However, together these all influence their developmental outcomes and impact on their learning journeys. In this respect, we imagine positioning learning beyond the 'business as usual' boxed-up, fixed and inflexible systems and spaces for learning and teaching, creating multi-paradigmatic learning opportunities and enabling 'liquid learning' (Savin-Baden, 2014, p. 210) to occur. Repositioning PBL as the engine of development of a learning ecology allows for both the recognition of these multiple learning spaces, as well as meaningful and proactive engagement with and in them.

As noted, Bronfenbrenner's ecological model is useful for mapping and visualising the complicated constellation of learning spaces involved in contemporary and future learning environments, but before we outline this model, it is important to identify what it is, fundamentally, about PBL that makes it, in our opinion, suitable to engage with twenty-first-century supercomplexity.

What Is PBL?

Howard Barrows is one of the key pioneers of PBL and has written extensively about the essentials of PBL since it was developed and first applied to medical education in the 1960s. Megan has had the privilege to learn PBL under the mentorship of the late Howard Barrows. We thought that for this section, which is about the essentials or non-negotiables of PBL, it might be best left to Howard Barrows himself to explain what PBL is. What follows next is an unpublished text (in its original form and in a different font to set it apart) which was written by Howard before his passing on March 25, 2011.

Problem-Based Learning Essentials
by Howard S. Barrows

Authenticity

Problem-based learning should be in the contexts of the environment where the learner will function after graduation. The problems presented to learners should be those that the learners will encounter in their work. The behaviours and skills required of learners in the learning process should be only those used and valued in their career. The problem-based learning process itself should parallel the process followed by expert professionals encountering problems in the learners' career field.

Problems should present as they do in the real world and permit free inquiry by learners

The problems should be in the form they will appear to the learners after graduation with only the information that would be initially available. The learner should be able to inquire about the problem through free inquiry, as occurs in the real world, to find the facts needed to build the problem into a case.

Problem-solving skill development

With problems that present as they do in work and designed to permit free inquiry, the learners should practise and develop effective and efficient problem-solving skills guided by tutors who understand and can facilitate the reasoning processes required.

Student-centered

The learners should be able to recall and apply the unique knowledge and skills they already possess to an understanding of the problem they are working with and determine what they each need to learn to more effectively understand and manage the problem. When the learners can build on the knowledge they already have, the understanding and recall of new information is enhanced.

Self-directed learning skill development

Under the guidance of the tutor, learners should become responsible for their own learning, able to determine what they need to learn and how to get the knowledge they need from a world of available resources (texts, libraries, journals, online, consultants, faculty experts). Since new knowledge is developed in all fields and new problems appear in the workplace, it is essential that the learners are able to update their knowledge and skills effectively and efficiently to meet new challenges on a just-in-time basis.

Integrated knowledge

In their self-directed learning and problem work, the learners should obtain information from all the subjects or disciplines related to the problem. They should be able to integrate that information to obtain an in-depth understanding of the problem and a fuller appreciation of the interrelation of information from all disciplines in contributing to the understanding and management of a problem.

Small group collaborative learning

Contemporary work of necessity involves teamwork, and graduates must learn how to work effectively in teams both as leaders and followers as the task requires, capable of learning from and teaching each other. The learners develop these skills through small group work with peer and self-assessment.

Reiterative

Following a period of self-directed study, what was learned must be applied back to the problem at hand and not just described. The learners must critique and revise their prior reasoning and knowledge about the problem and revise their decisions and inquiry on the basis of new learning through discussion and argumentation based on what was learned.

Reflective

When the learners have completed their problem work, they must review what they have learned and discuss its potential application to other problems. They need to reflect on what they had learned in prior, relate problems and consider what abstractions and generalisation might be developed. Developing a concept map that relates information acquired to the decisions about cause and management of the problem may often reveal errors in reasoning and holes in the learners' knowledge and understanding of the problem.

Self- and peer assessment

This should be practised at the end of every problem, where each learner assesses his/her own gain in knowledge, problem-solving skills, self-directed learning skills and interpersonal skills. Following such a self-assessment, the others in the group must then assess that learner. The ability to assess one's own performance and provide constructive feedback to others is an essential lifetime career skill. In problem-based learning, this developing skill can be used as a more accurate and detailed assessment of each learner's progress in the curriculum.

Skilled tutors

Trained tutors are skilled in facilitating learners as they problem-solve, identify what they need to learn, carry out self-directed learning, apply what they have learned back to the problem, work as a team and carry out peer and self-assessment as required. These are tutors that will not directly teach the learners, provide them with the information they need or tell them when they are wrong. They are the backbone of any problem-based learning curriculum and need to be specifically trained as this is a new and challenging teaching skill. The learners should not be dependent on the tutor for their learning, but on themselves.

Foundational

In problem-based learning, the learners are expected to become responsible for their own learning, determining what they need to learn, and to have the time to develop problem-solving and self-directed learning skills accessing the world's rich knowledge from many disciplines. The practice and development of these skills is central to their learning as is the acquisition of integrated information, not for its own sake, but for its usefulness in application to career problems. The learners are assessed with performance-based exams that require them to apply what they have learned to the solution of problems in their chosen field of practice.

These learners should not also be asked to learn in another part of the curriculum in separate subjects, where teachers provide them what they need to learn in lectures and reading assignments and expect learners to regurgitate that learning on exams that assess only their skills in memorising the required content. This is a totally different epistemology that is not aimed at producing a problem-solving, self-directed learner, who can assess his/her own learning needs and work effectively in teams. In addition, the demands of such a memorization/test curriculum rob the learners of the self-directed learning time they need.

Combining problem-based learning with traditional learning confuses both learners and teachers and weakens the effectiveness of problem-based learning.

When problem-based learning is the foundation of the curriculum, it is easy to incorporate lectures, seminars and laboratories for their own unique value and in a way that complements the problem-based learning approach.
January 13, 2002 (Source: H. S. Barrows, personal communication, January 13, 2002)

As to what constitutes a PBL problem, here again are Howard's unpublished thoughts written in 2000.

Problem
A problem occurs when the knowledge and/or actions you should undertake to accomplish an objective are not obvious or known.
A problem occurs when:

Something has failed and is broken, malfunctioning or not working correctly (equipment breakdown, technology failure, unsuccessful plan, patient with an illness, etc.).
You need an answer or explanation for a puzzle, mystery or unexplained phenomena.
You need to find a better way to accomplish something.
You need to design or create something.

A problem may have one or both of these challenges:

- The cause is unknown and needs to be determined.
- How to resolve the problem is unknown or uncertain. (Source: H. S. Barrows, personal notes, 2000)

Barrow's PBL Essentials in Action

According to Prawatt (1996), constructivism is a broad term that can be categorised into two groups of learning theories: modern or individual and postmodern or social learning theories. Modern or individual constructivism focuses on the structures of knowledge in students' minds and can be illustrated by the acquisition metaphor. It includes, among others, Piaget-based constructivism, information processing theory and cognitive schema theory. On the other hand, postmodernism or social constructivism rejects the concept that the locus of knowledge is in the individual. Instead it focuses on the distributed nature of cognition and students' participation in socially organised learning activities. Examples include situated cognition learning (Brown, Collins, & Duguid, 1989), community of practice (Lave & Wenger, 1991) and sociocultural constructivism (Vygotsky, 1978).

Even though these two approaches have different ontological bases, the goal is the same, which is the process of education. Therefore, to understand a complex phenomenon such as learning, both perspectives of constructivism are needed, as learning entails knowledge acquisition and construction, in line with the 'acquisition metaphor', *and* it entails the participation, illustrated by the 'participation metaphor', of the person and of the social world, in groups, communities and relationships (Sfard, 1998, p. 5).

Distilling Howard's writing on PBL, a set of PBL-based learning essentials can be formed, which amalgamates these two forms of constructivism, but leaning more towards social constructivism in a wider social cultural context where boundaries between social categories are more porous than ever before.

Learning Is Action Oriented, in Context and Just-in-Time

Action and situated learning afford students the ability to solve complex problems and to significantly increase the quality of learning. In PBL, students habitually seek, analyse, synthesise and apply information, with the guidance of the teacher, to resolve the problems presented to them at the outset.

Learning Is Motivating

Authentic problems are used so as to further fuel students' interest and motivation and to trigger inquiry. This means that problems will often be interdisciplinary and multifaceted, inherently triggering 'liquid learning', whereby different types of learning and learning contexts flow into each other.

Learning Needs Explicit Modelling and Scaffolding with Fading

Successful learning happens when there is a scaffolding process with fading. Scaffolding is a term first introduced by Wood, Bruner, and Ross (1976) and refers to those instances when appropriate assistance and support are provided, and learners can attain intended goals or engage in a practice that would otherwise be beyond their skill level. The notion of scaffolding is also consistent with Vygotsky's (1978) conception of the zone of proximal development (ZPD). However, scaffolding *without* fading (Pea, 2004) will not allow students to perform autonomously, and thus risks dependency instead. Therefore, it is essential that teachers avoid making the students dependent on them, but instead use the model-scaffold-fade approach to teaching (Kek & Huijser, 2011). That is, the teachers pose questions through modelling and scaffolding, to gradually but consciously remove the modelling (allowing the students to adopt the questioning role instead of the teachers) and scaffolds (support mechanisms for students) and to 'fade' themselves out of the picture, thereby ensuring that students become independent learners.

Learning Occurs in Groups, with Others and Peers

Knowledge is constructed collectively, physically and virtually, particularly in an increasingly digital world. It is through conversations with others about what each individual knows about the problem that learning occurs (Pask, 1976), and knowledge is shared and built (Hmelo-Silver & Barrows, 2008; Scardamalia & Bereiter, 2006). Collaborative learning in groups should therefore be embedded in the curriculum.

Learning Needs to Be Visible

An integral aspect of learning in groups through conversations is the need to externalise understanding (Pask, 1976). To be able to engage in a productive conversation, all members of the group, including the teacher, need to have a common understanding of the problem. Barrows' reasoning structure (Kek & Huijser, 2011) – facts (identify the facts), ideas (generate or explore possible ideas or hypotheses), learning issues (identify what you need to know to manage or solve the problem) and action plan (articulate an action plan to seek, evaluate, synthesise and apply information to the problem), also known as the FILA table – is a tool to scaffold learning by making thinking and reasoning processes visible and explicit to all parties in the PBL session, including students and teachers. FILA provides a structure for students, facilitated by teachers, to plan the best way to address a specific problem, as it purposively enables students to ask questions about what they already know and in turn what they need to learn.

Learning Requires Effective Feedback and Reflections: Self- and Peer Assessment

It is important to provide feedback and feedforward with reference to how every student in the group performs in PBL so that they can improve. It is also an important element in developing metacognitive skills. Providing and receiving feedback is another essential element of PBL. It is expected that the reflections form a part of structured learning activities or regular feedback sessions, usually at the end of each problem. The goal is to nurture the development of greater self-awareness of one's own strengths and weaknesses, an important skill of critical thinkers (Halpern, 1998) and, in particular, an essential skill in contemporary learning and professional contexts (Rotherham & Willngham, 2010). It facilitates the development of reflective practitioners (Schon, 1983).

Learning Requires Purposive Creation of Conditions and Contexts

Learning is not stable. Phenomenographic studies and research following the tradition of Marton and Saljo (1976), which focus on qualitative differences in individual approaches to learning, have established that a surface approach to learning is not necessarily inherent to students. Student approaches to learning studies using quantitative methods have also found students' learning to be associated with their perceptions of the learning contexts (Biggs, 2001) – teaching, learning activities and assessments. Biggs (1999) argued that only when the learning context involves a curriculum that is constructively aligned would students be 'entrapped in [a] web of consistency, optimising the likelihood that they will engage the appropriate learning activities' (p. 5). What this means is that to successfully implement PBL, the intentions of developing PBL higher-order thinking skills, such as critical thinking, problem-solving, reasoning and self-directed learning, while learning discipline knowledge or subject matter must be *intentionally aligned* to the learning outcomes, teaching, learning activities and assessment.

PBL as a Way-of-Being

The essential components of PBL form the staples to achieve the PBL educational objectives, regardless of disciplines (Barrows, 1998). However, the elements outlined above do not constitute a mere list of essentials or 'must haves' for PBL practices; rather they indicate an ontological space where students are afforded spaces in the curriculum (Barnett & Coate, 2004). This ontological space is also where students' learning approaches and ways of knowing, acquired through the PBL approach, later become an essential part of their way of thinking, doing and acting – a way-of-being. Polanyi (1983) has referred to this as 'indwelling', which is a familiarity with particular ideas (knowledge), processes (dispositions) and practices (skills) that is so ingrained that they become second nature to students. This way-of-being or 'dwelling' is internalised to the extent that it becomes the students' mental existence (Polanyi, 1969, 1983), forming a type of personal knowledge and disposition (Polanyi, 1962) that they will use on autopilot, to make sense of the world and to adapt, as they travel, socialise and negotiate with others. This includes an attitude and response to new tools and technologies; overall, it is the attitude in particular (as part of a way-of-being) that provides students as lifelong learners with ongoing choices in terms of where they would prefer to live and work in the world.

This is the dimension of PBL that provides an important nuance to our vision of agile PBL. PBL is seen here as the engine propelling the type of development whereby students, as part of PBL-based learning, become so familiar with actions of critical reasoning, reflections, collaboration and self-directedness and with unknown and uncertain problems that these elements become entrenched or ingrained in their everyday practice and disposition, like second nature, a way-of-being or a form of indwelling.

Similar to the reiterative cycles of PBL-based learning, indwelling is also adaptive to different environments, meaning that the PBL processes and practices that have become habitual or second nature are adaptive and responsive to changes in the environment, or indeed to changing environments themselves. These qualities are embodied in the lived, social experiences of students as they move through a PBL-based program, and ideally they would have become like a way-of-life upon graduation. This is responsive to Barrows' (2002) reminder that 'when the learners graduate, there will be no teachers to tell them … they will have to do that themselves. When they encounter … problems … changes in the way things are done … they will need to learn [or not] what [would] meet these new demands … they will need to determine when they are not performing [contributing] as well as they should and take the learning needed [or not] to improve' (p. 5).

Curriculum and Pedagogy in the Age of Supercomplexity

Our vision of developing a way-of-being enabled through PBL also echoes Barnett's 'being-for-uncertainty' (2004, p. 258), which embraces a kind of disposition that includes elements such as resilience, courage, humility, receptiveness and criticality. This is quite a departure from simply concentrating on functional attributes such as communication skills or discipline knowledge, but allows us instead to focus on long-term sustainability, rather than exclusively on short-term economic gains, both on the individual and societal levels. Savin-Baden (2008) warns in this respect that 'higher education has increasingly become colonized by an enterprising culture' and that 'these colonizing forms of enterprise in higher education reflect the market forces and the quick stance of commerce and industry. Higher education that only supplies "training" is unlikely to equip students to work in an uncertain world' (p. 141). Conversely, and most importantly, PBL students ultimately share a similar way-of-being that does enable them to live and work in a world of unknowns. Thus, the ideal of an agile form of PBL that we present in this book allows students and graduates who find themselves in situations where they do not have the relevant or necessary knowledge or skills to not be fearful of the challenges but to be able to draw on their PBL indwelling – knowledge, skills and dispositions – and their way-of-being as a matter of course, which would thus allow them to be productive citizens in an uncertain world (Barnett, 2004). This would also allow us to get away from a situation where 'gaining a degree is more about marginal advantage in the job market than about personal transformation' (Savin-Baden, 2008, p. 144). Agile PBL will allow for a whole lot more with a focus on the latter.

Barnett (2000) states that the development of 'a way-of-being' is crucial to universities in the twenty-first century, which he characterises as a 'radically unknowable world' (Barnett, 1999, p. 43). Barnett (2004) conceived of the term supercomplexity to denote a world in which 'the interactions between elements are

unclear, uncertain and unpredictable' (p. 249). Indeed, supercomplexity characterises a world that is not just 'radically unknowable' but also 'indescribable' (Barnett,
2004, p. 252). Hence, his argument is that this condition of uncertainty demands
curricula and pedagogy that must be founded on the principle that the learning process is both high risk and transformatory in character, wherein students and teachers
themselves are engaged as persons with 'openness, mutual disclosure, personal
risks and disturbance' (Barnett, 2004, pp. 257–258). Such curricula and pedagogy
engages students in developing three dimensions of knowing, acting and being, of
which being is the most significant (Barnett & Coate, 2004), that is, being truly and
actively engaged in the learning process and with others. Barnett and Coate add that
such active engagement can only occur when the students are afforded spaces in the
curriculum in which deep, reflective learning can take place. Agile PBL, with its
non-negotiables of working in groups, self- and peer assessment, critical thinking
and reasoning and students working on problems that are authentic or that mirror
the real world, affords continuous spaces for such deep, reflective learning. To some
extent this has been part of PBL since its initial conceptualization, but the difference
now is that it needs to be more flexible and agile in order to be able to engage productively with 'radically unknowable' contexts.

Similarly, where it is recognised that advances of technologies have penetrated
into every aspect of students' lives, the porous boundaries between the classroom
and life experience, formal and informal learning and curricular and co-curricular
experiences, along with connected learning, participatory web culture and integrative contexts, are reframing what is thought of as the formal curriculum in the 'post-
course era' (Bass, 2012, p. 24). The reframed curriculum, which leverages new
technologies, calls for a curriculum and pedagogy that afford students ways of
'learn[ing] to be' (Bass, 2012, p. 28) through both formal and informal experiences
and as early in the curriculum as possible. This is agile PBL.

Agile PBL for the Twenty-First Century

When PBL was first conceptualised in the 1960s, universities were decidedly different places for learning than what they are today. Furthermore, the context in which
they operate has altered quite radically since then. As Dede (2013) notes, 'new
media, insights from research, and alterations in organizational structures are changing long-standing assumptions that have shaped higher education' (p. 43). This in
turn has an impact on approaches to higher education and outcomes. Dede (p. 34)
identifies four key objectives in this respect, and each of them has direct relevance
to agile PBL:

1. Moving from thinking about expertise as something an expert 'knows' and can
   articulate to thinking about expertise as a complex mix of tacit (i.e. non-
   conscious) and conscious competencies

2. Moving from knowledge and skills localised in a student's mind to distributed understanding and performance
3. Moving from a focus on memorising and applying facts, simple concepts and straightforward procedures to 'higher-level' conceptual and analytical capabilities deployed adaptively in diverse contexts
4. Moving from a primary focus on the conceptual and procedural aspects of learner competencies that are often described as 'cognitive' to an equal emphasis on complementary aspects of learner competencies, 'noncognitive factors', which are instrumental to successful postsecondary learning, work and citizenship

This is an interesting set of objectives when we relate them to PBL, as PBL appears to be ideally suited to deliver precisely these outcomes, including 'distributed understanding and performance', which is encapsulated by PBL's emphasis on collaborative learning. This is not the only list of projected or desired outcomes that fit very well with PBL in its long-established guise. Marilyn Lombardi, for example, in her outline of what she calls 'authentic learning for the twenty-first century' lists the following ten design elements that again fit PBL perfectly (Lombardi, 2007, pp. 3–4):

1. Real-world relevance
2. Ill-defined problem
3. Sustained investigation
4. Multiple sources and perspectives
5. Collaboration
6. Reflection (metacognition)
7. Interdisciplinary perspective
8. Integrated assessment
9. Polished products
10. Multiple interpretations and outcomes

If we closed our eyes for a moment, we could almost hear Howard Barrows listing off what PBL was all about. Similarly, if we were to call this book simply 'PBL for the twenty-first century', this list would provide us with a ready-made contents page. However, it is not quite as simple as that. If PBL is the apparently perfect pedagogical and curriculum design approach for the twenty-first century, why is it only implemented selectively in relatively few tertiary education institutions, and why is it still often restricted to particular disciplines? The answer is complex and relates to a wide variety of factors, including institutional context factors, but importantly, the answer also includes the complexity of PBL itself, 'comprising multiple constantly changing elements' (Savin-Baden, 2014, p. 197). This complexity of tertiary education institutional contexts, as well as rapid changes in the wider societal context, in combination with the complexity of PBL itself, is an important reason for the development of our concept of agile PBL. Savin-Baden has identified a similar need and response and has come up with what she calls 'new constellations of PBL for the twenty-first century', and she identifies nine such constellations (Savin-Baden, 2014, pp. 202–203):

1. Constellation 1: Problem-based learning for knowledge management
2. Constellation 2: Problem-based learning through activity
3. Constellation 3: Project-led problem-based learning
4. Constellation 4: Problem-based learning for practical capabilities
5. Constellation 5: Problem-based learning for design-based learning
6. Constellation 6: Problem-based learning for critical understanding
7. Constellation 7: Problem-based learning for multimodal reasoning
8. Constellation 8: Collaborative distributed problem-based learning
9. Constellation 9: Problem-based learning for transformation and social reform

For each of these, she identifies design elements like 'problem type', 'level of interaction', 'focus of knowledge', 'form of facilitation', 'focus of assessment' and 'learning emphasis'. What this clearly shows is the complexity of problem-based learning and its implications for design, and this kind of breakdown is very useful for that reason, as it shows that there is no one-size-fits-all in PBL learning design. This further reinforces the importance of what we call 'agile PBL' in this book, which refers to both a response to constantly changing porous contexts, but importantly also a proactive agile approach to curriculum and pedagogy to embrace liquidity or Savin-Baden's (2014) liquid flow of knowledge and learning that are constantly on the move in the age of supercomplexity. Thus, agile PBL recognises the complexity of fast-changing contexts, and, by connecting these contexts across an entire learning ecology, it allows for the widening of access to learning for students, as argued by Ito et al. (2013). Then, designing appropriate 'constellar' PBL learning opportunities should provide students with what we have called above a 'way-of-being' that is sustained throughout the student's life course – during their university studies and beyond. This 'way-of-being' in turn becomes a 'practising what you preach' attitude too among teachers, university administrators and support staff, as we ultimately expect the same agility and proactive adaptability from our students and graduates. Savin-Baden, p. 213 draws on Siemens' concept of 'connectivist pedagogy', which is very useful for our purposes here as well, as most of its principles fit very well with the idea of agile PBL for connected learning:

- Learning and knowledge rest in diversity of opinions.
- Learning is a process of connecting specialised nodes of information sources.
- Learning may reside in non-human appliances.
- Capacity to know more is more critical than what is currently known.
- Nurturing and maintaining connections are needed to facilitate continual learning.
- The ability to see connections between fields, ideas and concepts is a core skill.
- Currency (accurate, up-to-date knowledge) is the intent of all connectivist learning activities.
- Decision-making is itself a learning process.
- Choosing what to learn and the meaning of incoming information is seen through the lens of shifting reality.

As becomes clear, many of these principles align very nicely with the spirit or essence of PBL, as espoused by Howard Barrows, while also recognising a fast-changing learning context. For our purposes here, a key observation is that for effective connected learning (Ito et al., 2013) to be fostered by using agile PBL, many of these types of learning that occur across multiple ecologies or environments need to be recognised and respected. We respond broadly by making deliberate and meaningful connections between formal and informal learning environments and between the university and the world beyond. In turn, this will create opportunities for design decisions that leverage such connections proactively and productively, rather than ignoring them. We will discuss the various elements of agile PBL throughout this book, but we will now turn to the ecology for learning in which agile PBL is the engine of development, by unpacking Bronfenbrenner's ecological model.

Towards an Ecology for Connected Learning

We have adapted Bronfenbrenner's (Bronfenbrenner, 1979, 2005b; Bronfenbrenner & Morris, 2006) ecological model for agile PBL. The dynamic and relational view of the process of human development provides us with a useful framework to explain agile PBL as a curriculum and pedagogy for connected learning in the twenty-first century, a concept strongly endorsed by Barnett and Coate (2004).

Bronfenbrenner's Human Ecology Model

Central to Bronfenbrenner's human ecology model (1979) is the evolving interconnectedness between individual characteristics and the environment in influencing human development. Bronfenbrenner conceived of the ecological environment as a set of nested, interdependent, dynamic structures ranging from the proximal, consisting of the immediate settings, to the most distal, comprising broader social contexts, such as social classes and culture. They can be viewed 'as a set of nested structures, each inside the other like a set of Russian dolls' (Bronfenbrenner, 1979, p. 3). Bronfenbrenner's ecology model entails micro-systems, meso-systems, exo-systems and macro-systems, linked together and interacting with each other to influence human development. If we apply this to a higher education context, it would involve the following:

1. At the innermost level are the students in what is known as the micro-system. 'A microsystem is a pattern of activities, roles and interpersonal relations experienced by the developing person [the students] in a given face-to-face setting with particular physical, social and symbolic features that invite, permit, or inhibit, engagement in sustained, progressively more complex interaction with, and

activity in, the immediate environment [the formal learning and teaching space]'
(Bronfenbrenner & Morris, 2006, p. 814).

2. The meso-system comprises 'the linkages and processes between two or more
   settings containing the developing person [such as the relation between university and the workplace, university and caring for the family, university and formal and/or informal social and peer groups]. In other words, a mesosystem is a
   system of microsystems' (Bronfenbrenner, 2005a, p. 148).

3. The exo-system is made up of 'the linkages and processes of settings taking
   place between two or more settings containing the developing person [the stu-
   dents], but in which events occur that influence processes within the immediate
   setting [formal learning and teaching space] that does contain that person [such
   as their teacher's work space, institutional student support or services, institution's quality and research decisions, plans and policies]' (Bronfenbrenner,
   2005a, p. 148).

4. The macro-system is 'the over-arching pattern of micro-, meso-, and exosystems
   characteristic of a given culture, subculture, or other broader social context, with
   particular reference to the developmentally instigative belief systems, resources,
   hazards, lifestyles, opportunity structures, life course options, and patterns of
   social interchange that are embedded in each of these systems' (Bronfenbrenner,
   2005a, pp. 149–150).

Underlying this human ecological model of the process of human development
are two key ideas or propositions, which are of relevance to agile PBL in a higher
education context. As explained by Bronfenbrenner and Morris (1998), a key proposition of the human ecological model states:

> Over the life course, human development takes place throughout life through processes of
> progressively more complex reciprocal interaction between an active evolving biopsycho-
> social human organism and the persons, objects, and symbols in its immediate external
> environment. To be effective, the interaction must occur on a fairly regular basis over
> extended periods of time. Such enduring forms of interaction in the immediate environment
> are referred to as proximal processes. (p. 996)

The second proposition states:

> The form, power, content, and direction of the proximal processes effecting development
> vary systematically as a joint function of the characteristics of the developing person; the
> environment – both immediate and more remote – in which the processes are taking place;
> the nature of the developmental outcomes under consideration; and the social continuities
> and changes occurring over time through the life course and the historical period during
> which the person has lived. (p. 996)

The two propositions for us mean that not only are the immediate learning space
and PBL proximal processes important in developing university students, but the
distal mechanisms beyond the immediate contexts could also influence the power
and direction of the proximal processes that affect students' connected learning
directly.

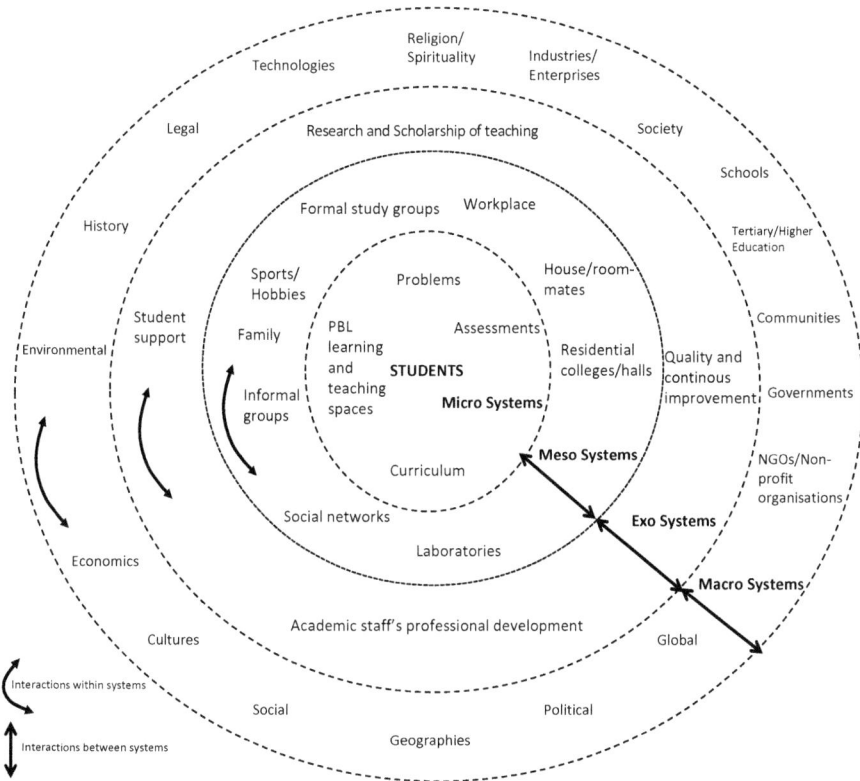

Fig. 2.1 An agile PBL ecology for learning

An Agile PBL Ecology for Connected Learning

We have adapted Bronfenbrenner's four systems and propositions to imagine an agile PBL ecology for connected learning, as shown in Fig. 2.1.

The model shows the university students as living in the micro-systems of PBL-based learning and teaching spaces, with their teachers and other students, but agile PBL is not limited to these micro-systems; rather, it flows over and through the porous boundaries between micro-, meso-, exo- and macro-systems. Exchanges between the students and their micro-systems are influenced by the connections with the meso-systems such as their relationships with their families and/or workplace, relationships with their peers, relationships with social and informal learning and the exo-systems where the students do not participate directly in the setting but are influenced by the linkages and processes of student support, academic development of academic staff, quality and research and the scholarship of teaching and learning. The patterns of behaviours can also be viewed from the macro-system vantage point, whereby the 'wider world' is seen as being in a reciprocal relationship with the tertiary education institution, not just as 'users' or 'receivers' of graduates, but as partnering with the university in developing students and as directly contributing to (and by extension benefitting from) the educational context. The dotted lines show the porousness of the boundaries between the different systems. The arrows show the possible dynamic interactions and interconnections at play between persons and the multilevel contexts.

This model helps to imagine education as facilitating learning that is fluid (Savin-Baden, 2014), through recognising the different systems in a learning ecology and responding by connecting these systems. This in turn enables various spaces (Savin-Baden, 2008) in the whole university and beyond for student learning, rather than being limited by one particular system such as the formal learning environment where teaching and learning commonly occur. Hence, there are chapters in this book about curriculum and assessment where formal learning and teaching take place (micro- and meso-systems). The chapters on quality, research and scholarship of teaching and learning, student support and academic development of academic staff recognise the distal ecology where the exo-systems are located. Even though students are not specifically located in these systems in most cases, they are indirectly or directly affected by the decisions and processes made in these spaces. More importantly, the ecology for learning model positions students as active agents contributing as producers of their own development throughout their lifetime. This is important as developing a way-of-being as students is a key learning outcome of agile PBL.

Overall then, this agile PBL ecology for learning is guided by imagining a space where learning and knowledge have no boundaries; where the contexts, values, and outcomes of higher education are better interconnected and integrated with 'external' environments; and where this connected learning will thus benefit students and the 'world'. The ecology for learning allows us to visualise the dynamic relationships between the different contexts and environments that are part of and impact on students' learning journeys. Agile PBL, in the way we develop the concept in this book, is a way of responding to these relationships and incorporating them into the learning design, in some cases literally. Ultimately, the ideal is towards building opportunities and a way-of-being capacity that allows students and graduates to approach life as problem-solvers, creators and reflective practitioners, benefiting both themselves as individuals, as well as their families, communities, society overall and 'the world'. In a dynamic and ever-changing environment, only an agile approach can fulfil this role, hence agile PBL.

References

Barnett, R. (1999). *Realising the university in an age of supercomplexity*. Buckingham, UK: SRHE and Open University Press.
Barnett, R. (2000). Supercomplexity and the curriculum. *Studies in Higher Education, 25*(3), 255–265.
Barnett, R. (2004). Learning in an unknown future. *Higher Education Research and Development, 23*(3), 247–260.

Barnett, R., & Coate, K. (2004). *Engaging the curriculum in higher education*. Berkshire, UK: Mc-Graw Hill Education.

Barrows, H. S. (1998). Essentials of problem-based learning. *Journal of Dental Education, 62*(9), 630–633.

Barrows, H. S. (2002). An overview of authentic problem-based learning. In K. N. L. Wee & Y. C. M. A. Kek (Eds.), *Authentic problem-based learning: Rewriting business education* (pp. 1–9). Singapore, Singapore: Prentice Hall.

Bass, R. (2012). Disrupting ourselves: The problem of learning in higher education. *Educause Review, 47*(2), 23–33.

Biggs, J. B. (1999). What the student does: Teaching for enhanced learning. *Higher Education Research and Development, 18*(1), 57–75.

Biggs, J. B. (2001). Enhancing learning: A matter of style or approach? In R. J. Sternberg & L. F. Zhang (Eds.), *Perspective on thinking, learning, and cognitive styles* (pp. 73–102). Mahwah, NJ: Lawrence Erlbaum Associates.

Bronfenbrenner, U. (1979). *The ecology of human development*. Cambridge, MA: Harvard University Press.

Bronfenbrenner, U. (2005a). Ecological systems theory. In U. Brofenbrenner (Ed.), *Making human beings human: Bioecological perspectives on human development* (pp. 106–173). Thousand Oaks, CA: Sage Publications.

Bronfenbrenner, U. (2005b). *Making human beings human: Bioecological perspectives on human development*. Thousand Oaks, CA: Sage Publications.

Bronfenbrenner, U., & Morris, P. A. (1998). The ecology of developmental processes. In R. M. Lerner (Ed.), *Handbook of child psychology* (5th ed., Vol. 1, pp. 993–1028). New York: Wiley.

Bronfenbrenner, U., & Morris, P. A. (2006). The bioecological model of human development. In W. Damon & R. M. Lerner (Eds.), *Handbook of child psychology* (6th ed., pp. 793–828). Hoboken, NJ: Wiley.

Brown, J. S., Collins, A., & Duguid, P. (1989). Situated cognition and the culture of learning. *Educational Researcher, 18*(1), 32–42.

Dede, C. (2013). Connecting the dots: New technology-based models for postsecondary learning. *Educause Review, 48*(5), 33–52.

Halpern, D. F. (1998). Teaching critical thinking for transfer across domains. *American Psychologist, 53*(4), 449–455.

Hmelo-Silver, C. E., & Barrows, H. S. (2008). Facilitating collaborative knowledge building. *Cognition and Instruction, 26*, 48–94.

Ito, M., Gutierrez, K., Livingstone, S., Penuel, B., Rhodes, J., Salen, K., et al. (2013). *Connected learning: An agenda for research and design*. Irvine, CA: Digital Media and Learning Research Hub. Retrieved from http://www.dmlhub.net/publications

Kek, M. Y. C. A., & Huijser, H. (2011). The power of problem-based learning in developing critical thinking skills: Preparing students for tomorrow's digital futures in today's classrooms. *Higher Education Research and Development, 30*(3), 317–329.

Lave, J., & Wenger, E. (1991). *Situated learning: Legitimate peripheral participation*. Cambridge, UK: Cambridge University Press.

Lombardi, M. M. (2007). Authentic learning for the 21st century: An overview. In D. G. Oblinger (Ed.), *Educause learning initiative 1* (pp. 1–12). Retrieved from https://library.educause.edu/~/media/files/library/2007/1/eli3009-pdf.pdf

Marton, F., & Saljo, R. (1976). On qualitative differences in learning – I: Outcome and process. *British Educational Research Journal, 46*(1), 4–11.

Pask, G. (1976). Styles and strategies of learning. *British Journal of Educational Psychology, 46*, 128–148.

Pea, R. D. (2004). The social and technological dimensions of scaffolding and related theoretical concepts for learning, education, and human activity. *Journal of Learning Sciences, 13*(2), 423–451.

Polanyi, M. (1962). *Personal knowledge: Towards a post-critical philosophy*. Chicago: The University of Chicago Press.

Polanyi, M. (1969). *Knowing and being*. Chicago: The University of Chicago Press.

Polanyi, M. (1983). *The tacit dimension*. Gloucester, UK: Peter Smith Publisher.

Prawatt, R. S. (1996). Constructivism, modern and postmodern. *Educational Psychologist, 31*(3/4), 215–225.

Rotherham, A. J., & Willngham, D. T. (2010). 21st century skills: Not new but a worthy challenge. *American Educator, 34*, 17–20.

Savin-Baden, M. (2008). *Learning spaces: Creating opportunities for knowledge creation in academic life*. Buckingham, UK: McGraw-Hill Education.

Savin-Baden, M. (2014). Using problem-based learning: New constellations for the 21st century. *Journal on Excellence in College Teaching, 25*(3&4), 197–219.

Scardamalia, M., & Bereiter, C. (2006). Knowledge building: Theory, pedagogy, and technology. In K. R. Sawyer (Ed.), *The Cambridge handbook of the learning sciences* (pp. 97–118). New York: Cambridge University Press.

Schon, D. A. (1983). *The reflective practitioner: How professionals think in action*. New York: Basic Books.

Sfard, A. (1998). On two metaphors for learning and the dangers of choosing just one. *Educational Researcher, 27*(2), 4–13.

Sharples, M., Adams, A., Ferguson, R., Gaved, M., Mcandrew, P., Rienties, B., et al. (2014). *Innovating pedagogy 2014: Open university innovation Report 3*. Milton Keynes, UK: Open University.

Vygotsky, L. S. (1978). *Mind in society: The development of higher mental processes* (M. Cole & S. Scribner, Eds.). Cambridge, MA: Harvard University Press.

Wood, D., Bruner, J. S., & Ross, G. (1976). The role of tutoring in problem solving. *Journal of Child Psychology and Psychiatry, 17*(2), 89–100.

Chapter 3
Agile PBL and the Next Generation of Learners

Introduction

In Chap. 2, we outlined our vision and model for an agile PBL ecology for learning. A key challenge we are aiming to address with agile PBL is the next generation of learners, both in terms of what skills they bring and what skills they need. This chapter explores the characteristics of a new generation of students and the idea of twenty-first-century skills. The particular emphasis here is how the two are, or should be, aligned and how an agile PBL provides opportunities to both draw on skills that a new generation of learners brings to the universities and empower these learners with the skills and attitudes they need to succeed upon graduation. An agile PBL ecology for learning allows us not only to recognise the myriad of factors, elements and layers that impact on learning but also to respond to these in both a responsive *and* proactive way, so that the learning environment is optimised for everyone involved.

With the first decade of the twenty-first century well behind us, the universities in general are facing a situation where they are expected to 'educate' more people from wider and more diverse backgrounds than ever before (Bradley, Noonan, Nugent, & Scales, 2008; James, Krause, & Jennings, 2010; Oblinger, 2010; Thomas, 2002). Yet, models of education in the university have arguably not changed in any fundamental way since the 1800s (Goodchild & Wechsler, 1989). As Tapscott and Williams (2010, pp. 18–19) argue, the current model of pedagogy, which is at the heart of the modern university, is fast becoming obsolete. In the industrial model of student mass production, the teacher is the 'broadcaster'. A broadcast is, by definition, the transmission of information from transmitter to receiver in a one-way, linear fashion. Broadcast learning may have been appropriate for a previous economic environment, and a previous generation, but increasingly it is failing the needs of a new generation of students who are about to enter the supercomplex world of uncertainties.

© Springer Science+Business Media Singapore 2017
M.Y.C.A. Kek, H. Huijser, *Problem-based Learning into the Future*,
DOI 10.1007/978-981-10-2454-2_3

Tapscott and Williams (2010) go on to develop their case for what they call 'collaborative learning', which they equate with 'social learning'. This creates an interesting link to PBL approaches to learning, which are inherently 'collaborative' and 'social'. PBL has been a notable exception to 'broadcast learning' since its introduction in the 1960s, and it was at a time of radical departure from the teacher-centred models. However, it has been relatively confined to particular disciplines, even if it is inherently designed to work on an interdisciplinary level. An additional element in the twenty-first century is the increasing ubiquity of digital technologies, both in the workplace and in educational contexts. It is urgent and crucial that universities adapt to changing patterns and contexts of education and work for two related reasons: firstly, to be able to adequately prepare their students for the needs of the twenty-first-century workplace and wider context and, secondly, to respond to and engage with the skills and characteristics that students bring to the educational environment. In short, it is urgent for universities to stay *relevant* and survive in a higher education context where online offerings are increasingly becoming the norm, which in turn means that universities can no longer depend on their physical location or traditional funding models to operate and add value to the society in which they are situated. Indeed, as we have begun to argue, they need to engage in much more deeper, responsive and agile ways to a wider learning ecology in which they are a part of and situated.

Barrows' PBL model is often lauded as an 'authentic' approach to learning (Wee & Kek, 2002) and 'authentic' in terms of our day-to-day environments, both at work and personal, and it has been increasingly characterised by a blend of face-to-face and technology-supported contexts. This fits with Barrows (2002) definition of PBL discussed in Chap. 2, which includes the central proposition that PBL is an education process that requires the learner to go through the same activities during learning that are valued in the real world. In other words, it is no longer a matter of *whether* to use technology to support PBL teaching approaches or PBL curriculum, but rather a matter of *how* to design a PBL curriculum, which entails the teaching approach, learning process, assessments, learning environment, problems (content) and evaluation, in the most effective manner *with* technology in an integrated manner. In other words, the question is how to rejuvenate PBL curricula for the twenty-first century and how to make it more agile, without compromising its fundamental principles. As Rotherham and Willingham (2010, p. 20) put it, 'devising a twenty-first century skills curriculum requires more than paying lip service to content knowledge'. This leads us to the central point of this book: fundamental PBL principles or spirit does not need to be compromised because they are very well suited to deliver the kind of learning outcomes that are generally considered to be needed for the contemporary *and* future workplace.

In terms of the latter, it is interesting, for example, that some educators are already beginning to talk about social media literacies (Rheingold, 2010), and new literacies will be needed as technologies continue to evolve at a rapid pace. In this twenty-first-century context, it is not important what students can do with a particular digital tool or suite of tools, but rather how fast they can learn to use new tools and adapt to fast-changing circumstances, including the ability to identify entrepreneurial ways of leveraging new technologies (Macmahon & Huijser, 2015). This is what we call a way-of-being or adaptive expertise throughout this book.

Research in learning sciences has emerged highlighting two major forms of expertise – routine expertise and adaptive expertise (Bransford et al., 2006). Adaptive expertise is a form of expert knowledge that can support 'continual learning, improvisation, and expansion' (Bransford et al., 2006) or, in short, open up innovations in society. Adaptive expertise is a concept first observed and studied by Hatano and Inagaki (1984). In contrast, a 'routine expert' refers to a person who is efficient and accurate and becomes even more efficient and accurate through time when addressing familiar problems. This form of expertise is developed through the repeated application of procedural knowledge on the same tasks or problems, i.e. with a well-established pattern or modes of processing a task or problem. However, this form of expertise is adequate in a context where the problems are similar, with familiar or constant variables surrounding the problems. The challenge here is around what happens if the student has not gone beyond procedural efficiency. Routine experts, even though they may have declarative knowledge and they may apply procedural knowledge repeatedly to address problems at hand, appear to perform without much understanding (nor reflection) and exploration or experimentation beyond the familiar (Hatano & Inagaki, 1984). This becomes a problem in an environment where the problems change continuously and, furthermore, where there is an increasing need to anticipate potential problems (and how to address them) either in advance or as part of entrepreneurial planning. This is where a 'way-of-being' becomes a salient part of becoming adaptive experts, which is what we would like to think of our graduates when they leave university.

Adaptive experts are more likely to go beyond routine competencies with variations, rather than in terms of speed and accuracy of solving familiar problems (Hatano & Inagaki, 1984). These experts apply their conceptual schemas in a more adaptive manner due to their understanding of why their procedures work; they also modify known procedures or even invent new procedures by responding in a flexible manner to contextual variations (Hatano & Inagaki, 1984), making them more flexible and innovative and indeed more agile. This is precisely what we want in twenty-first-century learners – to be adaptive and flexible as they traverse from the university to the supercomplex world of super uncertainties. However, it requires an educational landscape that allows them to actively explore, experiment and reflect (Hatano & Inagaki, 1984; Hatano & Oura, 2003) and that would eventually lead them to continually adapt to change (Hatano & Oura, 2003). However, for such learning to be reached and attributes to be developed, and to receive the full benefits from an agile PBL, we argue that it needs to be applied in a consistent manner across an entire curriculum, rather than in a piecemeal fashion or in isolated pockets. Naturally, this is not an easy task and requires a monumental shift in attitudes in the short term, but we argue that such a shift is ultimately inevitable and indeed desirable. By not focusing on a way-of-being, preparing students for future learning (Bransford & Schwartz, 1999), and by not changing the pedagogy and curriculum, we run the risk of educating pseudo-experts at best – students whose expertise does not mirror the expertise needed for real world, thinking inside or outside the academic disciplines and knowledges, and students who lack what Sternberg (2003) calls successful intelligence.

Why *Not* Problem-Based Learning in the Twenty-First Century?

It is relatively easy to make a theoretical argument about why PBL is a good approach to teaching in the twenty-first century as it appears to tick all the right boxes such as graduate attributes, learning outcomes, student engagement and student success and positive and significant educational student experiences. The key skill required in the twenty-first century is the ability to deal with a massive amount of information and turn this information into 'knowledge', that is, the ability to critically select and manipulate information and creatively repurpose it for whatever context it needs to be applied to. Moreover, it increasingly requires the ability to recognise and anticipate *potential* contexts for which that information may be repurposed, which calls for entrepreneurial skills. The latter does not necessarily mean 'to start an enterprise', but rather to have an entrepreneurial attitude in all aspects of life, including in a workplace. In an educational context, Jaros and Deakin-Crick (2007) explain it as follows:

> Instead of expending their learning power on rote-storing of solutions to eternal problems and 'facts', students must acquire methods of retrieving and manipulating knowledge and information. They must be able to recognize and manage their own learning processes and pathways, defining them in terms of simple local parameters, and sharing them with others on a time-scale dictated by the event itself. They must be able to learn while working on the problem and to use self-assessment to control the direction, intensity, and standard of their work. (p. 424)

This does not merely signify a minor change in education, which can be addressed by tweaking the way we teach and adjusting our approaches to teaching around the edges. Rather it signifies what some call a paradigm shift, as illuminated, for example, by Wee and Kek (2002) in their use of PBL to 'transform' marketing education to better prepare students for the world of marketing. Deakin-Crick (2007, p. 137) notes that 'this paradigm shift is towards a relational and transformative model of learning, in which the creation of interdependent communities of intentional learners provides a basis for the integration of "traditional academic" skills and outcomes with the learning dispositions, values and attitudes necessary to meet the demands of the emerging "networked society"'.

Similarly, Şendag and Odabaşi (2009, p. 132) argue that 'today's working conditions have required fundamental changes in the profiles of work power, which basically stemmed from the rapid change and transformation in the nature of information'. They expand on this by stressing the ability to think critically, especially in the context of technological change, for 'technological changes along with the changes in the workplace have made critical thinking abilities more important than ever before' (Sendag & Odabasi, 2009, p. 132), to which we can add the ability to creatively apply knowledge in ways it has not been applied before (Huijser & Kek, 2016).

The Partnership for 21st Century Skills collective has developed an extensive framework for twenty-first-century learning (2009) which outlines in great detail the kinds of skills, literacies and attitudes that may be required. They usefully split these into four main themes, with a series of related skills and literacies:

- *Core subjects and twenty-first-century themes*

    - Global awareness
    - Financial, economic, business and entrepreneurial literacy
    - Civic literacy
    - Health literacy

- *Learning and innovation skills*

    - Creativity and innovation
    - Critical thinking and problem-solving
    - Communication and collaboration

- *Information, media and technology skills*

    - Information literacy
    - Media literacy
    - Information, communications and technology (ICT) literacy

- *Life and career skills*

    - Flexibility and adaptability
    - Initiative and self-direction
    - Social and cross-cultural skills
    - Productivity and accountability
    - Leadership and responsibility

These themes, skills and literacies are echoed in the more recent 'Elements of the Creative Classroom Research Model' (Johnson, Adams Becker, Estrada, & Freeman, 2014, p. 4) which, as part of the *NMC Horizon Report: 2014 Higher Education Edition*, focuses on innovative pedagogical practices and details all the elements that are involved in such practices. The model has 8 themes and 28 related elements, which overall are consistent with what fundamentally characterises a PBL teaching and learning system:

- *Content and Curricula*

    - Emotional intelligence
    - Cross- and transdisciplinary
    - Open educational resources
    - Meaningful activities

- *Assessment*

    - Engaging assessment formats
    - Formative assessment
    - Recognition of informal and non-formal learning

- *Learning practices*

    - Learning by exploring
    - Learning by creating
    - Learning by playing
    - Self-regulated learning
    - Personalised learning
    - Peer-to-peer collaboration

- *Teaching practices*

    - Soft skills
    - Individual strengths
    - Multiple learning styles
    - Multiple modes of thinking

- *Organisation*

    - Monitoring quality
    - Innovative timetables
    - Innovating services

- *Leadership and values*

    - Innovation management
    - Social entrepreneurship
    - Social inclusion and equity

- *Connectedness*

    - Networking with real world
    - Social networks
    - Learning events

- *Infrastructure*

    - ICT infrastructure
    - Physical space

In the meantime, research on student development in higher education in general shows that the more time and energy students devote to educationally purposeful activities, the more they are engaged (Astin, 1993; Kuh, Kinzie, Buckley, Bridges, & Hayek, 2007; Pascarella & Terenzini, 2005). This research implies that the more universities can create purposively designed learning environments that channel students towards highly engaging learning and activities, the more these institutions would have created the conditions for their students' success, as it relates to student satisfaction, learning and development of learning outcomes and persistence (Astin, 1993; Pascarella & Terenzini, 2005). Chickering and Reiser's (1993) vector of development, which is an extension of Chickering's (1969) work on education and identity, suggests that students move through a number of psychosocial development phases termed 'vectors' during their university studies. Students navigate these vectors at different rates, often not sequential and often reiterative, but regardless, they do form 'major highways for journeying toward individuation' (Chickering & Reisser, 1993, p. 35). PBL learning processes and activities, when designed well, could also be seen as travelling along these vectors of development, requiring reiterative learning processes; complicated problems; going over the process again and again until it becomes second nature to students; representing the identities of PBL students as competent problem-solvers, independent and self-directed; and critically applying and creating knowledge to be able to manage today's world of complex and mixed demands of work, business, social and personal lives. However, the most convincing argument for why PBL ideally suits today's university contexts lies in Chickering and Reiser's 'three admonitions' of, firstly, the integration of work and learning; secondly, recognition and respect for individual differences; and thirdly, acknowledgement of the cyclical nature of learning and development.

In this way, PBL can be seen as having the potential to simultaneously facilitate and respond to the paradigm shift laid out above. An often cited strength of PBL initiatives is that they facilitate the development of transferable or 'soft' skills (sometimes called 'employability skills') such as teamwork, communication, information literacy, critical thinking, lifelong learning, problem-solving, self-management, planning and organisation and innovation and enterprise (Kek & Huijser, 2011; Moore & Poikela, 2011). On a global level, many employers identify such transferable skills as more important than technical skills or factual knowledge (Drohan, Mauffette, & Allard, 2011). PBL as a pedagogy and curriculum potentially opens the universities to better address these needs and to move away from more traditional transmissive models to learning and teaching, which are often purely focused on the transfer of declarative knowledges. Majoor and Aarts (2010, p. 249, our emphases) cite the following summary about higher education by the World Bank:

> The world today is increasingly dependent on knowledge and therefore on people who are capable of *generating* and *applying* knowledge. Thus, the potential of a society to develop is critically related to the comprehensiveness and quality of its educational system and rate of participation of the population in that system.

Again, the emphasis here is on *generating* and *applying* knowledge, rather than reproducing it, which is what more traditional transmissive approaches focus on. Majoor and Aarts (2010) further argue that the problem with traditional teaching approaches is not only that the knowledge thus acquired is static but more importantly that it is often outdated in a global context in which knowledge changes rapidly. They note that the qualitative challenges in education have their roots in the traditional transmissive tradition, which continues to dominate education in many developing countries and is not being adjusted to the changing needs of society (Davies, Fidler, & Gorbis, 2011; Majoor & Aarts, 2010), at least not fast enough.

Thus, there appears to be little debate about the proposition that PBL is a pedagogy and curriculum that has the *potential* to empower graduates with twenty-first-century skills, even if there is significant debate about whether the evidence actually supports this (Archetti, 2011). However, this raises two key questions: how do you ensure the desired learning for all students, and how do you integrate technology into this process in meaningful ways? In terms of the latter, Savin-Baden (2006, p. 10) has argued that 'problem-based learning and surfing the internet share similar qualities, for example the process of learning in problem-based learning teams is interactive, non-sequential, random, and often seems rather chaotic'. This in turn puts a significant amount of pressure on teachers: the PBL process has the potential to make teachers feel profoundly uncomfortable, and indeed it often does. Savin-Baden (p. 10) identifies the conflict for teachers as arising in the need for them to allow students 'freedom to manage knowledge, rather than keeping their previous roles and relationships with students as the controllers and patrollers of knowledge'.

For many teachers, PBL can mean a major 'culture shock' and requires a change in attitude and approach that goes to the core of their identity as teachers. This is precisely why PBL is difficult to implement in a consistent manner across an entire educational institution or, even less ambitiously, across a particular faculty, program or course. However, if we accept that PBL has the potential to develop twenty-first-century skills in students, then it is crucial that their teachers either already possess such skills themselves or are at the very least willing and open to 'teach' such skills or 'teach' a curriculum designed with a set of learning outcomes that comprise both skills, or procedural knowledge and declarative content knowledge, compared to a curriculum that teaches only the discipline knowledge or content. In other words, teachers need to be lifelong learners themselves and be comfortable opening up and operating in a world where there is an abundance of information, but which is at the same time 'non-linear, random and chaotic'. Şendag and Odabaşi (2009, p. 135) stress the importance of training teachers who have critical thinking, problem-solving, collaboration and networking skills, which they argue is 'a must in the current century'. This is important, because the role of teacher is often considered to be crucial in a PBL context (Kek & Huijser, 2011; Luck & Norton, 2004; Martyn, Terwijn, Kek, & Huijser, 2014; Omale, Hung, Luetkehans, & Cooke-Plagwitz, 2009), especially when students are first exposed to PBL. The preparation of teachers who are comfortable in both a PBL context and in online environments is therefore a vital part of ensuring that PBL delivers on its promise of developing students who are self-directed, lifelong learners, or what Black, Mccormick, James, and Peddler (2006) call 'intentional learners'. In a context where learning in higher education appears to be increasingly heading into learning and teaching environments rich with technologies (Davies, 2012; Johnson et al., 2014), blended forms of PBL learning environments, and various PBL constellations (Savin-Baden, 2014), offer the potential to prepare students for such significantly changed learning environments, and more importantly to equip them with the tools to get the most out of such learning environments. A related issue here concerns a new generation of students, and their characteristics; in other words, not only are current teaching practices outdated in many ways, and particularly in terms of their learning outcomes, but they may also be inappropriate in the way they target a new generation of students.

The Digital Generation

At this stage, it is important to draw attention to our use of the terms 'next generation of learners' and 'the digital generation'. It would be relatively easy to confuse this term with the widespread use of the terms 'digital natives' (Prensky, 2001) and 'net generation' (Oblinger & Oblinger, 2005). We will thus call this new generation of students the 'digital generation', to capture their engagement with, and immersion in, digital tools, rather than their age. As noted, much has been written about what is variously called Generation Y, the net generation (Oblinger & Oblinger, 2005), Millennials (Sankey, 2006) and digital natives (Prensky, 2001). Much of this writing however has a high 'hype factor', in that it presumes a radical break with the past. Prensky, for example, argues that 'our students have changed radically. Today's students are no longer the people our educational system was designed to teach' (para.1). He claims that 'today's students think and process information fundamentally differently from their predecessors' (2001, para. 4). This sets up a binary between students (digital natives) and teachers (digital immigrants). Ultimately, this then leads to his central question: 'should the digital native students learn the old ways, or should their digital immigrant educators learn the new?' (Prensky, 2001, para. 17). While this is clearly a deliberately provocative question, it has the unhelpful side effect of reinforcing an either/or binary, by simplifying both the category of 'student' and 'educator', thereby not only ignoring an increasingly diverse student population but also closing the door on the possibility that skills associated with digital natives could be acquired at a later stage, or at least appropriated in different, yet meaningful ways (Huijser, 2006), and that such skills could therefore also apply to mature age students, for example. Prensky and other proponents of the 'digital native thesis' have been widely critiqued for using overgeneralisations, but the key characteristics of digital natives that are identified include: digital natives prefer images over text; they prefer games over 'serious work'; they function best when networked; they can't pay attention (or choose not to); and finally, they have perfected their digital technologies-related skills (Koutropoulos, 2010; Oblinger & Oblinger). Some of these claims are supported with some evidence, even if it is somewhat tenuous. Sontag (2009), for example, draws attention to some evidence that social changes associated with technology use by teenagers (a 'generation of learners enmeshed in connective technologies', p. 1) impact on cognitive processes. The key point to make here, however, is that the next generation of learners is highly heterogeneous, in terms of access to digital technologies, use of digital technologies and applied skills in this regard. In other words, while there is clearly a highly divergent use of digital technologies, a basic level of use of digital technologies is nevertheless near-universal.

Basically, Prensky's argument is largely positional in nature and not based on specific empirical research (Koutropoulos, 2010), and it has attracted a lot of critique since it was first introduced (Bennett & Maton, 2010; Burton, Summers, Noble, & Gibbings, 2015; Jones, Ramanau, Cross, & Healing, 2010; Kennedy, Judd, Dalgarnot, & Waycott, 2010). As noted above, the idea that there is a homogeneous generation of students has been widely debunked as a myth, even if it persists as a popular notion. For example, Jones et al. (2010, p. 722) note that 'the generation is not homogeneous in its use and appreciation of new technologies, and there are significant variations amongst students that lie within the Net generation band'. More recently, empirical research is beginning to appear which cuts through some of the hype associated with this 'digital generation' (Kennedy, Judd, Churchward, Gray, & Krause, 2008; Kvavik, 2005), and it is beginning to show its heterogeneity in more detail (Czerniewicz & Brown, 2010; Harigittai, 2010; Oliver & Goerke, 2007). While these studies confirm that the digital generation has grown up in an environment 'saturated' by technology, they also suggest that there is much variation in terms of types of use, associated skills and, importantly for our purposes here, preferences for use in education. A large Australian study by Kennedy et al. (2008, p. 108) shows that 'many first year students are highly tech-savvy. However, when one moves beyond entrenched technologies and tools (e.g. computers, mobile phones, email), the patterns of access and use of a range of other technologies show considerable variation'. For example, while Kennedy et al. (2008) found a significant growth in students' general use of instant messaging, blogs and podcasting, they also found that the majority of students rarely or never used these technologies for study, and importantly, 'the transfer from a social or entertainment technology to a learning technology is neither automatic nor guaranteed' (Kennedy et al., 2008, p. 119). In a related study that builds on this evidence, Kennedy et al. (2010, p. 339) make a distinction, based on their empirical data, between what they call 'power users' (advanced technology users) (14 %), 'ordinary users' (27 %), 'irregular users' (14 %) and 'basic users' (45 %). The largest group, basic users, was 'rudimentary technology users, who used only standard web-based applications and mobile phones on a relatively frequent basis' (p. 339). In other words, the Prensky's (2001) 'digital natives' are more likely to be the exception rather than the rule.

However, in terms of outcomes, it is important that we strive for 'digital native'-like competencies. In other words, in the apparent scramble to appeal to the digital generation, there is often no direct engagement with what they *should* be able to do as part of their learning journey, and how this should be applied and adapted to work or entrepreneurial environments. As Koutropoulos (2010, p. 526, original emphasis) argues, for example, 'digital natives *should* also exploit that physical ability to learn to function in environments that don't necessarily have the tools that they are used to'. He goes on to question a range of other assumptions that are associated with the digital generation: 'the fact that one can mechanically go through the motions of searching for someone on Google doesn't mean that they possess the critical literacy and information literacy required to determine which results were quality results' (2010, p. 527). Interestingly, it is at that level of learning, and what we are calling twenty-first-century skills, that PBL is at its most powerful, because of two reasons: Firstly, an inherent part of the PBL process is identifying and exploring prior skills, as they are relevant to the PBL problem, so this means recognising the diverse skills that the digital generation brings to the classroom (e.g. those skills acquired in the meso- and macro-contexts of their learning environments) and leveraging those skills as part of the learning process. Secondly, the PBL process is outcomes driven, which means that a well-designed PBL program does not assume anything, but does clearly define the exit skills and actively works towards developing those skills.

Towards an Agile PBL

So far we have identified the potential relevance and outcomes of PBL and the need for teachers to acquire the skills to activate the type of learning to occur in a PBL context, on a theoretical level. However, there is a large gap between the theory and the practice, especially because PBL has the biggest potential impact if it is seen as a holistic pedagogy and curriculum, rather than as one of many teaching techniques that can be addressed in isolation. If we consider this in the context of an agile PBL ecology for learning, it becomes clear that nothing in such an ecology works in isolation. Thus, applying PBL in isolation would not have achieved any of the desired intentions that we are identifying here. Any rewards, however small, from PBL can be achieved by intentional design of the pedagogy and at the curriculum level. This is the key point and one that is often overlooked in the critiques of PBL. Most of the empirically based studies of PBL are based on individual units of study or courses. They are often case studies produced by teachers who are PBL enthusiasts or who are experimenting with PBL (Brodie & Gibbings, 2007; Huijser & Wali, 2012; Omale et al., 2009; Yeh, 2010). The results of such studies are often difficult to generalise, and they often create perceptions of benefits, rather than hard evidence about learning outcomes. It is therefore no coincidence that the main critiques of PBL are often levelled at the perceived lack of evidence for the benefits claimed (Eck, 2002; Sanson-Fisher & Lynagh, 2005). Archetti (2011), for example, asks the following provocative question: 'are teachers simply deriving the expected benefits from the characteristics of PBL activities rather than from the evidence of students' learning experience?' Our response to this question is twofold. Firstly, the question is based on an earlier mentioned traditional, and arguably outdated, conceptualisation of knowledge, rather than on the types of skills that most of the claims about PBL benefits relate to. This is what Jaros and Deakin-Crick (2007, p. 424, original emphasis) refer to when they discuss a 'new approach to curriculum structure and delivery, and a new style of benchmarking in which the competencies and the learning outcomes are *supported*, rather than led, by subject knowledge'. PBL is such an approach to both curriculum structure and delivery and should therefore be measured as such.

Secondly, the direct learning outcomes, in the form of transferable skills, are not the type of skills that can be developed in isolation in a single course or unit of study. Instead, they are the type of skills that will only be further developed progressively if a consistent intentional pedagogy, across an entire curriculum, is implemented, as they involve learning of knowledges, skills and dispositions that cannot be easily measured in the form of an exam in one sitting. A whole-of-institution approach is therefore a critical element of leveraging the potential benefits of PBL, but this demands significant organisational commitment and resources, and the types of critique outlined above, though flawed, create a barrier to such organisational implementation of PBL. Not only that, we argue throughout this book that an agile PBL pedagogy and curriculum do not just take place in a traditional classroom context but aim to move the PBL problems into authentic contexts (i.e. into the macro-context), such as workplaces, communities and society in general, as early in the curriculum as possible, and furthermore, it aims to involve employers and other external partners in the educational process as early as possible too. In an agile PBL context, the boundaries between the different spheres of the PBL ecology for learning are necessarily porous; the responsibility for learning concerns everyone involved, rather than just the teachers.

Implementing PBL in a course or program is often challenging enough, and of course, this challenge multiplies when it is a university-wide implementation. It often encounters major obstacles, ranging from professional learning needs to expectations about resource needs. In short, the theory behind PBL is convincing, but the link to practice is not always explicitly made. Therefore, we imagine an agile PBL ecology for learning as empowering a 'way-of-being' in students, opening the possibilities of ubiquitous learning. An agile PBL ecology for learning, leveraging a variety of technologies, provides a way to imagine the knowledge, skills and disposition 'flow' between the different ecosystems within the university environment, but also between the universities and the world outside the universities (macro-system) more seamlessly. This is crucial if the goal is to develop an agile PBL for a new generation of learners and to make their learning experience as 'authentic' as possible in relation to what they face during their studies or are likely to encounter in the world they will live and work in upon graduation.

Digital Technologies and the Digital Generation in an Agile PBL Context

A considerable amount of writing has emerged in recent years about the potential of new and emerging technologies for learning (Johnson, Adams Becker, & Hall, 2015). Such writing tends to advocate the use of mobile and social media for their potential affordances ('we will be able to do…' versus 'we have been able to do…') (Rheingold, 2010), but it is often characterised by a lack of empirical evidence to back up the claims. On a theoretical level, mobile and social media technologies appear to fit very closely with social constructivist conceptualisations of teaching and learning, which are widely regarded as most effective and which fit neatly with

PBL. However, despite the apparent momentum in the adoption of mobile and social media in formal (and informal) learning contexts, there is much less clarity about their effectiveness with regard to student learning and outcomes. For example, while we know that many education institutions and individual departments have their own *Facebook* pages, in what way does this contribute to student learning outcomes, and what is the evidence to support this? Engagement is one thing, but tangible learning outcomes is the area we, as educators, really need to focus on before substantial claims about a technology's usefulness can be made.

The key element here is that available technology should be used where relevant and in alignment with the pedagogical approach, rather than the other way around. For example, on a pragmatic level, Pepper (2009, p. 129) identifies the following key benefits of PBL:

- Students deciding on the information and skills they need to investigate issues while building on their current knowledge to synthesise then integrate new information
- Students taking responsibility for the learning that occurs within their group while instructors monitor and facilitate student learning
- Students engaging with the learning experience more fully

In terms of the first point, one of the main benefits of PBL is that it explicitly makes use of students' prior knowledge, thus often successfully manages to engage students, because the learning process starts from 'where they are at' (Brodie & Gibbings, 2007; Tate & Klein-Collins, 2012). This includes the use of online and mobile applications and environments that students are familiar with, especially if they are used in the authentic contexts in which students will engage with problems. The last point in particular is important and related to the other two points, and as Hu (2011) notes, 'student engagement is considered the pathway to success in college'. This engagement is further stimulated by group work, which is another central element of PBL. In relation to group work, and the development of learning communities, social media applications (such as *Facebook* or *Twitter*) can be used to develop such learning communities (Hall & Maugham, 2015; Yeh, 2010). Similarly, multi-user online environments (Omale et al., 2009) and even massive open online courses (MOOCs) (Davies, 2012) can be used, where relevant, for group work and the development of learning communities. There are no hard and fast rules around which tools to use and which not to use, or when and how. As Archetti (2011) argues, 'the effectiveness of PBL as a teaching and learning tool entirely depends on the context of its implementation' or, in other words, its agility to leverage on the complete ecology for learning, rather than isolated pockets of it. Similarly, the development of a technology-supported or 'blended' PBL learning environment should be responsive to where the learners are at and where they should be at the end of a particular unit of study. The latter refers both to how various technologies are relevant in the authentic workplace setting and to how to potentially create the opportunities to address authentic work-based problems. Getting that balance right is fundamental to the success of PBL as a pedagogy and curriculum, and to get that balance right ideally requires a whole-of-institution and a whole-of-curriculum approach, which includes sufficient and just-in-time professional learning for teachers so that they can activate their PBL groups with confidence, for as Savin-Baden (2006, p. 10) has argued, 'PBL online does require that tutors are supported'. This is crucial, especially when students are first engaged with PBL-based learning (and moreover, a blended PBL environment), which is when students often perceive a lack of guidance (Luck & Norton, 2004). As noted above, the teacher's facilitation role is a vital part of PBL, and this is not different in blended, technology-supported forms of PBL, nor is it that far removed from a mentor role in a workplace or business context.

'Whole-of-Curriculum' and 'Whole-of-Institution' Approaches

The implementation of successful technology-supported and blended PBL for the next generation of learners requires both a whole-of-curriculum and a whole-of-institution worldview, and by success, we mean that it will achieve the outcomes that are celebrated in the PBL literature and discussed above. This is not an easy task, that is in finding the right blend to what Pascarella and Terenzini (2005) refer to as the *interconnectedness* that are more likely to produce a more effective educational experience. We argue that this is the transformative element of an agile PBL ecology for learning. As noted in the introduction, this is very much a vision and a starting point in this book, rather than a blueprint for implementation, but we believe it is crucial to begin to imagine such a vision.

In short, it needs courage from those in senior management and educational administrative positions at the universities. It requires careful planning of PBL applications across the curriculum, as well as choices about technology to support the desired learning outcomes. Importantly, this is not a one-time process, but rather an ongoing process that is dynamic and adaptive to changing contexts, both internally and externally. Once the curriculum has been mapped or constructively aligned (Biggs & Tang, 2011) according to agile PBL spirit, learning needs of staff should be identified and acted upon and constructively aligned to their 'training' needs to effectively 'teach' in a technology-supported agile PBL context. This is particularly important when it comes to the incorporation of technology-supported applications, because the teachers need to be confidently able to facilitate the development of learning communities in online environments. The IT staff working in the background need to have their professional learning needs met as well, so that they can provide the appropriate support needed, at the appropriate time. Closely related to this is the recruitment of staff. As a learning organisation that is based on a transformative technology-supported agile PBL approach, new staff need to be recruited not simply based on the knowledge they possess, but rather on their willingness to learn and adapt on a continuous basis. In other words, they need to be able to model the same skills and attitudes that we expect students to learn. If the desired outcomes are students who are lifelong learners, then staff need to model what that means and embody the same principles. Again, this may sound straightforward, but it is far from it in reality.

An agile PBL allows organisations to design adaptive and blended problem-based learning environments that suit their specific student cohorts and their particular contexts. The suite of e-learning tools is potentially endless and ever growing. At the moment, it includes social networking tools (such as *Facebook*, *YouTube* and *Twitter*) that can be integrated into an agile PBL curriculum, along with e-learning tools such as online classrooms, blogs, wikis, multi-user virtual environments (MUVEs) and conferencing technologies. In addition, a series of mobile technologies, such as smart phones and tablets, can be explored for their potential affordances in an agile, blended problem-based learning environment. In each case, decisions need to be made about where and when it is most appropriate, and these decisions hinge, on the one hand, on what students, as the next generation of learners, bring to the learning environments and, on the other hand, on what they should be able to do at that particular stage of the curriculum. Agile PBL problems can thus be designed in such a way that they include both 'comfortable' technologies and 'new' ones in the educational process and indeed 'future' ones.

Conclusion

Overall, we have made a start in this chapter to imagine what an agile PBL context might look like and how it might suit a new generation of learners, both in terms of what they bring to the learning environment and in terms of the twenty-first-century skills they need to learn. The assumption from the beginning is that with regard to technology-supported PBL, it is not so much a question of *whether* anymore, but rather of *how best to*, and not a question of *whether* it will replace face-to-face PBL, but rather *how best to* blend it with face-to-face PBL, which not coincidently mirrors the 'real world' outside the university. The challenge is how to design a technology-supported agile PBL environment that stays true to the original intentions of PBL and that leverages technology to *enhance* the impact of learning, rather than reducing it. This is the challenge that we are taking up throughout this book. In the next chapter, we will therefore zoom in on the role and place of learning outcomes in an agile PBL ecology for learning.

References

Archetti, C. (2011). Friend or foe? Problem-based learning (PBL) in political communication. *European Political Science, 11*(4), 551–566. doi:10.1057/eps.2011.40.

Astin, A. W. (1993). *What matters in college? Four critical years revisited.* San Francisco: Jossey-Bass.

Barrows, H. S. (2002). An overview of authentic problem-based learning. In K. N. L. Wee & Y. C. M. A. Kek (Eds.), *Authentic problem-based learning: Rewriting business education* (pp. 1–9). Singapore, Singapore: Prentice Hall.

Bennett, S., & Maton, K. (2010). Beyond the 'digital natives' debate: Towards a more nuanced understanding of students' technology experiences. *Journal of Computer Assisted Learning, 26*(5), 321–331.

Biggs, J., & Tang, C. (2011). *Teaching for quality learning at university* (4th ed.). Maidenhead, UK: Open University Press.

Black, P., Mccormick, R., James, M., & Pedder, D. (2006). Learning how to learn and assessment for learning: A theoretical inquiry. *Research Papers in Education, 21*(2), 119–132.

Bradley, D., Noonan, P., Nugent, H., & Scales, B. (2008). *Review of Australian higher education*. Canberra, Australia: Department of Education, Employment and Workplace Relations.

Bransford, J. D., Barron, B., Pea, R. D., Meltzoff, A., Kuhl, P., Bell, P., et al. (2006). Foundations and opportunities for an interdisciplinary science of learning. In K. R. Sawyer (Ed.), *Cambridge handbook of the learning sciences* (pp. 19–34). New York: Cambridge University Press.

Bransford, J. D., & Schwartz, D. L. (1999). Rethink transfer. A simple proposal with multiple implications. *Review of Research in Education, 24*(1), 61–100.

Brodie, L., & Gibbings, P. (2007). *Developing problem-based leanring communities in virtual space*. Paper presented at the Connected: 2007 International Conference on Design Education, University of New South Wales, Sydney, Australia.

Burton, L., Summers, J., Noble, K., & Gibbings, P. (2015). Digital literacy in higher education: The rhetoric and the reality. In M. Harmes, H. Huijser, & P. A. Danaher (Eds.), *Myths in education, learning and teaching: Policies, practices and principles* (pp. 151–172). New York: Palgrave.

Chickering, A. W. (1969). *Education and identity*. San Francisco: Jossey-Bass.

Chickering, A. W., & Reisser, L. (1993). *Education and identity* (2nd ed.). San Francisco: Jossey-Bass.

Czerniewicz, L., & Brown, C. (2010). Debunking the 'digital native': Beyond digital apartheid, towards digital democracy. *Journal of Computer Assisted Learning, 26*(5), 357–369.

Davies, M. (2012). Can universities survive the digital revolution? *Quadrant Online*. Retrieved March 8, 2013, from http://www.quadrant.org.au/magazine/issue/2012/12/can-universities-survive-the-digital-revolution

Davies, A., Fidler, D., & Gorbis, M. (2011). In *Future work skills 2020* (pp. 1–14). Institute for the Future for the University of Phoenix Research Institute.

Deakin-Crick, R. (2007). Learning how to learn: The dynamic assessment of learning power. *The Curriculum Journal, 18*(2), 135–153.

Drohan, S., Mauffette, Y., & Allard, J. (2011). Employers' perspectives on problem-based learning initiatives. In T. Barrett & S. Moore (Eds.), *New approaches to problem-based learning: Revitalising your practice in higher education* (pp. 87–99). New York: Routledge.

Eck, C. J. (2002). *Assessing and researching problem-based learning*. Birmingham, UK: Samford University.

Goodchild, L. F., & Wechsler, H. S. (1989). *The history of higher education: Association of the study of higher education reader*. Boston: Glenn Press.

Hall, L., & Maugham, C. (2015). Going where the students are already: Reimagining online learning where students and lecturers co-create an interactive teaching and learning space. *The International Journal of Technologies in Learning, 22*(3), 51–61.

Harigittai, E. (2010). Digital na(t)ives? variation in internet skills and uses among members of the 'Net Generation'. *Sociological Inquiry, 80*(1), 92–113.

Hatano, G., & Inagaki, K. (1984). Two courses of expertise. *Research and Clinical Center for Child Development Annual Report, 6*, 27–36.

Hatano, G., & Oura, Y. (2003). Commentary: Reconceptualising school learning using insight from expertise research. *Educational Researcher, 32*(8), 26–29.

Hu, S. (2011). Reconsidering the relationships between student engagement and persistence in college. *Innovation in Higher Education, 36*(2), 97–106.

Huijser, H. (2006). Refocusing multiliteracies for the net generation. *International Journal of Pedagogies and Learning, 2*(1), 21–33.

Huijser, H., & Kek, M. Y. C. A. (2016). PBL and technology-supported learning: Exploring the right blend. In R. Henderson (Ed.), *Problem-based learning: Perspectives, methods and challenges*. New York: Nova Science Publishers. pp. At press.

Huijser, H., & Wali, F. (2012). *A PBL approach to teaching Bahraini perspectives at Bahrain Polytechnic*. Paper presented at the 3rd international PBL symposium: PBL and the problematization of teaching and learning, Singapore.

James, R., Krause, K.-L., & Jennings, C. (2010). *The first year experience in Australian universities: Findings from 1994 to 2009*. Melbourne, Australia: Centre for the Study of Higher Education, University of Melbourne.

Jaros, M., & Deakin-Crick, R. (2007). Personalized learning for the post-mechanical age. *Journal of Curriculum Studies, 39*(4), 423–440.

Johnson, L., Adams Becker, S., Estrada, V., & Freeman, A. (2014). *NMC horizon report: 2014 Higher education edition*. Austin, TX: The New Media Consortium.

Johnson, L., Adams Becker, S., & Hall, C. (2015). *2015 NMC technology outlook for Australian tertiary education: A horizon project regional report*. Austin, TX: The New Media Consortium.

Jones, C., Ramanau, R., Cross, S., & Healing, G. (2010). Net generation or digital natives: Is there a distinct new generation entering university? *Computers & Education, 54*(3), 722–732.

Kek, M. Y. C. A., & Huijser, H. (2011). The power of problem-based learning in developing critical thinking skills: Preparing students for tomorrow's digital futures in today's classrooms. *Higher Education Research and Development, 30*(3), 317–329.

Kennedy, G. E., Judd, T. S., Churchward, A., Gray, K., & Krause, K. (2008). First year students' experiences with technology: Are they really digital natives? *Australasian Journal of Educational Technology, 24*(1), 108–122.

Kennedy, G., Judd, T., Dalgarnot, B., & Waycott, J. (2010). Beyond native and immigrants: Exploring types of net generation students. *Journal of Computer Assisted Learning, 26*(5), 332–343.

Koutropoulos, A. (2010). Digital natives: Ten years after. *Merlot: Journal of Online Learning and Teaching, 7*(4), 525–538.

Kuh, G. D., Kinzie, J., Buckley, J. A., Bridges, B. K., & Hayek, J. C. (2007). Special issue: Piecing together the student success puzzle: Research, propositions and recommendations. *ASHE Higher Education Report, 32*(5), 1–182.

Kvavik, R. B. (2005). Convenience, communications, and control: How students use technology. In D. Oblinger & J. Oblinger (Eds.), *Educating the net generation* (pp. 7.1–7.20). Boulder, CO: Educause.

Luck, P., & Norton, B. (2004). Problem based management learning – better online? *European Journal of Open, Distance and E-Learning*. Retrieved December 10, 2012, from http://www.eurodl.or/index.php?article=156

Macmahon, C., & Huijser, H. (2015). 'We don't need no education?' Moving towards the integration of tertiary education and entrepreneurialship. In M. Harmes, H. Huijser, & P. A. Danaher (Eds.), *Myths in education, learning and teaching: Policies, practices and principles* (pp. 97–113). New York: Palgrave.

Majoor, G., & Aarts, H. (2010). A role for problem-based learning in higher education in the developing world. In H. J. M. van Berkel, A. Scherpbier, H. Hillen, & C. Van Der Vleuten (Eds.), *Lessons from problem-based learning* (pp. 249–257). Oxford, UK: Oxford University Press.

Martyn, J., Terwijn, R., Kek, M. Y. C. A., & Huijser, H. (2014). Exploring the relationships between teaching, approaches to learning and critical thinking in a problem-based learning foundation nursing course. *Nurse Education Today, 34*(5), 829–835. doi:http://dx.doi.org/10.1016/j.nedt.2013.04.023.

Moore, I., & Poikela, S. (2011). Evaluating problem-based learning initiatives. In T. Barrett & S. Moore (Eds.), *New approaches to problem-based learning: Revitalising your practice in higher education* (pp. 100–111). New York: Routledge.

Oblinger, D., & Oblinger, J. (2005). *Educating the net generation.* Retrieved from http://www. educause.edu/educatingthenetgen?bhcp=1

Oblinger, D. G. (2010). For the next generation. *Educause Review*, 76–98.

Oliver, B., & Goerke, V. (2007). Australian undergraduates' use and ownership of emerging technologies: Implications and opportunities for creating engaging learning experiences for the net generation. *Australasian Journal of Educational Technology, 23*(2), 171–186.

Omale, N., Hung, W., Luetkehans, L., & Cooke-Plagwitz, J. (2009). Learning in 3-D multiuser virtual environments: Exploring the use of unique 3-D attributes for online problem-based learning. *British Journal of Educational Technololgy, 40*(3), 480–495.

Partnership for 21st Century Learning. (2009). *Framework for 21st century learning.* Retrieved June 19, 2014, from http://www.p21.org/storage/documents/1._p21_framework_2_pager.pdf

Pascarella, E. T., & Terenzini, P. T. (2005). *How college affects students: A third decade of research.* San Francisco: Jossey-Bass.

Pepper, C. (2009). Problem-based learning in science. *Issues in Educational Research, 19*(2), 128–141.

Prensky, M. (2001). Digital natives, digital immigrants. *On the Horizon, 9*(5). Retrieved February 14, 2007, from http://www.marcprensky.com/writing/Prensky Digital Natives Digital Immigrants - Part1.pdf

Rheingold, H. (2010). Attention and other 21st century social media literacies. *Educause Review, 45*(5), 14–24.

Rotherham, A. J., & Willngham, D. T. (2010). *21st century skills: Not new but a worthy challenge* (pp. 17–20). Spring, UT: American Educator.

Sankey, M. D. (2006). A neomillennial learning approach: Helping non-traditional learners study at a distance. *International Journal of Education and Development Using ICT, 2*(4), 82–99.

Sanson-Fisher, W. R., & Lynagh, M. C. (2005). Problem-based learning: A dissemination success story? *Medical Journal of Australia, 183*(5), 258–260.

Savin-Baden, M. (2006). The challenge of using problem-basecd leanring online. In M. Savin-Baden & K. Wilkie (Eds.), *Problem-based learning online* (pp. 3–13). Maidenhead, UK: McGraw-Hill.

Savin-Baden, M. (2014). Using problem-based learning: New constellations for the 21st century. *Journal on Excellence in College Teaching, 25*(3&4), 197–219.

Sendag, S., & Odabasi, H. F. (2009). Effects of an online problem-based learning course on content knowledge acquisition and critical thinking skills. *Computers & Education, 53*, 132–141.

Sontag, M. (2009). A learning theory for 21st century students. *Innovate: Journal of Online Education, 5*(4). Retrieved January 25, 2016, from http://nsuworks.nova.edu/innovate/vol5/iss4/2

Sternberg, R. J. (2003). What is an expert student? *Educational Researcher, 32*(8), 5–9.

Tapscott, D., & Williams, A. D. (2010). Innovating the 21st century university: It's time! *Educause Review, 45*(1), 17–29.

Tate, P., & Klein-Collins, R. (2012). IT innovations and the non-traditional learner. In D. G. Oblinger (Ed.), *Game changers: Education and information technologies* (pp. 67–80). Bourlder, CO: Educause.

Thomas, L. (2002). Student retention in higher education: The role of institutional habitus. *Journal of Education Policy, 17*(4), 423–442.

Wee, L. K. N., & Kek, M. Y. C. A. (2002). *Authentic problem-based learning: Rewriting business education.* Singapore, Singapore: Prentice-Hall.

Yeh, Y. (2010). Integrating collaborative PBL with blended learning to explore preservice teachers' development of online learning communities. *Teaching and Teacher Education, 26*(8), 1630–1640.

Part II
Imagining an Agile PBL Curriculum for Learning

Chapter 4
Focusing on Learning Outcomes and Authentic Interdisciplinary Problems

Introduction

In Chap. 3, we have identified the challenge in designing a technology-supported agile PBL environment that stays true to the original intentions of PBL and that leverages technology to enhance the impact of learning in teams, rather than reducing it. We have also imagined what we called the 'next generation of learners' and began to identify the characteristics that they may bring to the formal learning environments. Of course, the flipside of considering student characteristics as they enter a particular learning environment is that we also need to define and clarify what we want them to learn and be able to do, once they have moved into and through this formal learning environment. In other words, what do we imagine their characteristics to be when they move out of the university? How do those characteristics align with what they are likely to encounter when they complete their university studies? And how do we ensure that we draw on students' prior learning and strengths while simultaneously empowering them with the skills, dispositions and knowledges to engage meaningfully and productively in the present and future twenty-first-century context?

PBL offers some solutions in this respect and in particular if we imagine an agile PBL, which draws on Savin-Baden's (2014) new PBL constellations for the twenty-first century. One of the key reasons for expanding PBL in this way is that PBL has traditionally been largely confined to disciplinary curricula. As Savin-Baden argues (2014), 'PBL is an approach to learning that is affected by the structural and pedagogical environment into which it is placed (that is, the discipline or subject, the instructors, and the organization)' (p. 198). As noted, many instances of PBL practice occur on the micro level of what we have termed an agile PBL ecology for learning (outlined in detail in Chap. 2). However, the meso-, exo- and macro-systems are of course also part of the overall ecology, and as with any ecology, none of these systems operate in isolation, but they are rather intimately related and feed into, and off, each other. Even though Savin-Baden's new PBL constellations can be seen as essentially a critique and a mapping exercise of the wide variety of approaches to PBL, we argue that these constellations can be employed for our

© Springer Science+Business Media Singapore 2017
M.Y.C.A. Kek, H. Huijser, *Problem-based Learning into the Future*,
DOI 10.1007/978-981-10-2454-2_4

purposes here to, firstly, allow for the recognition that students learn in an overall learning ecology that involves much more than the formal classroom environment and, secondly, to engage with the fact that they will move into a context upon graduation that is most likely interdisciplinary and characterised by high levels of uncertainty.

In this chapter then, we begin to imagine what curriculum design in an agile PBL context might look like, and we begin to imagine how interdisciplinary PBL problems may be conceived. This requires imagining a set of skills, dispositions, values, attitudes and knowledges that will be required, but without the certainty of knowing what the context will look like when such skills will ultimately be employed. In essence, this is the dilemma that we respond to in this book by employing the concept of agile PBL.

An Agile PBL Curriculum

Within the overall agile PBL ecology for learning, curriculum is positioned at the micro level, as it includes problems, assessment as well as PBL learning and teaching spaces in the formal university setting. To reiterate, we aim to extend the notion of strict boundaries between different levels of the ecology, which in turn means that each individual system in the ecology (e.g. the micro-system in this case) needs to be rethought. If we take curriculum as an example, we argue that it should not be confined to the level of disciplinary content, as this is too narrow a focus. This does not mean that highly specialised disciplinary knowledge and content cannot be part of the curriculum, but rather that in itself such knowledge is not enough. Specialised disciplinary knowledge increasingly needs to be adapted and applied in diverse and supercomplex environments, which brings in an additional set of skills. Furthermore, there are important ethical and moral dimensions to knowledge that require engagement and decisions that in turn require critical assessment of particular social and cultural contexts. In short, within an agile PBL ecology for learning, curriculum is imagined as connected to all other elements of the ecology, and this should be made explicit in curriculum frameworks.

In their critique of conceptualisations of 'the curriculum', Barnett and Coate (2004) identify that curriculum implications of learning and teaching strategies tend to be framed in unduly narrow ways. Their critique of current debates around the curriculum is summed up like this:

> Not only is it likely to lead to efforts that fall short of what is required even for capability in the disciplines, but it is also likely to lead to curriculum approaches that run counter to the understandings and practices that are necessary if higher education is to be in any ways adequate to the contemporary world. (p. 25)

If we look at the five elements that make up their critique, we can see that it aligns rather neatly to the key elements of our arguments which are in favour of agile PBL in this book. Firstly, by focusing on knowledges, dispositions, attitudes, values and skills in narrow, discipline-focused ways, more intractable dimensions of human development, such as human qualities and dispositions, are neglected. In this way, 'students are being reduced to the status of bearers of value beyond them-selves' (Barnett & Coate, 2004, p. 24). Secondly, the voice of students is largely absent from discussions about curriculum, and so student do not have an active and direct stake in it. This means by extension that the curriculum reflects its primary stakeholders, i.e. the academic community and employers in the labour market, while students, as stakeholders, are effectively excluded from the curriculum. In other words, the curriculum is 'done to them', reinforcing a sense of separation rather than a sense of ownership. Within this context, academics, employers and students are each discrete entities with discrete roles, rather than an integrated com-munity that negotiates the most desirable outcomes for all involved. Within an agile PBL ecology for learning, the boundaries around such discrete entities are imagined to be much more blurred, with employers and other external entities in the commu-nity and society being directly involved in teaching and teachers and students tra-versing in and out of formal university spaces, and thus crossing boundaries, in a much more seamless manner. Thirdly and fourthly, Barnett and Coate (2004) argue that the academic community does not reflect critically enough on curriculum design in a way that goes beyond the immediate curriculum environment or, in other words, beyond each semester's course surveys. Again, the argument here is that academics are locked within the boundaries of the micro-system, whereas they should look at the curriculum in its broader context and design their curriculum in such a way that it engages with, or indeed develops, 'higher forms of human devel-opment' (Barnett & Coate, 2004, p. 24). Of course, it is easy to be cynical about this, but we agree with Barnett and Coate that we should aim higher and that we should therefore imagine a curriculum that stimulates students well beyond the functional skills they need to 'get a job'. Their last point of critique is that the current narrow focus on skills and (functional) outcomes may come back to haunt universities, for 'the modern world may be such as to require human qualities and dispositions that are not easily caught in a language of skills and outcomes' (Barnett & Coate, 2004, p. 25). However, we will argue that focusing on employability is not wrong, and to ignore that it is an aspect and demand from the wide macro-system would be naïve. The fact that it is a part of the macro-system needs to be accepted, and serious con-siderations have to be taken into account for it, even if we should of course not be totally consumed by it. Thus, we believe that agile PBL can be the vehicle for imag-ining a curriculum and pedagogy that empowers and builds on such human qualities and dispositions, a way-of-being, as well as developing a functional skill set and knowledges in the process.

Agile PBL, Employability and Twenty-First-Century Learning Outcomes

More than a decade into the twenty-first century, much has been written about the kinds of skills that are needed in this century, and a variety of different frameworks has been developed. Some of these frameworks were beginning to be developed well before the turn of the century, such as multiliteracies, for example (The New London Group, 1996). Although the focus in their case was specifically on literacy, the framework of multiliteracies was based on a strong sense that teaching practices at the time were no longer suited for a fast-changing context of both education and employment. Thus, there is a strong pedagogy dimension to the multiliteracies framework, which includes four elements: situated practice, overt instruction, critical framing and transformed practice (Huijser, 2006; Kalantzis & Cope, 2001).

These four pedagogical elements are closely related and together have a strong emphasis on critical thinking and application of acquired knowledge in familiar and different contexts, rather than 'reproduction' of taught knowledge. This is in many ways the crucial element of employability skills for the twenty-first century: the centrality of what is variously called 'soft skills', 'generic skills' or 'transferable skills', or in the Australian higher education context, 'graduate attributes'. Cassidy (2006, p. 508) defines employability skills as skills that are 'not job specific, but are skills which cut horizontally across all industries and vertically across all jobs from entry level to chief executive officer'. In short, employability skills are skills that are not discipline specific nor content specific, but rather allow graduates to adapt quickly to new contexts and hit the ground running while also being able to learn continuously; to think about future applications or implications of whatever their current occupation is, whether that be as an employee or as a business and/or social entrepreneur; and to be self-directed as lifelong learners long after they move out of a university.

Another early example of an attempt to design a framework around the development of such transferable skills, and one that comes from a different angle, is Chickering and Reisser's (1993) seven vectors of college students' development (see also Chickering, n.d.; Foubert, 1980):

- Developing competence
- Managing emotions
- Moving through autonomy towards interdependence
- Developing mature interpersonal relationships
- Establishing identity
- Developing purpose
- Developing integrity

Here, the focus is more on personal attributes that students are expected to develop, but there are clear links with various versions of twenty-first-century skills and graduate attributes. In addition, and of particular importance for our purposes here, the development of these vectors can be mapped against an agile PBL program in that these vectors all relate to some extent to developing professional identities and productive relationships, which are an integral part of an agile PBL in the form of its emphasis on group or collaborative work in a professional context.

Since the turn of the century, work on various approaches to employability skills and frameworks for the development of twenty-first-century skills has accelerated, and this is no coincidence as there appears to be an urgent need for a rethink of approaches to higher education in the twenty-first century (Altbach, Gumport, & Berdahl, 2011; Bridges, 2000). This is consistent with feedback from employers who increasingly indicate that the graduates they 'receive' are not ready and often require long periods of 'retraining' when they enter the workplace and, therefore, stress the need for universities to make 'more explicit efforts to develop the "key", "core", "transferable" and/or "generic" skills needed in many types of high-level employment'(Mason, Williams, & Cranmer, 2006, p. 2). The difference that an agile PBL can potentially make here is that it requires employers to be actively involved bearing a level of responsibility for developing these types of skills, rather than waiting for universities (as completely separate entities) to 'deliver' such skills. In other words, agile PBL imagines the boundary between employers and academics to blur significantly when it comes to curriculum design, including the design of authentic agile PBL problems, as well as assessment tasks and evaluation.

It is important at this point to reflect for a moment on the historical context of calls for the development of transferable skills, as these are not exactly new and certainly not confined to the twenty-first century. For example, John Dewey wrote as far back as 1899: 'it is radical conditions which have changed and only a radical change in education suffices. Knowledge is no longer an immobile solid; it has been *liquefied*' (Dewey, 1980, p. 18, our emphasis). Dewey believed that the aim of twentieth-century education should not simply be the production of a labour force, but the enrichment of the individual and society by developing a child's 'social power and insight' (cited in Partnership for 21st Century Learning, 2007, p. 3). He saw the way to do that through learning by doing and a curriculum that involved the mind, hands and heart. Throughout the twentieth century, there was an ongoing debate around whether to focus on core academic subjects (or 'content') or on real-world knowledge and skills (or 'adapted' knowledge and 'transferable skills') (Partnership for 21st Century Learning, 2007). This dilemma is still at the heart of debates about twenty-first-century skills and learning outcomes. However, the difference now is the pace of change and the rapid rate at which existing pedagogical models appear to be outdated. This requires a 'liquefied' or flexible and adaptive pedagogy and curriculum, indeed a pedagogy and curriculum that are *agile*, rather than 'fossilised' and fixed. It is perhaps best imagined through the popular example of future proofing curriculum that is supposed to educate students for jobs that do not yet exist. We would argue that an agile PBL is ideally suited in this respect, because it requires educators to continuously look for relevance of the problems they design, which in turn allows for the development of relevant lifelong skills, rather than those that may be outdated by the time the students move out university. Furthermore, as noted above, this is not simply the responsibility of educators in the traditional sense of the word, but rather, agile PBL curriculum design requires employers, as stakeholders, to adopt an educator disposition. Of course, they do not necessarily possess the curriculum design skills, but we argue that they should at least be part of the conversation at the design level. This will ensure the agility and relevance of the curriculum.

In this chapter, we discuss various approaches to, and frameworks around, employability skills and develop some links between such frameworks and their potential application in education from an agile PBL perspective. We then provide some ideas on how to specifically incorporate and develop employability skills for the twenty-first century in an agile PBL educational space. Note that we deliberately use the term educational space, rather than classroom, as the idea here is to blur the boundaries between educational spaces and the spaces beyond the formal learning environment, as they all form part of the same agile PBL ecology for learning.

We draw on a number of different frameworks, each of which addresses employability skills for the twenty-first century in different ways:

- Framework for 21st Century Learning (Partnership for 21st Century Learning, 2007)
- The concept of learning power, combined with Effective Lifelong Learning Inventory (ELLI) (Deakin-Crick, 2007; Deakin-Crick, Broadfoot, & Glaxton, 2004)
- Future Work Skills 2020 (Davies, Fidler, & Gorbis, 2011)

This is by no means an exhaustive list, but as noted above, there is a certain amount of overlap between such frameworks, and the key element they have in common is the emphasis on transferable skills. As noted above, this is partly driven by commercial pressures (read: employer driven demands) for graduates who will not require long 'learning curves' when they start employment (Mason et al., 2006) as the employability skills employers stress they need are usually transferable skills, such as 'effective communication' or 'problem-solving'. As Mason et al. note:

> University responses to this agenda typically include modifications to existing course content (sometimes in response to employer suggestions), the introduction of new courses and teaching methods and expanded provision of opportunities for work experience – all intended to enhance the development of employability skills and/or ensure that the acquisition of such skills is made more explicit. In some cases university departments have sought to 'embed' the desired skills within courses; in other departments students are offered 'stand-alone' skills courses which are effectively 'bolted-on' to traditional academic programmes. (p. 4)

It could be argued, however, that such responses are 'tinkering around the edges' to some extent and do not fundamentally change the way skills development is approached, which makes their success questionable. Such responses are increasingly supported by lists of graduate attributes that universities draw up and proudly display in their marketing material (Barrie, 2007; Star & Hammer, 2008). We argue that there is a need to make more fundamental changes to the way curricula are designed. We believe that an agile PBL curriculum is ideally suited to a rapidly changing context that requires universities to not only respond to current employer demands for employability skills but also equip graduates with the skills to adapt to an employment context that does not yet exist and indeed equip them with the skills to help shape and design their future employment context.

In the context of the United Kingdom, employability is defined in the Dearing Report (1997) rather broadly as the ability of an individual to gain employment appropriate to his/her educational standard. Within that definition, Wickramasinghe and Perera (2010, p. 226) identify three key elements of employability:

- The ability to gain initial employment
- The ability to maintain employment and make transitions between jobs and roles within the same organisation to meet new job requirements
- The ability to obtain new employment, if required, by being independent in the labour market and able to manage employment transitions between organisations

Of course, the emphasis within this conceptualisation is still very much on employers seeking employees and employees meeting their demands. We would extend that and add a fourth element that is about having the skills to operate autonomously and either choose paid employment or start a business or social enterprise and/or move comfortably between the two at various times. Again, we believe an agile PBL curriculum has great potential to provide graduates with all three elements of employability: gain initial employment, maintain and transit between jobs and roles, obtain new employment whilst operating autonomously. The key focus of an agile PBL curriculum is therefore to empower students to have the courage to learn, unlearn and relearn as a 'way-of-being' and to open other possibilities for themselves in their personal and work lives.

Framework for 21st Century Learning

The Framework for 21st Century Learning was developed by the Partnership for 21st Century Skills, whose membership includes companies like Adobe Systems, AT&T, the LEGO Group and Pearson Education, among many others. The framework is divided into expected outcomes on four different levels:

- Core subjects and twenty-first-century themes
- Learning and innovation skills
- Information, media and technology skills
- Life and career skills

Each one of these levels is then further subdivided into more specific parts which ultimately allow you to drill down to the coalface. Thus, core subjects include English, reading or language, world languages, arts, mathematics, economics, science, geography, history, government and civics. Importantly, these are not only seen as discrete disciplinary subjects, but instead they are connected by twenty-first-century themes:

- Global awareness
- Financial, economic, business and entrepreneurial literacy
- Civic literacy
- Health literacy

This is important, because it ensures that the core subjects are not taught in isolation, but rather linked to 'real-world' or authentic contexts, because that is where the knowledge ultimately needs to be applied. As Bransford, Brown and Cocking (2000, cited in Partnership for 21st Century Learning, 2007, p. 8) note, 'transfer from school to the everyday environment is the ultimate purpose of school-based learning'. They go on to say that 'research indicates that students are more successful at doing this when instruction explicitly emphasises the process of transfer by using a real world context'. The question then becomes: what type of instruction would be most suited to achieve this effectively? In this framework, the authors suggest that '"teaching for transfer", that is instruction that helps students link their learning to the real world, can promote greater understanding of core subjects' (p. 9), and they see the use of projects as enabling students to make immediate connections between content and application. Of course, they are talking here about a school context, rather than a university context, but we believe that the principles are not different, and an agile PBL can be used to implement these principles at the appropriate level for where students are situated.

An agile PBL seems well positioned to be an intentional pedagogy, curriculum, assessment and learning environment – serving a bridging function (Stark, Renkl, Gruber, & Mandl, 1998) – to educate and prepare students in today's context for a world that is supercomplex, but increasingly digital and socially interconnected, complex and dynamic. Integrative learning, which is what the agile PBL ecology for learning is about, is learning in preparation for future learning (Bransford et al., 2006), preparing to apply adaptive expertise (Hatano & Inagaki, 1984; Hatano & Oura, 2003) which in turn is about responding flexibly to contextual variations and maximising transfer of learning in the workplace (Bransford & Schwartz, 1999). Furthermore, the twenty-first-century themes, when fully integrated, allow for interdisciplinary application, which is important because 'we know that we must draw on multiple knowledge domains to find solutions for many of today's problems' (Partnership for 21st Century Learning, 2007, p. 9). This dovetails nicely into our discussion about interdisciplinarity in this chapter.

Learning and innovation skills are subdivided into:

- Critical thinking and problem-solving
- Creativity and innovation
- Communication and collaboration

It is in this domain that any PBL-based approach appears perhaps most relevant, as each of these subdomains are central to the PBL process. However, each of them needs to be carefully rethought and adapted to ever-changing contexts. An agile PBL allows us to do precisely that. For example, problem-solving has obviously been an integral part of PBL since the 1960s, but 'successful problem solving in the twenty-first century requires us to work effectively and creatively with computers, with vast amounts of information, with ambiguous situations, and also with other people' (Partnership for 21st Century Learning, 2007, p. 14), either face to face or using computerised mediated tools, such as Skype, Zoom and many others. What we can see then is the blurring of the boundaries between each of these subdomains, whereby each of these attributes needs to be developed in context, because they do not exist in isolation. For example, work-based problems require creative and innovative solutions as well as the ability to cooperate and communicate about such solutions. In addition, they need a keen understanding of the social and/or ethical implications of potential solutions, which may draw on, for example, civic literacy and/or global awareness. Creativity in this context is not confined to traditional conceptualisations of 'the Arts' with a capital A, but rather refers to creativity in context and within the constraints of particular real-life situations and problems. Sir Ken Robinson (Robinson, 2006) has famously said that 'we do not grow into creativity, we grow out of it – or rather, we are educated out of it'. We imagine that an agile version of PBL educates creativity back into it.

The third domain, information, media and technology skills, is further subdivided into:

- Information literacy
- Media literacy
- Information, communications and technology (ICT) literacy

Within this framework, the inclusion of these subdomains is based on the recognition that 'the worlds of work, higher education, and personal life increasingly demand the ability to: (1) access information efficiently and effectively; (2) evaluate information critically and competently; and (3) use information accurately and creatively' (Partnership for 21st Century Learning, 2007, p. 18). We can begin to see the links between different domains, as of course these types of twenty-first-century literacies are based on the ability to solve problems through critical and creative thinking, as well as collaboration and communication. Importantly, using these types of literacies and skills at a sophisticated level does not stop at simply identifying a solution for a particular problem, but instead (and almost inevitably) includes what we might call 'future thinking', which involves thinking critically, creatively and analytically about future solutions to prevent problems from recurring.

The ability to learn continuously or what Cope and Kalantzis (2009) call 'ubiquitous learning' is arguably the most crucial 'employability skill' for the twenty-first century. Technology is both an enabler of this type of learning and a potential constraint if such skills are not explicitly taught. Moreover, it is not simply about teaching new technologies, but rather about developing self-directed lifelong learning skills. As noted in the explanation of this framework, it is critical that 'the workers of tomorrow develop the ability to use not just today's technologies, but be skillful enough to learn and adapt to the technologies of tomorrow, in other words, that they be ICT-literate' (Partnership for 21st Century Learning, 2007, p. 20). Again, we believe that an agile PBL ideally allows for the development of these types of skills, because the problems can be designed in such a way that in order to solve them, students would need to collaborate and learn how to use new tools that they may not have used before. Furthermore, an agile PBL provides a platform for what Bransford et al. (2006) call preparation for future learning, in the form of liquefied teaching and learning spaces that are not confined to the micro-system commonly found in traditional learning environments, which are fixed, bounded and restrictive.

The fourth and final domain of this framework, life and career skills, is further subdivided into:

- Flexibility and adaptability
- Initiative and self-direction
- Social and cross-cultural skills
- Productivity and accountability
- Leadership and responsibility

Limited versions of employability skills focus only on these 'soft skills', but they are not a separate skill set. Rather, they are about applied skills in authentic contexts. To many employers, applied skills are now so important that 'on all educational levels they trump basic knowledge and skills, such as reading comprehension and mathematics' (Partnership for 21st Century Learning, 2007, p. 22). What is needed then is an educational approach where the boundaries between these four domains are porous, and we believe that an agile PBL is ideal in this respect.

In their conclusion to the overview of their Framework for 21st Century Learning, the authors note that:

> Current research supports the effectiveness of pedagogical approaches such as cooperative learning, teaching for transfer, project-based learning, and real world teaching contexts – as well as the importance of educators' lifelong learning through professional development, professional learning communities, mentoring, and the like.

Although they do not specifically mention PBL, an agile PBL actually includes cooperative learning (and teaching), teaching (and learning) for transfer, problems and, ideally, learning in real-world contexts (rather than only scenario-based or simulated problems). The latter is crucial, for it is difficult to create a curriculum that is geared towards the development of employability skills for the twenty-first century if the teachers do not possess such skills themselves or are not prepared for a context of 'ubiquitous learning'.

Learning Power and Effective Lifelong Learning Inventory

Another framework that is based on the interpretation of large amounts of research data is that of learning power and its associated Effective Lifelong Learning Inventory (ELLI) tool. This was designed from the beginning to find out what the key elements are of effective learning in (and for) the twenty-first century.

Deakin-Crick (2007, p. 137) describes a need for a 'paradigm shift towards a relational and transformative model of learning, in which the creation of interdependent communities of intentional learners provides a basis for the integration of 'traditional academic' skills and outcomes with the learning dispositions, values and attitudes necessary to meet the demands of the emerging "networked society"'. The key term here is 'intentional learners', because it suggests lifelong learners who are able to identify what and when they need to learn and recognise how they will best be able to learn effectively for the goals and aims they set themselves. In other words, these are learners who take control of their own learning, who have an awareness of their own strengths and weaknesses and who use this awareness to both learn and grow their own learning capabilities. 'Learning power' provides a framework for highly learning-centred design of productive twenty-first-century learning programs, which we believe aligns well with an agile PBL program by adding a very deliberate self-reflection element to the learning process that ultimately leads to self-directed autonomous learners. In Deakin-Crick's (2007, p. 136) words, 'the concept of learning power and learning how to learn must be understood and contextualised as part of a complex system in which the formation of a learning identity, personal power to learn and competencies for managing life in the post-mechanical age are as important as the acquisition of knowledge'.

In the original learning power and the Effective Lifelong Learning Inventory (ELLI) research, Deakin-Crick et al. (2004) set out to identify the characteristics and dispositions of effective lifelong learners. Seven dimensions of 'learning power' emerged, via factor analysis, each with elements of 'thinking, feeling and doing'. Learning power reflects the kinds of attributes and skills graduates need to engage effectively with new learning opportunities. It is more than simply a style or a way of thinking or doing – it's a way of 'being a learner' that is appropriate for the twenty-first century (ELLI, n.d.).

The seven dimensions of learning power of ELLI are:

- Changing and learning – a sense of myself as someone who learns and changes over time
- Critical curiosity – an orientation to want to 'get beneath the surface'
- Meaning making – making connections and seeing that learning 'matters to me'
- Creativity – risk-taking, playfulness, imagination and intuition
- Learning relationships – learning with and from others and also being able to manage without them
- Strategic awareness – being aware of my thoughts, feelings and actions as a learner and being able to use that awareness to manage learning processes
- Resilience – the readiness to persevere in the development of my own learning power

Once they had identified these seven dimensions, Deakin-Crick and the original Bristol University research team developed what is now known as the Effective Lifelong Learning Inventory (ELLI) (Tew, Crick, Broadfoot, & Claxton, 2004). The learning inventory is an online questionnaire that is filled in by students according to how they see themselves as learners. The results provide a snapshot of the student's learning energy based on the seven dimensions of learning power (described above) which can be used as both a summative and a formative form of assessment. The assessment information is summative in that it sums up where a student is now, and it is formative because it provides impetus and direction for development, growth and change (Tew et al., 2004).

The figure below represents one snapshot or spider diagram for one individual as a learner – one form of feedback provided by the ELLI tool. The two coloured lines represent two different completions of the inventory. In between each completion, a range of interventions or strategies is implemented, designed to stretch learning power dimensions. The spider diagram provides a visual analytic which facilitates a conversation about an individual's learning story and their learning identity. It can also be used to track growth in learning power at two key stages (three stages are possible) in the learning journey (Fig. 4.1).

If we consider 'learning power' as a learning framework, then at least four broad categories are identified as making a substantial contribution (Jaros & Deakin-Crick, 2007, p. 430):

- Learning capacities: dispositions, awareness and skills
- Learning identity: the beliefs, values and attitudes about learning, self and knowledge held by the learner
- Learning story: the sociocultural formation of learners over time
- Learning relationships: the quality and substance of learning relationships

These are intimately related, and they hold different degrees of importance at different times and in different contexts. These broad categories in turn underlie the seven dimensions of learning power identified. Each of these can be 'assessed'

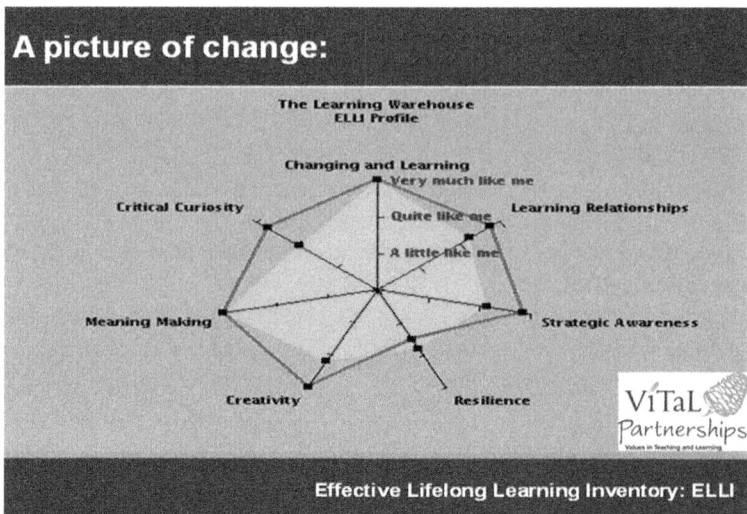

Fig. 4.1 Snapshot of an individual's lifelong learning inventory (Source: http://www.vitalpartnerships.com/elli/)

formatively and summatively within the learning process (Jaros & Deakin-Crick, 2007). This inventory can form a measurement instrument to assess and evaluate a student's lifelong learning skills in an agile PBL curriculum. The assessment and/or evaluation can either be conducted by a PBL teacher and/or by a peer within the PBL groups. The idea is that these assessments and/or evaluations are to be carried out regularly and at appropriate times during the learning journey of the students, and this then provides the opportunity for students to develop each of the four categories outlined above.

Although the learning power dimensions are not employability skills in the conventional sense of the term, we believe this aligns well with agile PBL, as it adds a metacognitive dimension which is a crucial part of employability skills for the twenty-first century. The ELLI tool can be integrated into an agile PBL curriculum with relative ease.

Future Work Skills 2020

While both the Framework for 21st Century Learning and the learning power framework are based on current understandings of what types of skills are needed in the twenty-first century, the Future Work Skills 2020 framework (Davies et al., 2011), designed by the Institute for the Future at the University of Phoenix, tries to move beyond this by making an educated guess about what kinds of skills would be needed in the 'future workplace'. This is important, because it helps us anticipate how we may need to change and adapt our curricula to both be responsive to ever-changing employment contexts and empower students with the confidence and skills to help shape future employment contexts.

Underlying their model, Davies et al. (2011) identify six drivers for change into the future:

- Extreme longevity – Increasing global lifespans change the nature of careers and learning.
- Rise of smart machines and systems – Workplace automation nudges human workers out of rote, repetitive tasks.
- Computational world – Massive increases in sensors and processing power make the world a programmable system.
- New media ecology – New communication tools require new media literacies beyond text.
- Superstructured organisations – Social technologies drive new forms of production and value creation.
- Globally connected world – Increased global interconnectivity puts diversity and adaptability at the centre of organisational operations.

Especially, the last two points take us well beyond approaching employability skills in a reactive manner and instead point us into the direction of a proactive approach to employability skills. In other words, graduates need to be able to engage with 'new forms of production and value creation', and indeed they need to be able to do some of this value creation themselves. In order to do so, they need to be creative, analytical, confident of their own strengths and weaknesses and, of course, able to deal with a context where diversity and adaptability is the norm; indeed, they need to be able to feel 'at home' in such a context, in order for them to thrive.

Within the framework, this leads to ten identified skills 'for the future workforce':

- Sense making – ability to determine the deeper meaning of significance of what is being expressed
- Social intelligence – ability to connect to others in a deep way, to sense and stimulate and desired interaction
- Novel and adaptive thinking – proficiency at thinking and coming up with solutions and response beyond that which is rote or rule based and familiar
- Cross-cultural competency – ability to operate in different cultural settings
- Computational thinking – ability to translate vast amounts of data into abstract concepts and to understand data-based reasoning
- New media literacy – ability to critically assess and develop content that uses new media forms and to leverage these media for persuasive communication
- Transdisciplinarity – literacy in and ability to understand concepts across multiple disciplines
- Design mindset – ability to represent and develop tasks and work processes for desired outcomes
- Cognitive load management – ability to discriminate and filter information for importance and to understand how to maximise cognitive functioning using a variety of tools and techniques
- Virtual collaboration – ability to work productively, drive engagement and demonstrate presence as a member of a virtual team

Interestingly, there is a fair amount of overlap with the two frameworks, but it takes most of the identified skills a little further, especially with regard to computational thinking and new media literacy. The crucial point for universities is that these skills (and attributes) do not necessarily develop unless you have a curriculum and pedagogy that is explicitly designed and intentionally taught to develop these skills and, more importantly, are flexible and agile enough to respond to ever-changing circumstances. As noted above, this is not a one-way street, where employers say they want graduates who can do this or that and educational institutions respond in kind. Rather, it should be an ongoing conversation that involves employers and partners outside the universities and students themselves in discussions about the curriculum in the design phase. Again, however, this needs to be systematically incorporated into curriculum design practices as part of an agile PBL approach.

Davies et al. (2011, p. 13) end their document with a set of anticipated changes in direction for educational institutions:

- Placing additional emphasis on developing skills such as critical thinking, insight and analysis capabilities
- Integrating new media literacy into education programs

- Including experiential learning that gives prominence to soft skills – such as the ability to collaborate, work in groups, read social clues and respond adaptively
- Broadening the learning constituency beyond teens and young adults through to adulthood
- Integrating interdisciplinary training that allows students to develop skills and knowledge in a range of subjects

At the risk of sounding rule bound and not flexible enough, an agile PBL curriculum appears to tick all of these boxes. However, to reap the full benefits of what an agile PBL can achieve in terms of employability skills for the twenty-first century, it is important that an agile PBL is integrated across an entire curriculum and designed in such a way that it is flexible enough to allow for interdisciplinarity and, also, that employers and entrepreneurial funding bodies are involved in discussions about (1) the structure of the agile PBL curriculum, (2) the design of authentic problems that incorporate future thinking elements and (3) the locations in which the problems are being addressed (i.e. where the learning occurs). The third point is particularly important, for if graduates are going to be work-ready to apply their twenty-first-century skills, they need to be familiar with the contexts in which they are to apply those skills (i.e. authentic workplace environments). As Mason et al. (2006, p. 25) point out, 'the strongly positive effects of student work experience on labour market outcomes serve as a reminder that many relevant employability skills are probably best learned in workplaces rather than in classroom settings'. Again, this draws attention to the importance of boundary crossing in the agile PBL ecology for learning.

Agile PBL and the Importance of Interdisciplinary

Interdisciplinarity is a key, but often neglected, implicit element of most PBL-based curriculum. Thus, the agile PBL ecology for learning that we are proposing ensures that this element is explicit and visible. An important reason for this is that authentic problems are increasingly interdisciplinary, and indeed they are often inherently interdisciplinary, or otherwise multi- or transdisciplinary, albeit to varying degrees. This is very important if we focus on learning outcomes of an agile PBL curriculum, because the ability to work in interdisciplinary teams and in cross-disciplinary contexts is a fundamental twenty-first-century skill. We would argue that a well-designed PBL curriculum develops a high level of comfort in working in interdisciplinary contexts in students as a way-of-being. However, this is certainly not an easy process as the architecture of many universities is still very much aligned to disciplinary, rather than interdisciplinary, structures. As Klein (2006, p. 10) notes, 'for most of the twentieth century, the dominant structure of education was the discipline-based department and school subject'. Despite rhetoric to the contrary, this is still very much the case in many universities. So we have Faculties of Engineering, Faculties of Arts and Faculties of Business, and the programs and courses they offer are largely fenced off from each other and largely confined to the micro-system of an agile PBL ecology for learning. And according to Hall and Weaver (2001, p. 867), 'this discipline-specific view of the world is taught and reinforced through the socialization processes of educational experiences'. Although we are beginning to see initiatives in the twenty-first century that make an attempt at blurring these disciplinary boundaries, this is clearly not a straightforward process and has potentially huge implications for rethinking of the curricula; in the case of an agile PBL, it requires a mindset or worldview capable of recognising that a paradigm shift is taking place.

One good example is the shift in some universities from a Faculty of Arts to a Faculty of Creative Industries (Flew, 2012, 2013; Hartley, 2005). This shift recognises the increasingly interdisciplinary nature of 'the arts' and expands the traditional boundaries around the individual arts disciplines to include, for example, design and architecture, but most importantly, it also includes more generic business skills such as entrepreneurial skills. However, while Creative Industries Faculties blur the boundaries to some extent, they are still organised around discipline-based schools, such as journalism, film and television, media and communication, and so on, with little interdisciplinary overlap beyond large first-year introductory courses, let alone interdisciplinary overlap within individual courses. This is a result and a historical legacy of what Petrie (1976, cited in Hall & Weaver, 2001, p. 867) has referred to as 'the professional's "cognitive map", i.e. the whole cognitive and perceptual approach embraced by the discipline. As these maps become entrenched through repeated use, communication with other disciplines can become increasingly challenging'. This is then followed by what Witz (1992, cited in Hall & Weaver, 2001, p. 871) has called 'external and internal closure', which is the process whereby 'professions tend to implement both procedures which separate other disciplines from their own and measures to restrict access to the discipline'. In other words, there is a process of entrenchment that actively works against interdisciplinarity, and this is structurally built into the way universities have been operating for hundreds of years. Of course, in 'the real world' of work and business, such strict disciplinary boundaries rarely exist, and knowledge in this context tends to be a lot more integrative.

We are currently on the cusp of a paradigm shift which will require profound changes in the way universities structurally operate (Tapscott & Williams, 2010), and if we take a closer look at the characteristics of disciplinary thinking, we can begin to see why this paradigm shift, which has been identified and discussed in previous chapters, is both needed and why it is likely to be met with fierce resistance from some corners.

From Disciplinarity to Interdisciplinarity

Disciplinary thinking is so ingrained into our modus operandi and woven into our DNA that it operates like common sense, and most of the time, we don't give it a second thought. For example, when we meet someone for the first time, one of the first questions we ask is 'what do you do for a living', and the answer we expect is a clearly defined disciplinary one, like an accountant, a journalist or a plumber. In other words, disciplinarity is like thinking in clearly delineated boxes, each with their own historical development, characteristics and language. In the context of the university, such characteristics become highly specialised and individual disciplines can become almost like individual cultures with their own languages and behaviours. For example, if you are an education academic and you accidently find yourself at a literary criticism conference, you will find that most presenters will literally read their densely theoretical academic papers in front of a live audience, and no one will blink an eyelid. In other disciplines, such as education, business or the STEM disciplines, this would be severely frowned upon, but no doubt these disciplines have their own quirks. One of the key twenty-first-century skills is the ability to move effortlessly between different disciplines and to be able to draw knowledge from different disciplines and synthesise and repackage that knowledge in different ways for different contexts. This is not a skill that students are taught in a purely discipline-based curriculum.

If we want to be clear on what we mean by interdisciplinarity, we should first zoom in on what characterises disciplinarity, and Klein (2006) very usefully identifies two sets of features in this respect: 'functional differentiation' and 'a system of power'. Functional differentiation is about creating disciplinary boundaries on a number of different levels:

- A subject matter and objects isolated for study
- A body of evidence, canon, content, laws and formalisms
- Example, models, paradigms and law
- Concepts and theories
- Methods, procedures, techniques and skills
- Explanatory modes, language and argument styles
- Ontologies and epistemologies (Klein, 2006, p. 10)

Each of these individual elements contributes to a unique disciplinary culture or ecosystem, which can become rather rigidified over time. Once disciplinary boundaries have been established, 'a system of power' guards the discipline through a number of structural and institutionalised practices:

- Departmental units of teaching and research
- Institutional structures of a profession
- Criteria of validity and legitimated practices
- A behavioural culture that shapes self and collective identities
- Patterns of education and training, publication and funding
- Accounts of disciplinary history
- Employment and labour markets
- Allocations of resources, privileges and prestige
- Economies of value with social, political and intellectual capital (Klein, 2006, p. 11)

In its purest form then, disciplinarity '[accentuates] stability and natural order, consistent realities, boundary formation and maintenance, normative social values, and homogeneity, with companion images of structure, foundation, compartmentalisation, and autonomous territorial regimes' (Klein, 2006, p. 11). This is firmly rooted in modernity and has clear links to Foucault's (1980) concepts of power and knowledge and the ways in which they are dynamically interrelated. This suggests of course that fundamental change will be characterised by a gradual erosion of the rigidity of disciplinary boundaries, and this process is well underway. The pressure comes from two different angles: the perceived inadequacy of discipline-based education in terms of outcomes and a perceived lack of alignment with the skills that students bring into the classroom, as discussed in Chap. 3. In terms of the former, there are many examples in medical education that decry the limited ability of graduates to work in interdisciplinary teams. As Fineberg, Wenger and Forrow (2004, p. 769) argue, '[non-PBL] medical education inadequately prepares students for interdisciplinary collaboration, an essential component of palliative care and numerous other areas of clinical practice'. The initial institutional response to the identified need for interdisciplinarity has been an array of new 'interdisciplinary' subjects, such as cultural studies, international studies, environmental studies, and even general studies. In some ways, these are related to what Newell (2010) calls integrative learning. However, they are not changing existing disciplinary curricula in any significant ways. Working towards that is a huge challenge, as 'the physical layout and traditional academic approach of universities are not conducive to interdisciplinary concepts' (Hall & Weaver, 2001. p. 873). The power elements outlined above also show that power is distributed, and so the resistance to change comes from guardians of various little fiefdoms that, put together, constitute a formidable force. Despite such structural barriers, there is an increasing pressure from different angles, including commercial ones, on disciplinary boundaries.

The focus on integrative learning outlined above has run parallel with an increasing interest in the development of generic skills, in the form of graduate attributes (Barrie, 2007; Bridgstock, 2009; Star & Hammer, 2008) which includes communication skills, critical thinking (Davies et al., 2011; Kek & Huijser, 2011), ability to work in teams (Beccaria, Kek, Huijser, Rose, & Kimmins, 2014) and collaboration (Tapscott & Williams, 2010) and of course problem-solving skills. As Klein (2006, p. 11) identifies, 'heightened demands for problem solving have fostered greater interest in collaboration and the ability to work with multiple sources of knowledge'.

So by now we can identify a number of interrelated themes that keep surfacing in debates about integrative learning and twenty-first-century skills, including communication, collaboration and problem-solving skills across disciplines. An agile PBL is ideally positioned to respond to the perceived need for such educational outcomes. The important point for our purposes here is that teachers should be seen as designers of learning experiences, and the design of problems is a crucial design element of an agile PBL. Moreover, we would argue that it is possible within an agile PBL context to design authentic problems that are inherently interdisciplinary and integrative and would thus stimulate and develop both collaborative skills and the ability to work with multiple sources of knowledge across different disciplines. We will return to the design of authentic interdisciplinary problems later, as we first need to establish what we actually mean by interdisciplinarity.

Not surprisingly, the idea of interdisciplinarity is not new and has a long history, mostly related to the development of schools, but the terminology is not consistent and includes concepts like 'integrated' and 'integrative' approaches, 'integration of studies' and since the 1920s also 'integrated curriculum' (Klein, 2006, p. 12). At various stages of the twentieth century, movements developed that were essentially trying to break through disciplinary boundaries and develop more holistic educational approaches that would have more generic learning outcomes. Broadly speaking, 'integration' was 'linked with the psychological process of holistic learning, personal integration, social integration, moral education, merging learning and work, a more relevant student-centred curriculum, teacher-student planning, preparation for participation in a democracy, a child-centred activity curriculum, and experience-based curriculum, and a broad-fields approach' (Klein, 2006, p. 12). We can draw clear links here to characterise elements of agile PBL, such as personal and social integration, holistic learning and an experience-based curriculum, otherwise known as experiential learning (Moon, 2013), but there are other links as well that may be relevant for an agile PBL, such as moral education and preparation for participation in a democracy, to which we can add ethical participation in a global economy. Each of these elements relies on the blurring of disciplinary boundaries to some extent. However, there are different levels of disciplinary 'integration', and each of these has a slightly different meaning. The three main contemporary terms that are widely used are multidisciplinary (Adamczyk & Twidale, 2007; Hooyman & Kiyak, 2008), interdisciplinary (Baldwin, 2007; Dillon, Noble, & Kaplan, 2009) and transdisciplinary (Clark & Button, 2011; Nicolescu, 2005).

Multidisciplinary approaches 'juxtapose disciplines, adding breadth and available knowledge, information, and methods. Yet, they speak as separate voices in an additive and encyclopedic mélange. Moreover, disciplinary elements remain intact' (Klein, 2006, p. 13). This is the 'postmodern' approach to blending disciplinary knowledge, otherwise known as the 'potpourri problem' (Jacobs, 2002). In other words, bits and pieces from different disciplinary knowledges are put together in this approach (but not necessarily people), which Jacobs argues diminishes the integrative focus and conceptual clarity. In other words, by juxtaposing different bits, students do not necessarily develop the ability to integrate these bits into a meaningful and rich whole. In fact, it may have the opposite effect of rigidifying the position of individual disciplinary bits. Similarly, even if you design collaborative tasks or problems that would require and bring together students from different disciplines, the problem in a multidisciplinary context would potentially create a jigsaw effect, whereby each disciplinary piece is simply added to the jigsaw by individual discipline-based students in a multidisciplinary team. In the worst multidisciplinary case scenario, none of the participants would have to cross-disciplinary boundaries.

This is different for interdisciplinary approaches, which go much further. The key here is integration of disciplines, which, in terms of curriculum design, is achieved through the use of themes, questions, ideas or problems. 'Subjects and disciplines become tools for studying a theme, a problem, a question, or an idea. Structures vary, from engaging two subjects in a single unit or course to a year-long program, or a student's entire educational experience in an "academy", "whole school", or "school-within-a-school"' (Klein, 2006, p. 14). Interdisciplinarity thus aligns very well with an agile PBL, and it is very possible to design authentic interdisciplinary problems that engage two subjects in a single unit or a year-long program. To do so, however, would require a blurring of disciplinary boundaries and programs and thus a collaborative and integrative approach to curriculum design, rather than a competitive, discipline-based one. With a full understanding of what is at stake, and with full support of the institutional hierarchy, along with a healthy dose of creative imagination, it is possible to design a fully integrated, interdisciplinary and scaffolded PBL curriculum that would be characterised by a balanced combination of shorter projects and longer projects at various points in the student learning journey.

Finally, transdisciplinarity goes one step further, in that it directly involves students in the design of the curriculum. Transdisciplinarity can be seen as a radically student-centred approach, whereby students participate in selecting the themes and problems they will study. Clearly, getting students involved in curriculum design, especially in an agile PBL context, is useful regardless of whether it is using a transdisciplinary approach. 'In university programs, transdisciplinary approaches are linked with new comprehensive frameworks that transcend the narrow scope of disciplinary worldviews through an overarching synthesis, such as general systems, policy sciences, feminism, cultural critique, and ecology and sustainability' (Klein, 2006, p. 14). We believe that at this stage a transdisciplinary approach is possible as an extension of an interdisciplinary program. It would call for genuine partnerships with students involving them in the educational process – curriculum, teaching, research and problem design – so that they are not just mere 'receivers' but become cocreators, co-teachers, co-learners and coresearchers (Healey, Flint, & Harrington, 2014). Therefore, if designed carefully and collaboratively with students, employers and partners outside the university, an agile PBL could potentially lend itself to a transdisciplinary approach or at least partially.

Overall, when we compare interdisciplinarity with discipline-based learning, the key distinction is that an interdisciplinary and integrative approach allows for integration and synthesis, or rather it demands integration and synthesis as learning outcomes, because these are an integral part of how the curriculum has been designed. As Klein (2006, p. 15) notes, 'interdisciplinary education at all levels intersects with innovative pedagogies that emphasize exploration and active involvement in the process of meaning making'. PBL can be seen as such an innovative approach that 'promotes dialogue and community, problem-posing and problem-solving, and critical thinking' (Klein, 2006, p. 15). Of course PBL is not the only student-centred approach that does this, and others, to varying degrees, include other forms of PBL such as project-based learning (Helle, Tynjala, &

Olkinuora, 2006) and anchored instruction (Hmelo-Silver, 2004), design thinking (Brown, 2008; Oka, 2010), service learning (Furco & Billig, 2002) and the learning factory (Lamancusa, Zayas, Soyster, Morell, & Jorgensen, 2008). However, the strength of an agile PBL is that it can potentially incorporate elements of all these approaches, especially when we consider Savin-Baden's (2014) new PBL constellations, such as the focus on authentic, contextualised learning, particularly through its problem design, and herein lies its potential.

With regard to interdisciplinarity, Klein (2006, p. 15) provides a useful list of structures, strategies and activities that are typically associated with interdisciplinary approaches, and these make for a useful comparison to the identified and documented characteristics of PBL:

- Team teaching and team planning
- Collaborative learning and learning communities
- Clustered and linked courses
- Core seminars at introductory and capstone levels
- Theme and problem focus in courses
- Proactive attention to integration and synthesis
- Models of interdisciplinary and integrative process
- Theories and methods from interdisciplinary fields
- Projects and case studies
- Dyads, triads and small groups for discussion
- Game and role playing
- Inquiry- and discovery-based learning
- Learning portfolios
- Experiential and service learning, internships and fieldwork
- Residential living-learning experiences

While perhaps not all of these apply directly to PBL in its more traditional sense, this can almost be seen as a 'tick list' for an agile PBL. For example, PBL is still too often applied by single teachers in their own courses. We are certainly not condemning this, as we know from our own experiences that implementing PBL across a whole curriculum, or indeed a whole institution, is a huge challenge, as suggested above. Even when it is applied across a whole institution, it may be quite a rigid and discipline-based version of PBL, as can be seen, for example, in the 'one problem per day' version of PBL at Republic Polytechnic in Singapore (O'Grady & Alwis, 2002; O'Grady, Yew, Goh, & Schmidt, 2012). Again, we are certainly not condemning this, as it has achieved good learning outcomes. However, our argument is that we need a much more flexible and interdisciplinary or what we call in this book an agile version of PBL in order to not only respond to twenty-first-century skills needs but to also empower students to shape twenty-first-century environments.

Possible Challenges

In an agile (and an admittedly imagined) version of PBL, teachers, students and problem designers from a variety of disciplines and with a range of specialised discipline-based expertise would work together to design the problems for the curriculum, and these problems would thus incorporate different disciplinary aspects that would need to be addressed in an integrated manner. Interdisciplinary team teaching would be a crucial part in its success, and this could take the form of different sessions being facilitated by different teachers, or in some cases, specific sessions being facilitated by two or three teachers with different specialised disciplinary expertise, and in really courageous cases partnering students in teaching. It is not hard to see how quickly this could become problematic within current university structures that are based on rigid units of time, workload and worldview, which has not changed in any fundamental way since the early Fordist factories (Amin, 2008). So yes, it would need considerable courage of university administrators, academics and educational leaders for a fully agile PBL version to be implemented.

The interdisciplinary problems thus designed would then be addressed through collaborative learning in collaborative learning communities or PBL teams. The interdisciplinary design team, which ideally would include employers, would have ensured that the problem is pitched at the right level and indeed that individual disciplinary elements are do-able at the level the students are at. Of course, it helps in this respect that exploring prior skills that individual students bring to the collaborative teams has always been an integral part of the PBL process (Dolmans & Schmidt, 2010), and indeed Schmidt and Moust (2010, p. 41) argue that 'a problem should be connected to the prior knowledge base students have'. Of course, this consideration can be managed if we involve students in the design of the problems in the first place. Still, this is a delicate balance, and the expectations about outcomes should be adjusted if the balance is not quite right. In the overall curriculum, these problems could be contained within individual courses, especially in the first year, but as students become accustomed to the PBL process, problems are more likely to become extended beyond individual courses, for example, through clustered and linked courses. This is particularly important when you begin to design increasingly authentic problems, as they cannot necessarily be contained in the neat and tidy 15-week boundaries of existing course structures. Indeed, they may run over a period of 1 year or even longer.

An interdisciplinary agile PBL curriculum needs to be carefully balanced, appropriately scaffolded with fading properties within and intercourses and time (year level). In other words, it needs to be intentionally planned and designed. So in most cases, it would be perfectly acceptable and appropriate to begin with scenario-based problems and short projects in the first year, accompanied by core seminars at introductory and capstone levels. However, even those scenario-based 'shorter' problems can have an interdisciplinary and integrative theme focus, rather than being purely discipline based. In this way, you would be paying conscious attention to integration and synthesis, and students would be stimulated from the beginning of their degrees to consider what kind of disciplinary knowledge they would require to address particular interdisciplinary projects, as well as how best to go about acquiring such knowledge. Moreover, they would be able to draw on their existing knowledge and skills, acquired in other parts of the agile PBL ecology for learning.

A well-facilitated PBL process already has built-in mechanisms to develop such skills and, in this way, models interdisciplinary and integrative process by requiring students to consider theories and methods from interdisciplinary fields. Again, the key here is the design of the problem, which then functions as the centre of the whole pedagogical process. The other crucial element is the facilitation, and as Klein (2006, p. 15) argues, 'teachers become "connection experts", not "subject experts"'. Of course, they are discipline experts as well, but their role lies primarily in connecting students to knowledge and activating learning rather than being mere providers and transmitters of knowledge.

Agile PBL Problems for the Twenty-First Century

The problems, regardless of whether they are case based, scenario based or authentic, require students to work collaboratively. Usually such integrative problems are addressed in teams of five or six students, and these teams would preferably be interdisciplinary in nature. Within such teams, tasks can then be assigned to individuals, dyads or triads. Depending on the problem and the envisioned learning outcomes, problems can involve game and role playing, for example, if a problem requires the delivery of a particular service in a high pressure context.

An example is a client-based marketing PBL program at a Singaporean polytechnic where the faculty, firstly, had to prospect for external industry partners as clients for marketing communications agencies, formed by students (Kek & Wee, 2000; Wee, Kek, & Kelley, 2003). The real clients contribute some funding to students to purchase materials and resources used to create appropriate products or artefacts related to the clients' problems. In the student groups, students will assume different roles such as account manager, strategic planning manager, media executive, creative directors, researchers and so forth. Students would attend an initial client briefing to obtain the issues or problems from the clients, which they would later clarify to find out what they already knew and what they needed to know and do about it. Subsequently, they learned to map their own strategies to accomplish the work at hand. Students become self-directed, working within authentic constraints of resources and time, but this varies with different client problems. During the client management, students learned crisis management as they had to learn to adapt their strategies when they faced unanticipated barriers or new information thrown at them by the clients, much like in the 'real world'. Students presented the final product or solution to the clients in the form of new creative campaigns with storyboards, developed advertisements, taxi ads, bill boards or product packaging. Both the faculty and industry partners graded the students' work. Thus, these problems are authentic, interdisciplinary and integrative, and they require a range of twenty-first-century skills, such as team work, communication and problem-solving.

In terms of the facilitation of these interdisciplinary teams, inquiry- and discovery-based learning approaches will be used by individual students after identifying the learning issues or knowledge to be sought and learned to solve the problem, and this is facilitated by PBL teachers. Integrative problems infer effective facilitation or teaching from PBL teachers. 'Inquiry teachers tend to use questioning techniques to promote deep thinking; as a result students are more active, but the teacher still leads the discussion, working towards global learning goals by choosing strategies on the fly' (Hmelo-Silver & Barrows, 2006, p. 23). The 'on the fly' bit may suggest a level of randomness, but this is not the case. It merely focuses on the importance of responding to where your students are at and probing in an appropriate but flexible manner to interrogate the problem as much as possible within the developmental stage of the group. That is, some groups will take longer than others. But all groups will learn about the integrated knowledge and integrative processes. At the same time though, 'it is critical for the facilitator to always keep the learning goals in mind' (Hmelo-Silver & Barrows, 2006, p. 29). In other words, while the facilitation of the team response to the problem is flexible, the outcomes are not, as they are contained in the design of the problem, which, if done well, should be pitched at the right level. It is clear however that the role of the teacher/facilitator in PBL is a crucial one and fades in time and not diminished, as is a common perception among those who are unfamiliar with the PBL process (Ribeiro, 2011).

Ultimately, in an agile PBL curriculum, the problems are as authentic as they can possibly be. Ideally, this means that the problems would involve some form of experiential and service learning, internships and fieldwork, as well as residential living-learning experiences where appropriate and relevant. When designing the curriculum, problems are the drivers to progress, extend and integrate student learning in an authentic context, drawn from partners in the macro-system. Indeed, some of these projects may even lead to start-ups, which would be another excellent outcome. Through working on numerous smaller and larger projects, and contributing to interdisciplinary teams, individual students can end up with a 'learning portfolio' of 'real' work of product and/or artefacts, demonstrating their knowledges, skills, attitudes, values and competencies. The products and/or artefacts students create in response to the authentic problems in an agile PBL context, and that they are able to show in the form of, for example, an (e-)portfolio, demonstrate the agile PBL outcomes about what they know and are able to do, as opposed to a list of discipline-based grades for exams and isolated assignments. In short, this is a 'living' and 'lived' portfolio that they can use well beyond their university degree and keep building when they move out of the university. At the same time, this is part of the development of their metacognitive skills and ability to reflect on their own practice, which is also a crucial twenty-first-century skill. If an agile PBL curriculum is well designed, the ultimate outcome, in Newell's (2002, cited in Klein, 2006, p. 15) words, would be 'a new category of interdisciplinary experts, capable of synthesising specialised insights of disciplinary experts into a comprehensive understanding of significant problems and solutions'.

Conclusion

As Schmidt and Moust (2010) rightly argue, the (agile PBL) problem needs to be pitched in such a way that it potentially links to prior knowledge and learning, on the one hand, even if this requires some careful teaching up front, but at the same time raises students' curiosity and challenges them to the right extent. Getting this balance right is probably the most important part of problem design, and the added complication is of course that the problems need to be as authentic as possible. However, while this is challenging, the rewards, in the form of twenty-first-century skills, and in particular the ability to address complex, interdisciplinary problems in diverse teams, are worth considering. As noted earlier, the use of problems and building a gradual increase in complexity into those problems is less challenging if PBL is an integrated pedagogy and curriculum throughout a student's learning journey. It would be very difficult if PBL is only applied in isolated courses and units. As we have argued, an agile PBL is an interdisciplinary and integrative pedagogy and curriculum, and within this imagined worldview, the problems should be as authentic as possible, cocreated with students and partners outside the university, and in this way, they will authentically position students for a twenty-first-century world which is no longer able to offer any level of certainty, but which instead requires confidence and creativity, with a healthy dose of interdisciplinary collaboration to function effectively and to improve things for those around them. The next question then becomes: how do you know that the learning outcomes are being achieved, and how do you assess the interdisciplinary skills in the context of an agile PBL ecology for learning. Thus, we will next shift our focus towards assessment in an agile PBL context in Chap. 5.

References

Adamczyk, P.D., & Twidale, M.B. (2007). *Supporting multidisciplinary collaboration: Requirements from novel HCI education.* Paper presented at the SIGCHI conference on human factors in computing systems.

Altbach, P. G., Gumport, P. J., & Berdahl, R. O. (2011). *American higher education in the twenty-first century: Social, political and economic challenges* (3rd ed.). Baltimore: The John Hopkins University Press.

Amin, A. (Ed.). (2008). *Post-Fordism: A reader.* Hoboken, NJ: Wiley.

Baldwin, D. C., Jr. (2007). Some historical notes on interdisciplinary and interprofessional education and practice in health care in the USA. *Journal of Interprofessional Care, 21*(S1), 23–37.

Barnett, R., & Coate, K. (2004). *Engaging the curriculum in higher education.* Berkshire, UK: Mc-Graw Hill Education.

Barrie, S. (2007). A conceptual framework for the teaching and learning of generic graduate attributes. *Studies in Higher Education, 32*(4), 439–458.

Beccaria, L., Kek, M., Huijser, H., Rose, J., & Kimmins, L. (2014). The interrelationships between student approaches to learning and group work. *Nurse Education Today, 34*(7), 1094–1103. doi: http://dx.doi.org/10.1016/j.nedt.2014.02.006.

Bransford, J.D., Barron, B., Pea, R.D., Meltzoff, A., Kuhl, P., Bell, P., et al. (2006). Foundations and opportunities for an interdisciplinary science of learning. In K.R. Sawyer (Ed.), *Cambridge handbook of the learning sciences* (pp. 19–34). New York: Cambridge University Press.

Bransford, J. D., Brown, A. L., & Cooking, R. R. (Eds.). (2000). *National research council: How people learn: Brain, mind, experience, and school: Expanded edition.* Washington, DC: National Academy Press.

Bransford, J. D., & Schwartz, D. L. (1999). Rethink transfer. A simple proposal with multiple implications. *Review of Research in Education, 24*(1), 61–100.

Bridges, D. (2000). Back to the future: The higher education curriculum in the 21st century. *Cambridge Journal of Education, 30*(1), 37–55.

Bridgstock, R. (2009). The graduate attribute we've overlooked: Enhancing graduate employability through career management skills. *Higher Education Research and Development, 28*(1), 31–44.

Brown, T. (2008). Design thinking. *Harvard Business Review, 86*(6), 84.

Cassidy, S. (2006). Developing employability skills: Peer assessment in higher education. *Education + Training, 48*(7), 508–517.

Chickering, A.W. (n.d.). The seven vectors: An overview. Retrieved April 26, 2014, from http://faculty.winthrop.edu/fullerb/QEP/7vectorsofdevelopment.pdf

Chickering, A. W., & Reisser, L. (1993). *Education and identity* (2nd ed.). San Francisco: Jossey-Bass.

Clark, B., & Button, C. (2011). Sustainability transdisciplinary education model: Interface of arts, science, and community (STEM). *International Journal of Sustainability in Higher Education, 12*(1), 41–54.

Cope, B., & Kalantzis, M. (2009). *Ubiquitous learning.* Champaign, IL: University of Illinois Press.

Davies, A., Fidler, D., & Gorbis, M. (2011). *Future work skills 2020* (pp. 1–14). Palo Alto, CA: Institute for the Future for the University of Phoenix Research Institute. Retrieved September 26, 2016, from http://www.iftf.org/uploads/media/SR-1382A_UPRI_future_work_skills_sm.pdf

Deakin-Crick, R. (2007). Learning how to learn: The dynamic assessment of learning power. *The Curriculum Journal, 18*(2), 135–153.

Deakin-Crick, R., Broadfoot, P., & Glaxton, G. (2004). Developing an effective lifelong learning inventory: The ELLI project. *Assessment in Education, 11*(3), 247–272.

Dearing, R. (1997). *Higher education in the learning society: Report of the National Committee of Inquiry into Higher Education.* Norwich, UK: HMSO.

Dewey, J. (1980). *The school and society.* Carbondale, IL: Southern Illinois University Press.

Dillon, P. M., Noble, K. A., & Kaplan, L. (2009). Simulation as a means to foster collaborative interdisciplinary education. *Nursing Education Perspectives, 30*(2), 87–90.

Dolmans, D., & Schmidt, H. (2010). The problem-based learning process. In H. van Berkel, A. Scherpbier, H. Hillen, & C. van Der Vleuten (Eds.), *Lessons from problem-based learning.* Oxford, UK: Oxford University Press.

Elli. (n.d.). *Learning power evaluations for pupils.* Retrieved April 27, 2014, from http://www.thelearningpartnership.com/elli-26082-0.html

Fineberg, I. C., Wenger, N. S., & Forrow, L. (2004). Interdisciplinary education: Evaluation of a palliative care training intervention for pre-professionals. *Academic Medicine, 79*(8), 769–776.

Flew, T. (2012). *Creative industries.* London: Sage.

Flew, T. (2013). *Global creative industries.* Cambridge, UK: Polity Press.

Foubert, M. (1980). *Power/knowledge: Selected interviews and other writings, 1972–1977* (Trans C. Gordon, C.). New York: Pantheon.

Foucault, M. (1980). *Power/knowledge: Selected interviews and other writings, 1972–1977* (Trans C. Gordon, C.). New York: Pantheon.

Furco, A., & Billig, S. (Eds.). (2002). *Service-learning: The essence of the pedagogy* (Vol. 1). Charlotte, NC: Information Age Publishing.

Hall, P., & Weaver, L. (2001). Interdisciplinary education and teamwork: A long and winding road. *Medical Education, 35*(9), 867–875.

Hartley, J. (2005). *Creative industries*. Oxford, UK: Blackwell.

Hatano, G., & Inagaki, K. (1984). Two courses of expertise. *Research and Clinical Center for Child Development Annual Report, 6*, 27–36.

Hatano, G., & Oura, Y. (2003). Commentary: Reconceptualising school learning using insight from expertise research. *Educational Researcher, 32*(8), 26–29.

Healey, M., Flint, A., & Harrington, K. (2014). *Engagement through partnership: Students as partners in learning and teaching in higher education* (pp. 1–76). New York: The Higher Education Academy, UK.

Helle, L., Tynjala, P., & Olkinuora, E. (2006). Project-based learning in post-secondary education-theory, practice and rubber sling shots. *HIgher Education, 51*(2), 287–314.

Hmelo-Silver, C. E. (2004). Problem-based learning: What and how do students learn? *Educational Psychology Review, 16*(3), 235–266.

Hmelo-Silver, C. E., & Barrows, H. S. (2006). Goals and strategies of a problem-based learning facilitator. *The Interdisciplinary Journal of Problem-Based Learning, 1*(1), 21–39.

Hooyman, N. R., & Kiyak, H. A. (2008). *Social gerontology: A multidisciplinary perspective*. New York: Pearson Education.

Huijser, H. (2006). Refocusing multiliteracies for the net generation. *International Journal of Pedagogies and Learning, 2*(1), 21–33.

Jacobs, H. (2002). Integrated curriculum design. In J. T. Klein (Ed.), *Interdisciplinary education in K-12 and college: A foundation for K-16 dialogue* (pp. 21–44). New York: College Board Publications.

Jaros, M., & Deakin-Crick, R. (2007). Personalized learning for the post-mechanical age. *Journal of Curriculum Studies, 39*(4), 423–440.

Kalantzis, M., & Cope, B. (2001). 'Multiliteracies' as a framework for action. In M. Kalantzis & B. Cope (Eds.), *Transformations in language and learning: Perspectives on multiliteracies* (pp. 19–32). Melbourne, Australia: Common Ground.

Kek, M. Y. C. A., & Huijser, H. (2011). The power of problem-based learning in developing critical thinking skills: Preparing students for tomorrow's digital futures in today's classrooms. *Higher Education Research and Development, 30*(3), 317–329.

Kek, Y.C., & Wee, L.K.N. (2000). *Triumphs and trials of using problem-based learning in marketing communications education: Perspectives from educators and students*. Paper presented at the International Advertising Association Conference, Miami, Florida.

Klein, J. T. (2006). A platform for a shared discourse of interdisciplinary education. *Journal of Social Science Education, 5*(2), 10–18.

Lamancusa, J. S., Zayas, J. L., Soyster, A. L., Morell, L., & Jorgensen, J. (2008). The learning factory: Industry-partnered active learning. *Journal of Engineering Education, 97*(1), 5–11.

Mason, G., Williams, G., & Cranmer, S. (2006). Employability skills initiatives in higher education: What effects do they have on graduate labour market outcomes? *Education Economics, 17*(1), 1–30.

Moon, J. A. (2013). *A handbook of reflective and experiential learning*. London/New York: Routledge.

Newell, W. H. (2010). Educating for a complex world: Integrative learning and interdisciplinary studies. *Liberal Education, 96*(4), 6–11. https://aacu.org/liberaleducation/le-fa10/LEFA10_Newell.cfm.

Nicolescu, B. (2005). Towards transdisciplinary education. *TD: The Journal for Transdisciplinary Research in Southern Africa, 1*(1), 5–15.

O'Grady, G., & Alwis, W.A.M. (December, 2002). *One day, one problem: PBL at the Republic Polytechnic*. Paper presented at the 4th Pacific Conference in PBL, Hatyai, Thailand.

O'Grady, G., Yew, E. H. J., Goh, K. P. L., & Schmidt, H. G. (Eds.). (2012). *One day, one problem: An approach to problem-based learning*. Singapore, Singapore: Springer.

Oka, H. (2010). *Design thinking: Integrating innovation, customer experience, and brand value*. bookforfree.us.

Partnership for 21st Century Learning. (2007). *Framework for 21st century learning*. Tucson, AZ: Partnership for 21st Century Skills.

Ribeiro, L. (2011). The pros and cons of problem-based learning from the teacher's standpoint. *Journal of University Teaching & Learning Practice, 8*(1), 4.

Robinson, K. (2006). How schools kill creativity. Retrieved April 27, 2014 from http://www.ted.com/talks/ken_robinson_says_schools_kill_creativity

Savin-Baden, M. (2014). Using problem-based learning: New constellations for the 21st century. *Journal on Excellence in College Teaching, 25*(3&4), 197–219.

Schmidt, H., & Moust, J. (2010). Designing problems. In H. van Berkel, A. Scherpbier, & C. van der Vleuten (Eds.), *Lessons from problem-based learning*. Oxford, UK: Oxford University Press.

Star, C., & Hammer, S. (2008). Teaching generic skills: Eroding the higher purpose of university, or an opportunity for renewal. *Oxford Review of Education, 34*(2), 237–251.

Stark, R., Renkl, A., Gruber, H., & Mandl, H. (1998). Indeed, sometimes knowledge does not help: A replication study. *Instructional Science, 26*(5), 391–407.

Tapscott, D., & Williams, A. D. (2010). Innovating the 21st century university: It's time! *Educause Review, 45*(1), 16–29.

Tew, M., Crick, R. D., Broadfoot, P., & Claxton, G. (2004). *Learning power: A practitioner's guide*. Manchester, UK: Lifelong Learning Foundation.

The New London Group. (1996). A pedagogy of multiliteracies: Designing social futures. *Harvard Educational Review, 66*(1), 60–92.

Wee, L. K. N., Kek, M. Y. C. A., & Kelley, C. A. (2003). Transforming the marking curriculum using problem-based learning: A case study. *Journal of Marketing Education, 25*(2), 150–162.

Wickramasinghe, V., & Perera, L. (2010). Graduates', university lecturers' and employers' perceptions towards employability skills. *Education + Training, 52*(3), 226–244.

Chapter 5
Assessing Agile PBL

Introduction

As suggested in Chap. 4, the learning outcomes we imagined for an agile PBL ecology for learning in this book, do not only include (inter)disciplinary skills and knowledge, but instead constitute a whole way-of-being, which includes an attitude and disposition. Agile PBL serves as a curricular and pedagogical vehicle to facilitate the development of this way-of-being among students so that they learn and develop adaptive expertise while in their current studies and beyond the microcontext of the university as lifelong learners. This also brings with it the need to reconceptualise assessment, as it raises the question of how we can, or should, assess such learning outcomes, in particular the intangible ones such as 'attitude' and 'disposition', which are notoriously difficult to measure. We are not suggesting to rethink assessment for its own sake as a new curricular reform agenda, but rather that current assessment practices are so entrenched in traditions of psychometrics in a testing culture that it has been immune to changes, even though the concept of learning has significantly evolved and reconceptualised in the past few decades (Boud, 2000; McDowell & Sambell, 1999; Segers, Dochy, & Cascallar, 2003). The traditional testing assessment paradigm and practices do not align with Barrow's essentials of PBL conceptualised 50 years ago, particularly not as they relate to the continuous and reiterative participation of students in the teaching and learning process and activities, in assessment activities and in authentic assessment problems or tasks. They align even less with agile PBL.

The one end point, high-stakes examinations, is not only unfit for the intentions of agile PBL, but it fails to recognise that learning in agile PBL is an integral part of assessing and vice versa. That is, students are constantly assessing themselves and their peers in the learning and teaching process and activities. Authentic problems or tasks and activities are used to motivate and engage students to share their present knowledge, share alternative ideas or hypotheses, search for information and evaluate and develop reasoned arguments to support, or disagree with, proposed solu-

© Springer Science+Business Media Singapore 2017
M.Y.C.A. Kek, H. Huijser, *Problem-based Learning into the Future*,
DOI 10.1007/978-981-10-2454-2_5

tions. And where possible, students and partners outside the university in the macro-system cocreate the problem. Throughout the learning process and at the end of a problem, students reflect through self- and peer assessment on their developing knowledge and competencies so as to support transfer of learning (Salomon & Perkins, 1989). Research has continuously found that PBL students, when compared to traditional forms of learning and teaching, are better able to transfer knowledge to new problems (Lu, Bridges, & Hmelo-Silver, 2014; Strobel & Van Barneveld, 2009; Xian & Madhavan, 2013); in agile PBL, this ability can be accelerated. In another words, agile PBL students are considered to be more apt as adaptive experts, having the opportunities to learn and developed a way-of-being that is flexible, and adapt to future contexts, both within and beyond the university. Part of the reason for this is that these two domains are not seen as separate but instead are seamlessly intertwined in an agile PBL ecology for learning. As discussed in the previous chapters, agile PBL serves to bridge the university and the world beyond, to transition students from current university studies (micro-context) to future contexts of supercomplexity, where their ability to deal effectively and efficiently with novel or new situations and problems is the ultimate form of assessment.

In agile PBL, we imagine assessment to be enmeshed in learning and teaching activities, and the intention is to assess a way-of-being as an integral part of an overall set of learning outcomes that also includes (inter)disciplinary knowledge and skills. From our perspective, these three agile PBL components – outcomes, learning and teaching process and assessment – are interrelated and interdependent or, as Biggs (Biggs & Tang, 2011) termed it, in constructive alignment. That is, if the outcomes are about enabling student to become lifelong learners, not only do the teaching, curriculum and learning outcomes have to focus squarely on knowledge, skills and dispositions that can sustain students beyond current university studies, but the assessment practices and methods must also engage and facilitate students to *be*(come) lifelong learners. Messick (1994) referred to such assessments as having consequential validity, that is, a measure of the consequences of assessment on learning. The mode of assessment that is required as part of agile PBL puts the students and consequences on learning squarely in the centre and can be termed as 'assessment for learning' to distinguish it from the more traditional 'assessment of learning', which is part of the measurement paradigm.

In this chapter, we will discuss the challenges faced in transforming assessment practices, recent thinking around assessments that are aligned to agile PBL's intentions and goals of developing a way-of-being and the tensions and possibilities associated with assessments for learning. Central to all of this, again, is the position of assessment in the context of an overall agile PBL ecology for learning.

Importance of Assessment

Assessment is a powerful tool in higher education as it plays a major role in student learning, to the extent that, for some, assessment is the actual curriculum (Ramsden, 1992) and, for others, it embodies the success of an institution (Tinto, 2012).

Regardless, assessment is one of the distinct features of student approaches to learning (Marton & Saljo, 1997), as it drives learning (Gibbs, 2006a; Ramsden, 1992) and is a necessary condition of student success (Tinto, 2012). Assessment has been found to engage students and stimulate them into taking a deep approach to learning (Entwistle & Tait, 1990; McDowell, Wakelin, Montgomery, & King, 2011) and to support learning outcomes, teaching, pedagogy and curriculum that focus on 'what students can do in the world' (Boud & Soler, 2015, p. 2). Assessments influence what and how students learn, and they act as a motivator for learning. Yet sadly, much evidence has indicated that students mostly tend to learn surface declarative discipline-based knowledge rather than show a deep understanding and use of higher-order thinking skills, unlike the experts in their area of study or at work (Biggs & Tang, 2011).

Undesirable backwash or wash-back effects of assessments on student learning have long been recognised and have been one of the reasons for developing closer alignment between teaching and assessment to learning outcomes, otherwise known as Biggs' principle of constructive alignment (Biggs & Tang, 2011). It is only through constructive alignment that students are:

> … entrapped in a web of consistency, optimising the likelihood that they will engage the appropriate learning activities … where assessment is not aligned to the intended or other desired outcomes, or where the teaching does not directly encourage the appropriate learning activities, students can easily escape by engaging in inappropriate learning activities, which become a surface approach to learning.… (Biggs & Tang, 2011, p. 99)

If assessment is such a powerful tool for students, assessment should also be a powerful tool for teachers to leverage and use productively, rather than being used against them as backwash. Thus, whatever we claim as the intended learning outcomes, and no matter how well the agile PBL curriculum and authentic problems are designed, and how excellent the teaching is, it is the assessment that is viewed by students as the driver of their learning (McDowell & Sambell, 1999; Sambell, McDowell, & Montgomery, 2013). Therefore, what we claim as our intended educational goals and/or learning outcomes must be reflected in what we assess – providing the *evidence* to us as teachers and to other important constituents or stakeholders of the institution and beyond, that our students know *and do* what we claim they know and are able to do. However, to be able to do this, students must perceive the time, efforts and emotions invested in doing the assessments NOT to be just about gaining good grades and/or just about acquiring the 'right' disciplinary/technical or professional declarative knowledge. So what are the barriers for institutions and teachers in designing and practising assessment for learning?

Challenges in Transforming Traditional Assessment Practices

Traditional assessment practices are deeply entrenched in a long history of the testing culture that reflects the psychometric-quantitative paradigm (Birenbaum, 2003). The testing culture subscribes to traditional theories of learning and teaching and is behaviouristic in nature. Students are broadly viewed as empty vessels, passively receiving knowledge transmitted by their teachers. As the term psychometric-quantitative connotes, testing culture is heavily reliant on psychometric models in developing tests, strongly guided by objectivity and fairness in testing and scoring, and thus requires a high level of standardisation.

According to Baartman, Bastiaens, Kirschner and van der Vleuten (2007), testing culture emerged at the start of the industrial revolution in the 1920s, when efficient and cheap tests were needed to detect individual differences in achievement. During those days, teaching and assessment were two separate activities in education. That is, the teachers carried out the teaching, and assessment experts were the ones to develop the assessment tools to be used by the teachers. The assessment tools were commonly comprised of multiple-choice questions, true/false or matching items. They were mostly paper-and-pencil tests, taken in class, and usually as a big summative exam at the end of a course or year. The assessments were also conducted under tight surveillance such as strict time limits, and external resources such as books, reading materials and tools at the examination halls were not allowed. Assessments were norm referenced whereby students were compared across student cohorts. The development of the tests and the criteria used to judge the students were not made known to students. The tests mostly addressed the basic and lower-level skills and were mostly based on rote learning and memorisation of what was taught in the classrooms or read from textbooks (Birenbaum, 2003). What is assessed in this model is only the product. The processes of getting to the end product are not taken into account.

Even though we wrote about such assessment practices above in the past tense, the same testing culture, assessment tools and practices remain relatively unchanged today, in PBL and non-PBL programs alike. Many teachers may observe that some assessments are not appropriately assessing what they should, but they may not know, firstly, that the assessments they are using are legacies of outdated testing traditions and, secondly, how to actually change the assessment in meaningful ways. Moreover, there are other contextual factors (especially emanating from the exo- and macro-systems) that impede institutions, and these spiral down to teachers and students, which in turn renders such assessments effectively the status quo.

According to Gibbs (2006b), some of the reasons for maintaining traditional assessment tools and subscribing to a conservative, testing mindset could be attributed to:

- Declining resources to the higher education sector by governments, which leads to increased pressure on teachers to increase research productivity, resulting in less time allocated to teaching and interactions with students.
- Increasing class sizes, which makes computer-aided assessment marking more efficient; however, teachers continue to design low-level questions relying on students' recall and memorisation because it is much easier to design and it is commonly thought that MCQs are more objective.

- Worries of declining standards have inadvertently resulted in many institutions of higher education being overly cautious about approving changes to assessment policies that relate to learning or innovative assessments.

Similarly, Kvale (2007) offers a perspective from the sociopolitical functions of assessment to explain why testing culture and traditional assessment practices have continued to be a mainstay in today's educational system. Reasons include:

- The increased formal legal requirements and continued reference to objectivity or psychometric criteria in tests have pushed teachers to continue using assessment for certification and selection purposes.
- The domination properties in traditional assessment where teachers can maintain power, authority and control of the discipline or knowledge they are teaching. This idea also echoes Savin-Baden's (2004) study where the impact of assessment at four British universities implementing four different PBL curricula was explored. She concluded that '... many of our current assessment practices are hegemonic practices whereby ideas, structures and actions are constructed and promoted by the powerful to maintain the status quo' (p. 232).
- Assessment is used as censorship where examinations are constantly used to define for students what knowledge is worthy of acquiring.

In short, many assessment practices today still focus on assessment of learning, instead of assessment for learning (Boud, 2007), contributing to differences in academic tribes and territories (Becher & Trowler, 2001). Moreover, in this way, they remain squarely confined to the micro-system, thus reinforcing the boundaries within the overall ecology for learning, rather than traversing between them, as an agile PBL ecology for learning aims to do.

To summarise, traditional assessment tools and practices are currently too limited in scope in preparing students for future learning needs, application of knowledge, skills, dispositions and competencies deemed important for the twenty-first century:

- They test predominantly disciplinary knowledge or declarative knowledge with less attention to skills, competencies and dispositions.
- They drive teaching for assessment instead of teaching for learning.
- They treat assessment as a separate, post-teaching activity instead of integrating assessment into teaching and curriculum at the program level.
- They focus only on individual achievement instead of group interactions and group achievement.
- They focus on artificial constraints such as a prescribed length of time; high-stakes, big final exam at the end of the study period; and most of the time students must attempt the exam individually.

What Should Assessment for Learning Look Like Instead?

If the traditional assessment practices and tools are insufficient to provide the evidence, what should the 'new' assessment look like, particularly ones that would be aligned with twenty-first-century experiences and/or requirements? Assessment culture, as opposed to testing culture, appears much more suitable. Segers et al. (2003) state that the concept of learning has transformed today based on new insights and developments from various disciplines. New insights into learning have led to a movement towards rethinking and reframing assessment, in ways that converge more directly with learning.

Many insights into learning can be found in our earlier chapters so we will not repeat them here. However, the thesis is that students are not passive receivers of knowledge and that they share responsibilities for the learning process. In this twenty-first century, students not only need (inter)disciplinary knowledge, but they need to be able to think critically, analyse, synthesise, communicate, solve problems, work with others and technologies and innovate and create new products or knowledge. More importantly, they need to be able to perform and adapt knowledge when encountering a new problem, task or novel situation that is not 'taught' in schools. This means they will not necessarily have the knowledge domain ready in hand, but they will have the indwellings, a way-of-being – they have the skills, competencies and dispositions to formulate problems, propose possible ideas or hypotheses, search for information and problem-solve. This comes from being used to interacting with others, texts, technologies and tools effectively and as a result being able to judge the best solutions or approaches in any particular circumstance.

The fundamental belief of this new assessment culture is that the final grade or score normally obtained in the testing culture does not represent the developmental competence of a student, which is assumed to change over time (Baartman, Bastiaens, et al. 2007). This is to be expected of a beginning novice student in contrast to a later year expert student engaging in an agile PBL curriculum. Thus, the new assessment modes are generally less standardised than the ones used in the testing culture, and they have the following aspects (Baartman, Bastiaens, et al., 2007):

- Assessments are carried out without time pressure.
- Tools or resources used in real life are used in tandem.
- Assessments are interesting and authentic to engage students in meaningful learning processes.
- Assessments assess both product and processes.
- Summative assessments are not only used, but formative assessments are frequently carried out to guide students through the provision of prompt and constructive feedback on the product and processes.
- Assessment criteria and standards are communicated and shared with students and even codeveloped or developed and assessed by students.
- There are multiple assessments (a suite or program) instead of one single assessment to measure the multidimensional aspects of competencies.

The major changes differentiating assessment and testing cultures could be summarised in continua related to the following seven characteristics of assessment (Segers et al., 2003, pp. 3–4):

1. Authenticity – from decontextualised, atomistic to authentic, contextualised
   Refers to a shift from objective tests with item formats such as short answer, fill in the blanks, multiple-choice questions and true/false *to authentic, performance- or competence-based assessment.*
2. Measures – from single to multiple
   Refers to depicting a student's competence with one single measure such as a mark or grade *to portraying a student's competence based on multiple measures showing the various aspects of a student profile.*
3. Level of comprehension – from low to high
   Refers to the move from mainly assessing reproduction of knowledge *to assessing higher-order skills and processes.*
4. Dimensions of intelligence – from few to many
   Refers to recognising that intelligence is more than cognition; *it implies metacognition and also affective, social and psychomotor skills.*
5. Relation to learning process – from isolated assessment to integrated assessment
   Refers to the move from one, isolated assessment *to integrating assessment in the learning process, emphasising assessment as a tool for ongoing learning.*
6. Responsibility – from teacher to student
   Refers to a move from focusing on teachers only in assessment *to the increased involvement of students in the assessment process, seen through the increasing implementation of self and peer student assessment.*
7. Use of assessment – from assessment of learning to assessment for learning
   Refers to a move from using assessment to measure learning achievement to *using assessment as a tool for learning through provision of prompt and constructive feedback.*

Even though this summary list shows the *differences* between traditional and new assessment practices, it is interesting that the new assessments *closely resemble* the way people are assessed on a daily basis in the workplace (e.g. by managers, clients, peers, etc.). The relation to employability skills, learning outcomes and competencies has been discussed in Chap. 4.

Variants and Synonyms for a New Mode of Assessment for Developing Way-of-Being

Assessment for Learning (AfL)

Assessment for learning or AfL, a term that has become familiar and popular in many UK universities and in UK policies of the Quality Assurance Agency for Higher Education, grew from long-standing scholarship on assessment at the

University of Northumbria and its joint leadership of the European Association for Research on Learning and Instruction (EARLI). A tangible product from research on formative assessment and feedback is a seminal practical guide on assessment for learning, called *Assessment for Learning in Higher Education* (Sambell et al., 2013).

They argued that *all* assessments should contribute to helping students to learn and to succeed. They wanted to dispel the myth that assessment for learning only comprises formative assessments and that they are only about giving effective feedback. Assessments should inform both students and teachers about what students know and can do, and this should in turn inform the planning of future learning activities, and help students and teachers to improve their learning and teaching, respectively. In today's assessment landscape, the question of whether to use formative or not, or whether summative assessment is better than formative assessment, is pointless because learning and developing to be adaptive lifelong learners 'encompass[es] both formative and summative assessment and in some applications these two are indistinguishable' (Sambell et al., 2013, p. 3).

Their view of assessment for learning is a holistic model representing an overall approach to assessment, rather than a set of techniques that can be bolted on. This view aligns quite closely with an agile PBL ecology for learning, which is based on an integrated approach to learning and developing present knowledge, skills and dispositions for current and future learning. The crucial factor is that it traverses the various systems in the ecology, rather than being confined to the micro-system. Assessment for learning is based on the following six core conditions for effective assessment for present and future learning:

- Authentic and complex assessment tasks are emphasised.
- Appropriate balance of summative and formative assessment.
- Extensive opportunities to build confidence and practice.
- Students' abilities to evaluate own progress and direct own learning are developed.
- Rich in informal feedback.
- Rich in formal feedback (Sambell et al., 2013, pp. 6–7).

Sustainable Assessment

Our view of agile PBL as developing a way-of-being where students can not only operate in the present formal education context but also in a supercomplex future is echoed by Boud's (2000) sustainable assessment. He termed it sustainable assessment for future learning because the current assessment practices are perceived to be more focused on meeting the specific and immediate goals of a course or program, and/or certification requirements, rather than preparing students for the longer term.

He argued that assessment needs to be reframed in such a way that the idea of informing judgement is central and that learning is foregrounded rather than certification (Boud, 2007). Informed judgement is salient in sustainable assessment, and it encompasses the abilities required to undertake activities that necessarily accompany learning throughout life beyond the universities (Boud, 2000) so that students can meet their own future learning needs (Boud & Soler, 2015). In fact, Boud and Falchikov (2006) have argued that there should be more assessments that can foster future learning after graduation because in their view the purpose of assessment is to measure achievement (summative assessment) and to engender learning (formative assessment). Again, this fits the agile PBL context well, because it suggests authentic assessments, set in a rich variety of contexts that may contain elements from micro- to macro-systems, and everything in between.

Assessment as Learning and Empowerment

This future learning is also echoed in Rodriguez-Gomez and Ibarra-Saiz's (2015) concept of assessment as an instrument for learning and empowerment that 'enables students to take charge of their own learning within an academic context, but beyond that, students will also become empowered with extra-academic – professional and personal contexts' (p. 2), i.e. macro-systems. They added that educators must leverage technology by not asking 'how technology should be incorporated into educational practice but rather what kind of technology should be developed and stimulated so that in all our higher education institutions students are faced with high quality assessment tasks, participate in their assessment and receive feedback in a manner which ultimately help them learn *how to learn*' (Rodriguez-Gomez & Ibarra-Saiz, 2015, p. 18).

There are ten conditions for effective assessment as learning and empowerment:

- Credibility – assessment is systematic and expresses the extent the work produced by students is a result of learning based on reasoned, effective and valuable judgements.
- Dialogue – assessment produces both formal and informal dialogue between participants.
- Improvement – assessment offers opportunities for learning and progress.
- Participation – assessment involves all participants – students, peers and teachers – in a shared, collaborative and responsible process (and we will add employers and/or partners outside the university to the mix here).
- Reflection – assessment is a learning activity that promotes reflection, analysis and critique through substantial tasks that also enable one's own performance and that of others to be evaluated.
- Regulation – assessment develops autonomy and independence, promoting empowerment and initiative in the learning process which can be transferred to extra-academic, professional and social contexts.

- Challenge – assessment provides engagement with challenging, authentic tasks, providing demanding and motivating assignments that require use of increasingly high level of skills and performance.
- Sustainability – assessment encourages learning for life, offering opportunities to develop skills and abilities in a range of contexts and throughout one's life.
- Transparency – assessment is carried out against a set of transparent criteria and standards to guide students to achieve the required learning outcomes.
- Transferability – assessment is undertaken in a way that is coherent, interrelated and integrated within the course, program, module or subject matter such that it avoids segmentation and disconnection from learning (Rodriguez-Gomez & Ibarra-Saiz, 2015, p. 4).

Integrative Assessment

The debate in higher education on whether assessments should be summative for the purposes of certification or whether assessments should be formative to facilitate learning, autonomy and future learning can be abated if there is a clearer distinction between them (Crisp, 2012). Crisp proposed using the term, integrative assessments whose:

> Primary purpose is to influence students' approaches for future learning by providing activities that define and track strategies that students use to assess their own learning abilities and problem-solving capabilities, the quality and standards of student responses and how students might adapt their learning to future scenarios. (Crisp, 2012, p. 39)

The main purpose for this distinction is so that teachers and academic developers can be aided in curriculum design that will enhance both current and future learning because the distinction provides greater clarity around the proposed outcomes and reward mechanisms related to the assessment tasks and feedback. The key characteristics of integrative assessment, which can be either in summative or formative mode, are that its primary purpose is to 'influence students' approach to future learning, and the reward mechanisms in place for students will reflect an analysis of approaches to learning, rather than learning itself' (Crisp, 2012, p. 41).

Students are viewed as active partners in integrative assessments, which provide them with opportunities to:

- Make judgements about their own learning or performance.
- Define standards and expectations in their responses.
- Track and analyse their approaches to responding to a problem, issue, situation or performance.
- Integrate prior or current feedback into their response.
- Engage with meaningful tasks that have inherent worth beyond just an assessment activity.
- Be rewarded for the quality of their analysis of their metacognitive abilities, rather than factual knowledge or a specific performance (Crisp, 2012, p. 41).

Commonalities in Assessments for Learning

All assessments for learning, regardless of the variants, are closely aligned with agile PBL because they intentionally cultivate habits of mind or a way-of-being a lifelong learner. From the outset, assessments for learning are framed from the perspective that the learning has to encompass declarative knowledge, skills and dispositions. In this way, students can learn how to be competent, adaptive and flexible during their studies so that it becomes like 'indwelling' or a way-of-being to be competent, adaptive and flexible in future contexts. In this view, students are not passive learners, empty vessels to be 'equipped' with domain or disciplinary declarative knowledge and related professional or disciplinary skills, in order to certify them in the hope that they then become competent individuals *after* graduation.

There are a number of important commonalities between the essentials of agile PBL and features of assessments for learning, including the positioning of students, developing metacognition to allow for productive self-regulated learning, creating iterative processes and opportunities for learning and providing feedback and authenticity in assessments. There might be other features for each, but these are the ones that we consider as the most powerful features – philosophically and practically.

Positioning of Students in Assessments

Student engagement is a generic term related to the extent of students' involvement in their learning, as measured in terms of their time, effort, interest and emotions. Student engagement is a term that has evolved in North America over the last 40 years and in recent years has been associated with student success or retention. It is now used to describe the effort and time that students invest in meaningful educational experiences (Kuh, 2003, 2004, 2009). It is a measure used in the National Survey of Student Engagement (NSSE) in the United States and a similar version called Australasian Survey of Student Engagement in Australia and New Zealand (AUSSE). The American version focused more on the cognitive and behavioural aspects of learning, such as time and effort, while the British and Europeans have focused more on the qualitative essence of learning, from students' perspectives, for example, in the form of interests and emotions (Zepke, 2013).

Regardless of the versions, when applied to assessments for learning, teachers must position students in the centre of the assessment design and tasks, because only when assessment tasks are educationally purposive, that is, pedagogically or educationally aligned with the intended future learning outcomes, would students be stimulated to engage meaningfully with the tasks by investing their time, effort and emotions, as they see the value and benefits to them personally. They are thus stimulated into going beyond surface learning. When students' interests are triggered, they are more likely to want to delve deeper into the subject matter, as compared to just doing the assessments because they have to with the assessment pieces just being regarded as for markers or teachers (McDowell & Sambell, 1999; Sambell et al., 2013).

Engaging students in the assessment tasks and processes directs students' attention to learning, thereby reaping the inherent benefits from learning. This applies in particular to learning in groups – acquiring, collaborating, sharing, dialoguing, conversing, experimenting, exploring, analysing, judging, evaluating and contributing. These are the skills or competencies and dispositions that would enable and empower them in future contexts. Students involved in an agile PBL ecology for learning acquire knowledge and skills from their peers, their own performances and those of their peers, integrate what they have learned into their own world views and other academic and social experiences and form their identities – personal (Baxter Magolda, 2001; Chickering & Reisser, 1993), professional and academic (Zhao & Kuh, 2004). Student engagement is greater when academic and social support are available (Tinto, 2012). In particular, students who are academically unprepared benefit the most from engagement with peers because of the social and academic support they receive (Trowler & Trowler, 2010). In other words, peers serve as instrumental resources for one another (William, 2011). The role and importance of student support in an agile PBL ecology for learning is discussed in more detail in the next chapter.

Metacognition, Self-Regulation and Reflection

Self-regulated learning refers to the active control and monitoring by students of some aspects of their own learning, such as setting learning goals and monitoring and regulating progress to achieving these goals (Pintrich, 1995; Zimmerman, 1990). Students' capacity to monitor their own work, rather than rely on others telling them what to do, and students' capacity for independent judgement and critical reflections are considered important in the work and social contexts that they are likely to meet in the future and are thus important to develop (Boud & Falchikov, 2006). In order for students to engage in self-regulated learning, they must first engage in metacognition productively, where metacognition is thinking about the contents and processes of one's mind (Winnie & Azevedo, 2014, p. 63). Winnie and Azevedo further argue that students (and teachers) must realise that they need multiple forms of strategies and tactics for learning, as well as having declarative knowledge. Declarative knowledge by itself is insufficient.

Self-assessment is a common assessment task to engage students' metacognition and develop abilities as judges of their own and others' performances and to promote awareness that they are responsible for their own learning because after graduation they need to drive their own learning (Fastre, Van Der Klink, Sluijsmans, & Van Merrienboer, 2013). To be able to self-regulate and critically reflect promotes autonomy (Knight & Yorke, 2003) and self-directed learning skills (Tan, 2007).

More precisely, when explicit reflection activities are demanded of students in the assessment tasks, students retrospectively consider a learning event or their own learning, evaluate the effectiveness and engage in 'forward-reaching' transfer by making decisions about how to approach similar tasks in the future (Salomon & Perkins, 1989, p. 126). It is this form of 'mindfulness' (Salomon & Perkins, 1989, p. 124) or way-of-being, which is central to an agile PBL teaching and learning environment, that facilitates their capacity to make informed judgement that is valuable for future learning (Boud, 2007). Informed judgement is 'informing the capacity to evaluate evidence, appraise situations and circumstances acutely, to draw sound conclusions and act in accordance with this analysis' (Boud, 2007, p. 19). Boud further argues that the idea is to put learning in the centre where students learn to form judgements, as well as learn about the act of forming judgements, about learning.

Iterative Processes and Opportunities for Learning

For students to learn, they need to be in a social setting where social participation and interactions occur frequently enough for them to practise applying skills and knowledge before they learn to become 'experts' themselves in the future (Wenger, 1998). The testing assessment paradigm where students 'cram' and sit for one, big, high-stakes examination at the end of their course simply does not afford students the iterative 'spaces' for them to develop and learn. Formative assessments placed throughout the course or program before the 'the big one' would create the opportunities or affordances for students to practise, rehearse and build knowledge and skills. This is reflective of the way in which people are 'evaluated' and 'assessed' in the workplace, and it is precisely for this reason that we imagine the involvement of employers in assessment design, thus blurring the boundary between the micro- and macro-systems in an agile PBL ecology for learning.

Creating opportunities for iterative practice means engaging students in a more active, all-encompassing social space where they learn to make sense of the subject matter, organise knowledge and skills and progressively develop their own interpretations and judgements. They also learn the practices of their disciplines or professions and in the process build evolving personal and professional identities (Lave & Wenger, 1991). The learning community space also provides a pathway for students to traverse, much like a training ground, while gaining the requirements for full participation (Lave & Wenger) in (inter)disciplinary or professional communities in the future.

Another reason for creating iterative processes and opportunities for students is learning from mistakes or errors. Mistakes, misconceptions or incorrect responses can be, and should be, made, and they should be considered a good thing. There are lessons to be learned because mistakes are forms of feedback to students that 'something is wrong', and they afford feedforward to students about why it is incorrect and how to improve and progress (Black, 2007). Feedforward can be provided by peer students and teachers but, more importantly, by students themselves through observation, self-awareness, critical reflection and judgement.

Feedback

Feedback is important in the development of students' self-regulated learning so that they can be self-directed learners (Nicol & Macfarlane-Dick, 2006). Students generate internal feedback when they monitor engagement with learning activities from assessment of how they are performing. Feedback can also be generated externally from peers and teachers. Both of these types of feedback are valuable ingredients for fostering and developing self-regulated learning because how else will students learn to regulate and self-correct if they do not receive feedback on the achievement or performance and feedforward on what and how to self-correct?

Nicol and Macfarlane-Dick (2006) have identified the following seven principles of effective feedback from the research literature:

- Helps clarify what is good performance
- Facilitates development of reflection and self-assessment in learning
- Delivers high-quality information to students about their learning
- Encourages teacher and peer dialogue around learning
- Encourages positive motivational beliefs and self-esteem
- Provides opportunities to close the gap between current and desired performance
- Provides information to teachers that can be used to shape their teaching

Authenticity in Assessment

The other recurring theme in the new assessment paradigm is authenticity and authentic assessment, which we propose are closely aligned with agile PBL. Authenticity is the level or degree of resemblance to the criterion situation (real or actual situation) or fidelity. It is the underlying motivator for active student engagement and involvement. When an assessment is authentic, students can see the relevance and meaning of the assessment to their future professions; and for non-professional programs or studies, they can see the resemblance to complex disciplinary ways of thinking and practising and/or be personally involved through having the opportunity to have a hands-on experience (Sambell et al., 2013). Students are not just engaged cognitively but also affectively; they also develop their personal and professional identities. Increasing student engagement or involvement in assessments means that students would invest more time, effort and emotions on really learning because they know that they are learning to adopt a professional identity and way-of-being in future contexts or professions while still being supported in the educational context.

So, What Is Authentic Assessment?

Many authors have viewed authentic assessment as performance assessment (Baron & Boshchee, 1995; Hart, 1994; Torrance, 1995; Wiggins, 2011), while there are some who emphasise the realistic value of the task and the context of the authentic assessment (Herrington & Herrington, 1998). The difference really is a question of its fidelity (Reeves & Oakley, 1996). This refers to the extent the tasks and conditions of the assessment task resemble the tasks and conditions under which the performance would normally occur. In other words, while fidelity is not a factor in performance assessment such as playing the piano or dance, authentic assessment has high fidelity. That is, every authentic assessment is a performance assessment, but not vice versa (Meyer, 1992).

There are other terms used interchangeably for authentic assessment such as competence assessment, outcomes-based assessment and holistic assessment. Even though there are a number of definitions or opinions on what constitutes authenticity and authentic assessment, all of them share a commonality. That is, authentic assessment enables teachers to determine students' skills, knowledge, disposition and competence and to provide evidence that values learning per se and, for students, authentic assessment provide a more engaging and effective way to promote understanding and value the process of learning (Newton, 2009). Within an agile PBL ecology for learning, authentic assessment ideally blurs the lines between teachers and employers, between teachers and students and between classrooms and contexts outside the university such as the workplace. In other words, ideally students, employers and partners outside the university are involved in both the assessment design and the actual assessing, as students would be assessed when they move beyond the university, e.g. at their work in the workplace. Indeed, it is in the workplace that the assessment would ideally take place, however defined.

The term authentic in the context of learning and assessment first appeared in 1988 and was coined by Newmann and Archbald (Archbald, 1991). Authentic assessment's major goal is to 'cultivate the kind of higher-order thinking and problem-solving capacities useful both to individuals and to the society. The mastery gained in school is likely to transfer more readily to life beyond school …' (Newmann & Archbald, 1992, p. 75).

According to Archbald (1991), the notion of learning beyond classrooms has been largely absent in the testing and psychometric paradigm of assessment. For Newmann and Archbald (1992), an authentic assessment has the following components:

- Construction of knowledge: Students organise information using higher-order skills and consider alternatives instead of reproduction or response only to the produced work of others.
- Disciplined enquiry: (Inter)disciplinary content, processes and communications to elaborate understanding.
- Value beyond assessment: Connecting problems to the world beyond the classroom.

The *value beyond* assessment, a characteristic of authentic assessment, is at the heart of the new assessment paradigm and all assessments for learning. More importantly, it is also an element in our imaged agile PBL ecology for learning. The agile PBL ecology for learning also suggests that learning permeates through all levels of contexts. Thus, assessments in agile PBL need to go beyond the classroom to future contexts where future learning needs of students are drawn and actors or players in future contexts would be involved in the assessment process in the form of being providers of authentic problems or providers of cases for students to solve, as co-assessors with teachers and students to provide feedback and judgement on merit and worth of assessment products or solutions or ideas and ultimately also as co-learners with students. The liquid flow of knowledge through assessment tasks and interactions between these actors would mutually benefit the educational system (teachers, students, and administrators) and the community and society at large (products and solutions deployed in society). This is in essence what the agile PBL ecology for learning is all about.

Challenges and Possibilities of Assessments for Learning

We acknowledge that there are challenges and tensions in shifting the much entrenched testing assessment paradigm to an assessment for learning paradigm by institutions and teachers. In the following, we have considered a number of frequently asked questions or statements that can be seen as barriers hindering wider use and practices of assessment for learning, along with possible suggestions to overcome them.

1. It's impossible for assessments to measure intended learning outcomes relating to a 'way-of-being' or lifelong learning skills and dispositions!

   Assessments for learning comprise both formative and summative assessments, and contrary to what many people think, they do not only consist of formative assessment activities, and they are not just about providing feedback to students. Formative assessments can be graded and marked akin to summative assessments. Assessment per se, regardless of its form, summative or formative, connotes students submitting to standards and criteria that judge the worth or merit of their performance in relation to the intended learning outcomes. On the other hand, the more generic learning outcomes of developing a 'way-of-being' or becoming lifelong learners are about students discovering self, others and the world or progressing to a 'state of authentic being' (Barnett, 2007, p. 25).

   Herein lies the tension: can we imagine assessment that can measure this educational state of authentic being? We believe the answer is a firm yes and that the tension can be overcome with formative assessment practices because the educational properties inherent in formative assessments provide the space and affordances to students to learn and develop in a safe, supportive learning environment. This happens in an agile PBL environment with a PBL teaching approach and an explicit curriculum that comprises disciplinary knowledge and skills and dispositions related to future learning. If this is the case, however, can summative assessment, which is still widely practised and has an important role to serve to the public as a tangible certification of quality, perform this formative role simultaneously to develop students in a more holistic and interdisciplinary sense?

Sambell et al. (2013) suggest that this is possible by (1) enhancing learning by doing in summative assessment; (2) learning from guidance on summative assessment, e.g. meetings or sessions between teachers and students to discuss the summative assessment tasks and requirements before the submission date; and (3) learning from feedback associated with summative assessment, e.g. teachers give generic but timely information before students complete the assignment by reporting on key feedback points of previous students who took the same assignment or type of assignment.

2. Formative assessment takes too much time –for academics and students!

For the academics, the common challenges are that they spend a vast amount of time on marking and providing feedback; that the department or institution workload formula only allocates X amount of time for marking, which is insufficient for marking a final exam *and* marking formative assessments; or that having too many formative assessments will take time away from research activities. For the students, the common perception is that there are too many assessments. As a consequence, time-poor academics will often favour summative assessment over formative, and even if they provide feedback on summative assessment, the quality and quantity of the feedback can be questioned, as it is often inconsistent and not provided in a timely manner. From the students' perspective, formative assessments are designed to develop students, but they often create the perception that the teachers are not supporting them because the feedback does not tell them much about anything or it comes too late for them to respond to. Moreover, the emotional stress due to a large number of assessments can for some students be a barrier and a hindrance to learning and progress.

Jessop, El Hakim, and Gibbs (2014) suggest taking a more programmatic approach, rather than a piecemeal approach to assessment and feedback design and practice. Their suggested strategies include (1) developing a shared collegial culture of marking, e.g. establish collaborative team discussions to generate and review criteria, staff and student marking workshops, mentoring for new markers and collaborative online marking so that comments are open and visible to all markers to enable sharing of good practice, and (2) mapping assessments across the program to create connections, sequences, timing and logical flow of assessment tasks. The goal here is to find a balance between summative and formative assessments to engender meaningful and purposive learning.

The 'problem' of too many assignments or assessments will still be there, but if students find meaning and relevance in the assessment tasks, students report that they will invest the time, effort and emotions into doing them because they can see the link to their profession or disciplinary practices and know that it is for their future (Sambell et al., 2013). The answer is in the assessment design from the outset.

3. When can I involve students in assessment for learning tasks?

Healey, Flint, and Harrington (2014) have argued that the process of involving students as partners in learning and teaching can be made in the assessment component of learning and teaching in higher education. According to Rodriguez-Gomez and Ibarra-Saiz (2015), they can be involved at any of the three stages of the assessment process: (1) during planning when students can be involved in selecting and defining the criteria, choosing assessment tasks, designing the assessment instrument and weighting of components in the marking rubric; (2) during execution when students can be involved in self-, peer and co-assessment with students, teachers and external assessors such as employers and receivers/audience of the assessments; and (3) during the formal evaluation and analysis stage when students can be involved in self-, peer and co-reflection and feedback on the final results.

4. Authentic assessments are not appropriate for academic disciplines that are not professional or vocational oriented!

We acknowledge that designing authentic assessment can be perceived as more of a challenge for teachers in academic disciplines that are not traditionally professional or vocational oriented, such as the humanities, the social sciences, and the pure sciences, in contrast to programs that are traditionally considered to be 'professional', such as engineering, business, nursing and education. Does that mean that such disciplines are not developing skills required for the uncertain age of supercomplexity or that they should not? We argue that despite the perceived difficulties in practising authentic assessments, the notion of learning or acquiring knowledge, skills and dispositions in authentic contexts is a useful notion. In other words, the perception is based on what we would consider an artificial binary between 'academic' disciplines and 'professional' disciplines. The boundary between the two is largely imagined to be dissolved in an agile PBL ecology for learning, as to us, 'pure science in a lab' is just as 'professional' as a marketing department of a business school. As a result, students in each will benefit from developing an agile PBL way-of-being.

Sambell et al. (2013) similarly suggest that *all* disciplines can embed authenticity into their assessment tasks by (1) enhancing students' perceptions of the meaning and relevance of assessment, e.g. specifying a 'real' audience for the assessment tasks by prompting students that they are being asked by someone other than the teacher (marker) to develop an artefact, communicate or explain a concept; (2) drawing on and linking the assessment to the real world, e.g. working on problems with real-world significance, getting students to perform working practices such as working in groups rather than performing individually; and (3) developing a sense of personal engagement, e.g. explicitly build opportunities for students to draw on their personal experience, explicitly build in opportunities to discuss assessment tasks with others, explain and defend their ideas to others or present their solutions or ideas to others.

5. But authentic assessment is not reliable!

One common criticism of authentic assessment is that reliability is compensated with validity. Reliability is concerned with the degree to which consistent results are obtained at different occasions or by different assessors. In testing within the psychometric paradigm, reliability concerns the accuracy of the measurements, because the ultimate goal is to be able to identify the high achievers from the failures (norm referenced).

However, authentic assessment is about making a judgement of a student's competence (technical knowledge, skills and disposition) and not evidence of learning (criterion referenced). Applying the same psychometric traditional testing approaches to authentic assessment would be inappropriate because the tasks are often complex and open ended and it is unavoidable to use decisions that are based on multiple scores and assessors (Cronbach, Linn, Brennan, & Haertel, 1997). Cronbach et al. (1997) have indicated that acceptable levels of reliability across multiple assessors can be reached in any assessment format, provided multiple assessments are used. Therefore, the reliability issue in authentic assessment can be managed by providing multiple assessment tasks and formats so as to reach acceptable levels of reliability across multiple assessors. Gipps (1995) reminded us that even with standardised tests, greater reliability cannot be guaranteed!

In the overall assessment paradigm, the issue of constructing validity is mainly of interest within a testing culture where the issue of reliability is of primary concern. This applies in particular to a concern with the consequences of test use and test scores for students known as the consequential validity (Messick, 1994). Research in the student learning field has shown that student approaches to learning are driven by assessment. Consequential validity addresses this issue by investigating whether the actual consequences of assessment are also the expected consequences (Gielen, Dochy, & Dierick, 2003). Gielen et al. (2003) have pointed out that provision of constructive feedback plays an important role in determining that the actual consequence is as expected. Teachers should provide their students with quality information about their performance and product and support them in reflecting on the learning outcomes and the learning processes that they are expected to demonstrate. As such, the assessments can serve as tools *for learning*, instead of just tools *of teaching*. This has been demonstrated in a study by McDowell et al. (2011) whose findings revealed that the overall student experience is more positive in courses where assessment for learning approaches is used and, by extension, students are more likely to employ a deep approach to learning.

6. Is this really authentic?

There also have been concerns about student perceptions of assessment in that the true intention of developing authentic assessment can be construed by students as artificial and this helps to create unintentional consequences such as assessment backlash or wash-back. Cumming and Maxwell (1997, p. 10) observed, for example, that some authentic assessments are disguised as 'authentic' assessments, either in the implementation or design stages.

These assessments, which are disguised as authentic assessment, would have the opposite effect in that they would only make the assessment appear to be more superficial, artificial and contrived to students (Cumming & Maxwell, 1997), rather than authentic. Cumming and Maxwell argued that such assessment is not fair because it only aids to distract students from the real intention and underlying expectations of the teachers and assessors. However, they contended that assessments disguised as authentic assessment occur when the content of the assessment is not carefully considered, where assessment is limited in that it is not open ended or unbounded with real-world complications and unexpected contingencies and consequences of assessment and where the students being assessed are not accountable for the outcomes.

Therefore, Cumming and Maxwell (1997) advise teachers and academic developers to identify the most salient characteristics of learning (i.e. the learning outcomes) that are intended to be fostered and assessed and then ensure that these characteristics are enveloped in the assessment tasks. By doing so, the emphasis is on the 'important critical aspects of the criterion situation or knowledge and skills that are inferred, at a sufficient level to resemble the real world, so that relevant differences and changes in the performances or variables assessed can be detected' (Messick, 1994, p. 17). As such, these assessments 'are authentic in that they replicate the challenges and standards of real-world performances and are representative of the ways in which knowledge and skills are used in real-world contexts, even though they do not simulate all the complexity of real-world functioning' (Messick, p. 17). We would take this a step further and suggest that, as students move through a program, the assessment should get increasingly 'authentic' and indeed draw on the 'complexity of real-world functioning', including the ways in which such functioning gets assessed, for example, by clients or managers. Again, this would significantly blur the boundaries between 'the university' and 'the workplace', and thus fit neatly into the agile PBL ecology for learning.

7. How to design authentic assessments in a technology-rich environment?

Lombardi (2007, pp. 3–4) provides ten design elements for learning for a twenty-first-century environment that is rich with technology and tools to support and aid authentic assessment processes. She proposes using the following elements as checklists, and they can be adapted to any subject matter or discipline, which, not coincidently, also resembles an agile PBL ecology for learning:

- Authentic assessment tasks and activities match real-world tasks of professionals in practice as nearly as possible. Learning progresses to the level of authenticity when students are asked to work actively with abstract concepts, facts and formulae inside a realistic and highly social context, imitating the ordinary practices of the discipline and/or the workplace.
- Authentic assessments are relatively undefined and open to multiple interpretations and solutions, requiring students to identify for themselves the tasks and subtasks needed to complete the major task. Challenges cannot be easily solved by the application of existing algorithms.

- Authentic assessments comprise complex tasks to be investigated by students over a period of time, requiring significant time and intellectual resources. Problems cannot be solved in a matter of minutes or even hours.
- Authentic assessment provides the opportunities for students to examine the task from a variety of theoretical and practical perspectives, using a variety of resources, requiring students to distinguish relevant from irrelevant information in the process.
- Authentic assessments make working with others or collaboration an integral aspect of assessment, both within the walled gardens of formal learning and in the real world. Success cannot be achieved by an individual student working alone.
- Authentic assessments enable learners to make choices and reflect on their learning, both individually and as a team.
- Authentic assessments have consequences that extend beyond a particular discipline, culture and walls of classrooms, encouraging students to adopt diverse perspectives and roles and think in interdisciplinary terms. Relevance is not confined to a single discipline or domain or subject matter.
- Assessment is not merely a summative piece but is woven seamlessly into the major task in a manner that reflects real-world evaluation processes.
- Authentic assessment culminates in the creation of products, not merely exercises in preparation for something else.
- Authentic assessment allows for diverse interpretations and competing solutions, rather than yielding a single correct answer.

8. How can I evaluate authentic assessment?

Baartman, Prins, Kirschner, and van der Vleuten (2007, p. 261) have proposed 12 quality criteria for authentic assessment, based on Messick's (1994) construct validity as a unified and overarching validity concept that aligns with an authentic assessment paradigm. Their framework also incorporated Gulikers, Bastiaens, and Kirschner's (2004) work on assessing the level of fidelity between the assessment and the criterion situation, which is helpful to eliminate possible disguises (Cumming & Maxwell, 1997) that can occur in authentic assessment and, thereby, innocently and inadvertently sabotaging intended learning.

We have transformed Baartman, Bastiaens et al.'s (2007) quality framework into evaluation questions to guide teachers and academic developers and to be used as self- and/or peer assessment activities. The responses to these questions would illuminate the areas of limitations in the suite of authentic assessments and prompt corrective actions to improve the assessments. This also serves as a checklist of sorts to ascertain whether the assessment design aligns with an agile PBL ecology for learning.

- How much does the authentic assessment resemble the criterion situation (workplace or disciplinary practice)?
- How does the authentic assessment relate to the future professional life or disciplinary practice and reflect higher cognitive skills?

- How does the authentic assessment provide opportunities for students to demonstrate their abilities and maximise their potential?
- What is the significant value of the authentic assessment to teachers, students and employers/disciplinary community of practitioners?
- How confident are all the stakeholders with the authentic assessment?
- How clear and comprehensible are the criteria and standards of the authentic assessment to all stakeholders?
- What are the effects of the authentic assessment on learning and teaching?
- Are there multiple authentic assessments, carried out by multiple assessors and on multiple occasions, across multiple disciplines?
- Are the authentic assessments conducted consistently and responsibly?
- Is the authentic assessment practical in terms of efficiency and cost?
- Is the authentic assessment aligned to intended learning outcomes, curriculum, and teaching and learning?
- How do the authentic assessments stimulate self-regulated learning of students?

Conclusion

An authentic assessment paradigm that fits into an agile PBL ecology for learning, or at least in its spirit, is a lot of work. So the question for many inevitably will be: is it worth it? We argue that it is, in particular when we consider the future contexts of students and the anticipated demands of those contexts, in combination with how entrenched existing assessments often are, which means they are increasingly misaligned with those demands. Assessment for learning has the promise to meet the demands of society in which students will be employed or where they will be employers themselves. Today's students must be comfortable with the complexities, uncertainties, ill-defined and complex problems found in an increasingly competitive society, as well as a volatile and fluid sociocultural environment. The greater exposure students have to assessment-related learning, in tandem with an agile PBL curriculum, while they are in university, the better prepared they will be in dealing with ambiguities and ubiquitous technologies and resources beyond university. Better still, if these students are already engaging with the realities of the world, and solving real problems, learning and developing cannot get any more authentic! Therefore, it seems to us that to teach and develop a way-of-being and becoming a lifelong learner, it matters that students are assessed as authentically as possible so that the knowledge, skills and dispositions that they require for their future can be put to practice now as current *and* future practitioners. The cooperation between various stakeholders (students, teachers and employers) is a vital part of this, and they are seamlessly interwoven in an agile PBL ecology for learning.

Although there seems to be progress in the assessment field, moving assessment away from the traditional assessment paradigm is not without its challenges and tensions. We have presented the challenges and tensions faced and the possibilities to overcome them. We acknowledge that it is not a comprehensive list nor do we have all the answers, but it is clear that the old way of thinking about and using assessment has shifted in the last decade, and with further research and scholarship into new forms of assessment, challengers and sceptics might be won over. However, until that time comes, to realise the intention and goal of developing a way-of-being, learning outcomes should remain the focal point to reframe assessment as part of agile PBL teaching and an agile PBL curriculum for future learning.

References

Archbald, D. A. (1991). Authentic assessment: Principles, practices, and issues. *School Psychology Quarterly, 6*(4), 279–293.

Baartman, L. K. J., Bastiaens, T. J., Kirschner, P. A., & Van Der Vleuten, C. P. M. (2007). Evaluating assessment quality in competence-based education: A qualitative comparison of two frameworks. *Educational Research Review, 2*(2), 114–129.

Baartman, L. K. J., Prins, F. J., Kirschner, P. A., & Van Der Vleuten, C. P. M. (2007). Determining the quality of competence assessment programs: A self-evaluation procedure. *Studies in Educational Evaluation, 33*(3/4), 258–281.

Barnett, R. (2007). Assessment in higher education: An impossible possible? In D. Boud & N. Falchikov (Eds.), *Rethinking assessment in higher education: Learning for the longer term* (pp. 29–40). Milton Park, UK: Routledge.

Baron, M. A., & Boshchee, F. (1995). *Authentic assessment: The key to unlocking student success.* Lancaster, PA: Technomic Publishing Company.

Baxter Magolda, M. B. (2001). *Making their own way: Narratives for transforming higher education to promote self-development.* Sterling, VA: Stylus.

Becher, T., & Trowler, P. R. (2001). *Academic tribes and territories.* Buckingham, UK: The Society for Research into Higher Eduction and Open University Press.

Biggs, J., & Tang, C. (2011). *Teaching for quality learning at university* (4th ed.). Maidenhead, UK: Open University Press.

Birenbaum, M. (2003). New insights into learning and teaching and their implications for assessment. In M. Segers, F. Dochy, & E. Cascallar (Eds.), *Optimising new modes of assessment: In search of qualities and standards* (pp. 13–36). Dordrecht, The Netherlands: Kluwer Academic Publishers.

Black, P. (2007). Full marks for feedback. *Journal of the Institute of Educational Assessors, 2,* 18–21.

Boud, D. (2000). Sustainable assessment: Rethinking assessment for the learning society. *Studies in Continuing Education, 22*(2), 151–167.

Boud, D. (2007). Reframing assessment as if learning is important. In D. Boud & N. Falchikov (Eds.), *Rethinking assessment in higher education: Learning for the longer term* (pp. 14–25). Oxon, UK: Routledge.

Boud, D., & Falchikov, N. (2006). Aligning assessment with long-term learning. *Assessment and Evaluation in Higher Education, 31*(4), 399–413.

Boud, D., & Soler, R. (2015). Sustainable assessment revisited. *Assessment and Evaluation in Higher Education.* doi:10.1080/02602938.2015.1018133.

Chickering, A. W., & Reisser, L. (1993). *Education and identity* (2nd ed.). San Francisco: Jossey-Bass.

Crisp, G. T. (2012). Integrative assessment: Reframing assessment practice for current and future learning. *Assessment and Evaluation in Higher Education, 37*(1), 33–43.

Cronbach, L. J., Linn, R. L., Brennan, R. L., & Haertel, E. H. (1997). Generalizability analysis for performance assessments of student achievement or school effectiveness. *Educational and Psychological Measurement, 53*(3), 373–399.

Cumming, J. J., & Maxwell, G. S. (1997). Contextualising authentic assessment. *Assessment in Education: Principles, Policies and Practices, 6*(2), 177–194.

Entwistle, N., & Tait, H. (1990). Approaches to learning, evaluations of teaching, and preferences for contrasting academic environments. *Higher Education, 19*, 169–194.

Fastre, G. M. J., Van Der Klink, M. R., Sluijsmans, D., & Van Merrienboer, J. J. G. (2013). Towards an integrated model for developing sustainable assessment skills. *Assessment and Evaluation in Higher Education, 38*(5), 611–630.

Gibbs, G. (2006a). How assessment frames student learning. In C. Bryan & K. Clegg (Eds.), *Innovative assessment in higher education* (pp. 23–36). London: Routledge.

Gibbs, G. (2006b). Why assessment is changing. In C. Bryan & K. Clegg (Eds.), *Innovative assessment in higher education* (pp. 11–22). Abingdon, UK: Routledge.

Gielen, S., Dochy, F., & Dierick, S. (2003). Evaluating the consequential validity of new modes of assessment: The influence of assessment on learning, including pre-, post- and true assessment effects. In M. Segers, F. Dochy, & E. Cascallar (Eds.), *Optimising new modes of assessments: In search of qualities and standards.* Dordrecht, The Netherlands: Kluwer Academic Publishers.

Gipps, C. (1995). Reliability, validity and manageability in large-scale performance assessment. In H. Torrance (Ed.), *Evaluating authentic assessment.* Buckingham, UK: Open University Press.

Gulikers, J. T. M., Bastiaens, T. J., & Kirschner, P. A. (2004). A five dimensional framework for authentic assessment. *Educational Technology Research and Development, 52*(3), 67–86.

Hart, D. (1994). *Authentic assessment: A handbook for educators.* Menlo Park, CA: Addison-Wesley Publishing Company.

Healey, M., Flint, A., & Harrington, K. (2014). *Engagement through partnership: Students as partners in learning and teaching in higher education* (pp. 1–76). York, UK: The Higher Education Academy, UK.

Herrington, J., & Herrington, A. (1998). Authentic assessment and multimedia: How university students respond to a model of authentic assessment. *Higher Education Research and Development, 17*(3), 305–322.

Jessop, T., El Hakim, Y., & Gibbs, G. (2014). The whole is greater than the sum of its parts: A large scale study of students' learning in response to different programme assessment patterns. *Assessment and Evaluation in Higher Education, 39*(1), 73–88.

Knight, P., & Yorke, M. (2003). *Assessment, learning and employability.* Maidenhead, UK: SRHE/Open University Press.

Kuh, G. D. (2003). What are we learning about student engagement from NSSE. *Change* (March/April), pp. 24–32.

Kuh, G. D. (2004). The National Survey of Student Engagement: Conceptual framework and overview of psychometric properties. http://nsse.iub.edu/nsse_2001/pdf/framework-2001.pdf

Kuh, G. D. (2009). The National Survey of Student Engagement: Conceptual and empirical foundations. *New Directions for Institutional Research, 2009*(141), 5–20.

Kvale, S. (2007). Contradictions of assessment for learning in institutions of higher education. In D. Boud & N. Falchikov (Eds.), *Rethinking assessment in higher education: Learning for the longer term* (pp. 57–71). Abingdon, UK: Routledge.

Lave, J., & Wenger, E. (1991). *Situated learning: Legitimate peripheral participation.* Cambridge: Cambridge University Press.

Lombardi, M. M. (2007). Authentic learning for the 21st century: An overview. In D. G. Oblinger (Ed.), *Educause learning initiative 1* (pp. 1–12). Retrieved September 26, 2016, from https://library.educause.edu/~/media/files/library/2007/1/eli3009-pdf.pdf

Lu, J., Bridges, S., & Hmelo-Silver, C. E. (2014). Problem-based learning. In K. R. Sawyer (Ed.), *The Cambridge handbook of the learning sciences* (2nd ed., pp. 298–318). New York: Cambridge University Press.

Marton, F., & Saljo, R. (Eds.). (1997). *Approaches to learning* (2nd ed.). Edinburgh, UK: Scottish Academic Press.

McDowell, L., & Sambell, K. (1999). The experience of innovative assessment: Student perspectives. In S. Brown & A. Glasner (Eds.), *Assessment matters in higher education: Choosing and using diverse approaches*. Buckingham, UK: Society for Research into Higher Education and Open University Press.

McDowell, L., Wakelin, D., Montgomery, C., & King, S. (2011). Does assessment for learning make a difference? The development of a questionnaire to explore the student response. *Assessment and Evaluation in Higher Education, 36*(7), 749–765.

Messick, S. (1994). The interplay of evidence and consequences in the validation of performance assessments. *Educational Researcher, 23*(13), 13–23.

Meyer, C. A. (1992). What's the difference between authentic and performance assessment? *Educational Leadership, 49*(8), 39–40.

Newmann, F. M., & Archbald, D. A. (1992). The nature of authentic academic achievement. In H. Berlak, F. M. Newmann, E. Adams, D. A. Archbald, T. Burgess, J. Raven, & T. A. Romberg (Eds.), *Toward a new science of educational testing and assessment* (pp. 71–83). Albany, NY: SUNY Press.

Newton, R. (2009). Authentic assessment. In E. F. Provenzo & A. B. Provenzo (Eds.), *Encyclopedia of the social and cultural foundation of education* (pp. 64–66). Thousand Oaks, CA: Sage Publications.

Nicol, D. J., & Macfarlane-Dick, D. (2006). Formative assessment and self-regulated learning: A model and seven principles of good feedback practice. *Studies in Higher Education, 21*(2), 199–218.

Pintrich, P. R. (1995). *Understanding self-regulated learning*. San Francisco: Jossey-Bass.

Ramsden, P. (1992). *Learning to teach in higher education*. London: Routledge.

Reeves, T. C., & Oakley, J. R. (1996). Alternative assessment for constructivist learning environment. In B. G. Wilson (Ed.), *Constructivist learning environment: Case studies in instructional design* (pp. 191–202). Englewood Cliffs, NJ: Educational Technology.

Rodriguez-Gomez, & Ibarra-Saiz, M. S. (2015). Assessment as learning and empowerment: Towards sustainable learning in Higher Education. In M. Peris-Ortiz & J. M. Merigo Lindahl (Eds.), *Sustainable learning in higher education, innovation, technology, and knowledge management* (pp. 1–20). Cham, Switzerland: Springer International Publishing.

Salomon, G., & Perkins, D. N. (1989). Rocky roads to transfer: Rethinking mechanism of a neglected phenomenon. *Educational Psychologist, 24*(2), 113–142.

Sambell, K., McDowell, L., & Montgomery, C. (2013). *Assessment for learning in higher education*. Abingdon, UK: Routledge.

Savin-Baden, M. (2004). Understanding the impact of assessment on students in problem-based learning. *Innovations in Education and Teaching International, 41*(2), 223–233.

Segers, M., Dochy, F., & Cascallar, E. (2003). The era of assessment engineering: Changing perspectives on teaching and learning and the role of new modes of assessment. In M. Segers, F. Dochy, & E. Cascallar (Eds.), *Optimising new modes of assessment: In search of qualities and standards* (pp. 1–12). Dordrecht, The Netherlands: Kluwer Academic Publishers.

Strobel, J., & Van Barneveld, A. (2009). When is PBL more effective? A meta-synthesis of meta-analyses comparing PBL to conventional classrooms. *Interdisciplinary Journal of Problem-Based Learning, 3*(1), 44–58.

Tan, K. (2007). Conceptions of self-assessment: What is needed for long-term learning? In D. Boud & N. Falchikov (Eds.), *Rethinking assessment in higher education: Learning for the longer term* (pp. 114–127). Milton Park, UK: Routledge.

Tinto, V. (2012). *Completing college: Rethinking institutional action*. London: The University of Chicago Press.

Torrance, H. (1995). *Evaluating authentic assessment*. Buckingham, UK: Open University Press.

Trowler, V., & Trowler, P. (2010). *Student engagement evidence summary*. York, UK: The Higher Education Academy.

Wenger, E. (1998). *Communities of practice: Learning, meaning, and identity*. Cambridge: Cambridge University Press.

Wiggins, G. (2011). A true test: Toward more authentic and equitable assessment. *Kappan Magazine, 92*(7), 81–93.

William, D. (2011). What is assessment for learning? *Studies in Educational Evaluation, 37*(1), 3–14.

Winnie, P. H., & Azevedo, R. (2014). Metacognition. In K. R. Sawyer (Ed.), *The Cambridge handbook of the learning sciences* (2nd ed., pp. 63–87). New York: Cambridge University Press.

Xian, H., & Madhavan, K. (2013). Building on and honouring forty years of PBL scholarship from Howard Barrows: A scientometric, large-scale data, and visualization-based analysis. *Interdisciplinary Journal of Problem-Based Learning, 7*(1), 132–156.

Zepke, N. (2013). Student engagement: A complex business supporting the first year experience in tertiary experience. *The International Journal of the First Year in Higher Education, 4*(2), 1–14.

Zhao, C., & Kuh, G. D. (2004). Adding value: Learning communities and student engagement. *Research in Higer Education, 45*(2), 115–138.

Zimmerman, B. J. (1990). Self-regulated learning and academic achievement: An overview. *Educational Psychologist, 25*(1), 3.

Part III
Imagining an Agile University for Learning

Chapter 6
Agile Student Development and Engagement for Learning

Introduction

As has become clear by now, within an agile PBL ecology for learning, there are four interrelated systems or environments that feed into each other and depend on each other. In this chapter, we turn our attention to the exo-environments surrounding the students' immediate formal micro-environment where learning, teaching and assessment interconnect to initiate the development of students' ways-of-being and them becoming change ready for supercomplex future contexts. Our imagining of the 'new' university for learning will not be complete if we do not discuss these environments and systems. While students are not directly situated in them, the decisions and actions of actors and systems situated in exo-environments can influence the development of their 'ways-of-being' by enhancing student engagement.

In this chapter, the focus is on student development and engagement and how the whole university environment – people, policies, tools and systems – academic teachers, professional staff, administrators and managers must be interconnected and take a whole-of-university approach to be able to codevelop a way-of-being and becoming. The future university for learning must consider the whole development of a student – emotions and affect as well as cognitive and performative development in terms of learning knowledges, competencies, dispositions and skills. Thus, this would involve the continuous interaction between the various systems of the agile PBL ecology for learning.

Based on this model, a university for learning applies an integrative, rather than an add-on or bolt-on, approach to engage students. By interconnecting the four university environments for learning, consequential, immediate and micro level student success, in the form of learning and development outcomes, can be achieved. Furthermore, consequential, distal and institutional student success, in the form of retention, progression and completion rates, can be achieved as well. It is only when the micro-system, i.e. the curricular environment, and the exo-system, the non-curricular environment, are interconnected and viewed as a totality that we are able

© Springer Science+Business Media Singapore 2017
M.Y.C.A. Kek, H. Huijser, *Problem-based Learning into the Future*,
DOI 10.1007/978-981-10-2454-2_6

to say that the university for learning is *mattering* (Schlossberg, 1989). A mattering institution sends a clear signal to the students that they matter, which then propels them to engage in their learning and development, and this in turn is part of fostering development of the self and of professional and/or academic identities, precisely because they feel they mattered. In return, mattering institutions would expect to experience high student success, in the form of retention and educational outcomes such as lifelong learning (Kuh et al., 2005; Pascarella, Seifert, & Blaich, 2010; Schlossberg, Lynch, & Chickering, 1989; Trowler & Trowler, 2010).

This chapter draws primarily on the student development literature, which covers the factors that play a crucial role in facilitating growth in university students (Evans, Forney, Guido, Patton, & Renn, 2010). We discuss integrative theories that address student development and student engagement and in particular theories and frameworks that examine a range of contexts that affect students emotionally and academically, in line with our discussions in this book of an agile PBL ecology for learning. Ultimately then, we discuss strategies and practices in student development and engagement in pursuit of developing a 'way-of-being' and of becoming an agile PBL university that is serious about its position in the overall ecology and recognises its associated responsibilities.

Student Development

We have considered the literature on student development for guidance to understand what students experience when they enter and graduate from universities. Student development is 'the ways that a student grows, progresses, or increases his or her developmental capabilities as a result of enrolment in an institution of higher education' (Rodger, 1990, p. 27, as cited in Evans et al., 2010). It is a philosophy that is concerned with the development of the whole person, where interventions, programs and services are focused on encouraging learning and student growth. Citing Miller and Prince (1976, as cited in Evans et al., 2010), Evans et al. explain that most of the student development programs and services in higher education apply human development concepts, particularly in the North American higher education sector. A central view shared by most human development theories is that every student can be expert in increasingly complex developmental tasks and strive to be self-directed and autonomous. Similar to an agile PBL ecology for learning, it is also underpinned by concepts from human development – where Bronfenbrenner's bioecological model of human development (Bronfenbrenner & Morris, 2006) was mostly used.

Student Identity

One of many human development concepts that are important to agile PBL ecology for learning and our central premise underlying agile PBL teaching, learning and assessment is students' formation of their identities during their undergraduate experience. Inherent in agile PBL's becoming or way-of-being is a student's sense of identity. The seminal work on student identity by Chickering (1969) is crucial here. He introduced seven vectors of development that contribute to the formation of identity, based on a psychosocial perspective. The term vector is used here to depict the direction and magnitude of development, expressing that the progression of development is not linear but full of twists and turns during a student's journey in higher education. This progression of development is applicable to adult, mature students and traditional high-school leavers, as well as to face-to-face or virtual and online learning environments. However, it is based on the recognition of the interconnectedness presented in an agile PBL ecology for learning.

In the updated theory by Chickering and Reisser (1993), the seven vectors present a more contemporary and comprehensive picture of the psychosocial development of a student during their time at university:

• Developing competence

   Competence is expressed as a three-tined pitchfork, the three tines being intellectual competence, physical skills and interpersonal competence. Intellectual competence involves acquisition of knowledge and skills related to the disciplinary or professional academic subject matter, as well as development of intellectual, cultural and aesthetic sophistication and critical thinking and reasoning ability. Physical competence comes from participation in athletic, recreational activities, artistic and manual activities and wellness programs. Interpersonal competence includes communication, leadership and collaborative skills. The handle, if the tines are doing their work as imagined, comes from students' sense of confidence that they can cope and achieve goals successfully.

• Managing emotions

   During their time in higher education, students develop the ability to recognise and accept emotions, how to express them appropriately and how to control them. They will also learn to act on those feelings in a responsible manner. This vector includes a range of feelings, including anxiety, depression, anger, shame, guilt, caring, optimism and inspiration. This is sometimes referred to as emotional intelligence (Bar-On & Parker, 2000; Boyatzis, Stubbs, & Taylor, 2002; Gross & Thompson, 2006).

• Moving through autonomy towards interdependence

   This vector is about students developing increased independence from a need for a constant supply of reassurance or approval from others to 'instrumental independence' (Evans et al., 2010, p. 68), which is characterised by self-direction, problem-solving and mobility. As they move through their programs, students learn the importance of interdependence, of being interconnected with others.

- Developing mature interpersonal relationships

  This vector is about the development of intercultural and interpersonal tolerance, respect of differences and appreciation of commonalities. It includes the capacity to build and sustain rich and healthy relationships with others.
- Establishing identity

  This vector is an extension of the vector about developing mature interpersonal relationships. Student identity development also includes 'comfort with body and appearance, comfort with gender and sexual orientation, a sense of one's social and cultural heritage, a clear self-concept and comfort with one's roles and lifestyle, a secure sense of self in light of feedback from significant others, self-acceptance and self-esteem, and personal stability and integration' (Evans et al., 2010, p. 68).
- Developing purpose

  The sixth vector concerns students developing clear career goals, making meaningful contributions to specific personal interests and establishing strong interpersonal commitments. This includes making purposive, intentional decisions in the face of opposition or barriers.
- Developing integrity

  The last vector is a three-sequential, overlapping stage of student identity that involves humanising values, personalising values and congruence. First, students progress from a usually rather rigid and moralistic view of others to development of a more humanised value system where interests of others are viewed and balanced with their own interests. Next, a personalised value system is formed, acknowledging and respecting beliefs of others. Over time, these values and actions become more salient as their self-interests are balanced by a sense of social responsibility.

Chickering and Reisser's (1993) seven vectors serve to remind us that one of the many responsibilities, and indeed the purpose of universities as creators and implementers of educational environments, is to develop and support the development of student identities, as well as disciplinary or professional declarative knowledge as students move in, move through and move out of a university for learning and move into a future supercomplex society. It is important to keep in mind that while this implies a neatly packaged block of 'time at university', we do not consider it to be a fenced-off block of time; instead, time at university in an agile PBL ecology for learning is seamlessly linked to learning environments inside and outside the university, formal and informal learning and curricular and co-curricular activities and thus forms a continuum, rather than a separate experience. However, this does not mean that the formal educational environment is not important and contributes in crucial ways to developing lifelong learners. Indeed, it is Chickering and Reisser's proposition that the educational environment is the most powerful influencing factor on student development, even if it was written before the 'digital revolution':

- Clear and specific institutional objectives to make the values of the institutions evident to students and staff, which then leads to greater consistency in policies, programs and practices.
- Meaningful opportunities for involvement and significant participation in campus life and consequently more satisfaction with the university experience.
- Extensive and varied student-faculty relationships facilitating development.
- A relevant curriculum that is sensitive to individual differences, offering diverse perspectives and helping students make sense of what they are learning.
- Teaching strategies should include active learning, student-faculty interaction, timely feedback, high expectations and respect for individual learning differences to affect cognitive development in the form of active thinking and integration of ideas, encouraging interdependence, cooperation and interpersonal sensitivity.
- Peer and student communities provide significant interactions to encourage development along all seven vectors. Communities can be formal or informal groups. To have maximum positive benefit, the community should interact regularly, offer opportunities for collaboration, include people of diverse backgrounds, be small enough so that no one is left out and serve as a reference group. The student-to-student communities and interactions are so important that Chickering and Reisser (1993, p. 392) claimed that 'a student's most important teacher is often another student'.
- Faculty and student services staff working collaboratively, which is necessary to provide developmental programs and services for students.

Adapting to Changes Throughout a Student's Learning Journey

Schlossberg (Goodman, Schlossberg, & Anderson, 2006, 1981, 2008), a human development theorist with specialisation in counselling, observed that every individual, young or old, continually experiences transitions during their lifetime – where life stage is more important than chronological age of the individual. These transitions do not occur sequentially nor does everyone experience transitions in a similar manner, but such changes often result in new roles, relationships, routines and assumptions. She also noted that adapting to transitions is often complicated, and students have to be supported to adjust to transition changes, from entry to a program and an institution through to graduation.

Transition is defined as 'any event or non-event that results in changed relationships, routines, assumptions, and roles' (Goodman et al., 2006, p. 33). An individual's reactions to transitions depend on the type of transition, the context in which it occurs and its impact on their lives.

- Types of transition
    Transitions can be predicted, which is known as anticipated transition. Such transitions are usually major life events such as entering university, graduating from a university or starting a first job. Unanticipated transitions are often

disruptive events that occur unexpectedly, such as falling really ill during studies, a serious car accident or surgery. Non-event transitions are the expected events that fail to occur, such as not getting into a preferred program of studies and not getting admission to the desired university. The individual's perception of the transition plays a more important role than the transition itself, that is, the transition only exists if the transition is defined by the person experiencing it (Schlossberg, 1981, p. 5).

- Context
    Context of the transition refers to the relationship of the individual to the transition and setting in which the transition occurs (Goodman et al., 2006, p. 40). The transition may be related to the self, friends, family, work, health or finances/economic well-being.
- Impact
    For an individual undergoing transition, it is not the event or non-event that matters, but its impact – the degree to which the transition changes one's daily life (Goodman et al., 2006, p. 37), in terms of relationships, routines, assumptions and roles.

Stages of Transition

Transition is a process that takes time and has no end point. Essentially, the individual moves from a preoccupation with the transition to an integration of the transition. Schlossberg described the transition process or cycle as a process over time that includes moving in, moving through and moving out (Goodman et al., 2006; Schlossberg, 1997, 2008; Schlossberg et al., 1989). Each of these three phases has their own issues and challenges.

The move-in phase is when individuals move into a new situation, leaving their known contexts behind. In the higher education context, we identify this phase with groups of students moving into a university or higher education context to pursue a degree, also known as commencing students. In this phase, students start the process of 'learning the ropes' (Schlossberg, 1997, p. 94). They need to be familiar with the rules, regulations, norms and expectations of the new environments, including the university in general, and the programs and/or courses of studies. Institutions are encouraged to devote a great deal of time to orientation, a process designed to help individuals know what is expected of them (Goodman et al., 2006), and many institutions do so, that is, in the form of an institution-wide or faculty-wide orientation for first year and commencing students. Again, we need to keep in mind that the idea of a neatly packaged time frame for a degree is eroding and that for a considerable number of students, doing a degree is increasingly becoming a fragmented experience, whereby they move in and move out of their studies at different stages of their lives.

After moving in to a new experience, once the students know the ropes, the moving-through or 'in-between' (Goodman et al., 2006, p. 50) phase begins. Students begin the process of adjustment, balancing and managing their day-to-day life that includes work and studying, family, university life and so on (i.e. it spans the four systems of an agile PBL ecology for learning). The moving through can be described as a 'hang-in-there' phase (Schlossberg, 1997, p. 96). This is a phase where students face many tasks, issues and challenges, such as the ones posited by Chickering and Reisser (1993). Therefore, students in this phase require continuing support to sustain their commitment, goals, confidence, motivation and persistence in learning and staying on in the institution.

The last phase, moving out, is a process associated with passing or exiting the familiar university or higher education environment (graduation) and beginning a move into some new setting such as starting postgraduate studies or work. According to Schlossberg (Goodman et al., 2006), students at the moving-out phase experience feelings of grief, and they might be fearful of the unknowns because they are leaving behind familiar surroundings, people and structures that they have grown accustomed to. However, this only applies if these two phases are conceptualised as separated by rigid boundaries. Within an agile PBL ecology for learning, the 'exiting' phase is imagined to be much more drawn out as the world outside the university (macro-system) is a seamless part of the ecology. Thus, the boundaries between the micro- and meso-systems on the one hand and the macro-system on the other are significantly blurred, thereby reducing the feeling of grief, traditionally associated with this phase.

Student Engagement: Connecting Students to 'Becoming'

The two student development concepts show that students' learning journeys when they enter university to gain their degrees are not a simple matter of just acquiring academic or subject matter knowledge or just doing a degree to get a 'job', even if this is often an important reason for obtaining a degree. However, in an agile PBL ecology for learning, these students learn the skills, competencies, attributes and values, in tandem with declarative professional and/or disciplinary knowledge, so that they learn a 'way-of-being' and become an individual of 'potential' – their personal and professional/disciplinary identities – as they interact and navigate the social settings in the university and beyond, progressing through their university studies as contributing members of society (Hinchliffe & Jolly, 2011; Holmes, 2013; Lairio, Puukari, & Kouva, 2013).

Much like the 'liminal space' in Meyer and Land's (2005, p. 375) threshold concept, it refers to a transitional space students encounter when they move in and out of learning. It is a metaphor to describe 'the conceptual transformations students undergo, or find difficulty and anxiety in undergoing, particularly in relation to notions of being 'stuck'' (Meyer & Land, 2005, p. 377). Students go through a process of epistemological transformation, which ultimately leads to a state of '"becoming": becoming disciplinary experts, and perhaps, most importantly becoming more fully themselves' (Timmermans, 2010, p. 16). The interconnected and multiple layers and contexts where students are situated in the agile PBL ecology for learning mean that there are many liminal spaces that students encounter and support needs to be provided to them. This does not just relate to curricular or subject matter support – as in the curricular – teaching, learning and assessing. As Chickering and Reisser (1993) noted, the learning and developing trajectories of university students can be nebulous and learning can be ubiquitous, and they bleed into contexts outside the formal curricular spaces. In a student's learning journey, these liminal spaces are therefore naturally found in the transitional stages in their university progression, starting when they first move into the university through to when they move out beyond their university life upon graduation, again keeping in mind that the boundaries between these stages are porous.

The liquidising element between the curricular and non-curricular boundaries is what the students 'do' or 'engage' with, in relation to other people, tools and systems in the university environment (micro- and exo-systems) and outside of the university (macro-system), and what matters most. A term commonly used to refer to what students do is student engagement, which is commonly used to describe the effort and time that students invest in meaningful educational experiences (Kuh, 2003, 2004, 2009) and is measured in the National Survey of Student Engagement (NSSE) in the United States. Similar versions of NSSE are known as the Australasia Survey of Student Engagement (AUSSE) in Australia and New Zealand and, in China, the National Survey of Student Engagement – China (NSSE-C). At the same time and more so in recent years, British and European versions of student engagement have also emerged. They focus more on the qualitative essence of learning from students' perspectives, for example, in the form of interests and emotions, while the American version focused on the quantitative behavioural and cognitive aspects of learning, in the form of time and effort (Zepke, 2013).

Within an agile PBL ecology for learning, teaching and assessing, a way-of-being and becoming is not just a matter of students being engaged with the explicitly stated skills, competencies and knowledge, but they are in 'a transitional process of boundary crossing' (Hager & Hodkinson, 2009, p. 635). Students encounter liminal spaces and engage with troublesome knowledge or threshold concepts (Meyer & Land, 2005) throughout their learning journeys as they transit to a way-of-being. Students are also engaged in forming their personal and professional or disciplinary identities during undergraduate studies, which again will change when they move beyond university. In many workplaces beyond the university, employers highly value students who (1) have values referring to personal ethics, awareness of social and cultural diversity and ability to recognise and act on opportunities; (2) have a creative intellect and the ability to adapt and broaden thinking and reflect on learning and development; (3) perform in a way that displays the ability to self-check and revise their work; and (4) engage in a way that is 'outward looking' (Hinchliffe & Jolly, 2011, pp. 575–581). However, they tend to rely on universities to 'deliver' graduates with those attributes and qualities. Within an agile PBL context, we argue instead that employers should be part of the learning process and thus take a certain level of responsibility to develop those qualities in learners, thereby blurring the rigid boundaries between 'the university' and 'the real world'. Moreover, engaging students in agile PBL is not just about performance-based economic outcomes, where skills and functional performance are the primary focus. Student engagement encompasses engaging students in their sense of being and becoming, not only engaging them cognitively and behaviourally but also emotionally and affectively (Solomonides, 2012; Trowler & Trowler, 2010; Wimpenny & Savin-Baden, 2013). It is not a matter of either-or; it is both.

To us, student engagement is what students do – cognitively, behaviourally and emotionally – which matters in their learning and developing towards a way-of-being or becoming, both for their current educational purposes and for their future learning. Our educational goal and purpose is to support them through our teaching, learning, assessing and the business of running a university. Student engagement from our perspective must be conducted and embedded in the different contexts of the university and beyond. In other words, it must be cognisant of the different systems in the agile PBL ecology for learning and the relationships between them. Thus, this does not just apply in the curricular spaces where agile PBL learning, teaching and assessment occur but also in non-curricular spaces, because learning, developing and knowing are liquid and cross boundaries within the university contexts and beyond (Hager & Hodkinson, 2009; Savin-Baden, 2014).

Student engagement must be present in all the phases of the transition process, crossing boundaries between curricular/academic and non-curricular/professional, to enable and empower students in their journeys of learning and developing. A 'mattering institution' attuned to student engagement – cognitively, behaviourally, emotionally – will enable students to traverse smoothly and signal to them that they 'matter' (Schlossberg, 1989). Students would then experience a great sense of belonging and not feel alienation and disjunction as they move through the transitions. The sense of feeling that they matter (Barron & Corbin, 2011; Hager & Hodkinson, 2009; Holmes, 2013; Trowler & Trowler, 2010; Wimpenny & Savin-Baden, 2013) can only fuel students to be more engaged in their learning and developing, resulting in a high sense of loyalty and in return in high retention and progression outcomes desired by institutions (Chickering, 2006; Chickering & Kuh, 2005; Coates & Ransom, 2011; Kuh et al., 2005; Pascarella et al., 2010; Pascarella & Terenzini, 2005; Schlossberg et al., 1989).

Strategies and Practices for Student Engagement

This section deals with the strategies and practices for a more holistic, whole-of-university approach to student engagement.

Moving-In Practices

Agile PBL practitioners need to recognise that students moving in have just moved out of a learning experience or environment that may have been rather traditional and totally different. Many of the frustrations experienced by students in the move-in phase are about adapting to and coping with PBL, especially when they have moved from a very different educational environment. Therefore, we need to respond by guiding students to be ready to invest the time, energy and emotions required for a successful transition. Students in the move-in phase need to be familiar with the rules, regulations, norms and expectations of the new, PBL environment. Orientation is the most common practice in higher education to ease commencing students into the university environment. However, it is regarded to be especially crucial to prepare students for a PBL (and an agile PBL) environment, whether it is a program or a single course/unit (Brouwer & Kruithof, 2010; Hung, Harpole Bailey, & Jonassen, 2003; Moust, Van Berkel, & Schmidt, 2005; Uden & Beaumont, 2006). This preparation or orientation is so important at this move-in stage that the longevity and sustainability of an agile PBL learning and teaching program can be at risk if you fail to do it effectively (Moust et al., 2005). A critical component of the orientation program must be about clarifying the reasons and benefits for an agile PBL approach to future learning. This is because students need to understand why a PBL educational approach is taken in terms of the theoretical ideas, underlying principles and philosophy behind agile PBL (Brouwer & Kruithof, 2010; Moust et al., 2005). Involving students' support systems such as parents, guardians, spouses, life partners, children from the meso-system and employers and alumni graduates from the macro-system in some engagement activities at this stage can help to create a 'bridge' for students between the curriculum and the future by stressing the benefits of agile PBL as a way-of-being and becoming. Research has shown that persons in the meso-system still have prevailing influence on students even when they invest time, effort and emotions in the immediate micro-system of a PBL university (Kek & Huijser, 2011; Kek, Darmawan, & Chen, 2007).

Moving-Through Practices

In this phase, students are in what is described as 'hang-in-there' mode. An agile PBL university needs to recognise that this is a phase where students face many tasks, issues and challenges and that they need continuing support post-orientation. The purpose of responses in this phase is so that these students can sustain their commitment, confidence, motivation and persistence. Bearing in mind social forms of support are the most effective mechanisms in this transition stage, it is important to purposively consider engaging students as partners in the development of non-curricular as is for curricular activities (Healey, Flint, & Harrington, 2014).

Some form of student-peer or students-supporting-students communities can be established such as a buddy system (Brouwer & Kruithof, 2010). Another powerful student learning community that can be developed is some form of peer-assisted learning (PAL), also known as supplemental instruction, which was first conceptualised in the University of Minnesota in the United States. According to Kimmins (2014, p. 109), student-peer learning communities do not function like they do with academic tutors or mentors. Rather, the PAL student leaders support students, usually low-achieving or at-risk students, by engaging them in disciplinary learning through group participation with their peers and improving learning skills such as thinking and reasoning, independence and reflection.

However, we argue that these student learning communities should also be widened and extended beyond 'moving-in' students where learning communities are commonly found to 'moving-through' students where such student learning communities are few in existence. We propose that these student-peer learning communities serve as an inclusive student engagement response that can lead every student in the university to sustain their confidence, commitment and persistence. For example, the Meet-Up Student Community (MUSC), a variant of PAL, a non-disciplinary-specific student-peer learning community that focuses on generic learning skills to support students regardless of their disciplines and stages of their learning journey, is being trialled at the University of Southern Queensland (USQ), a regional, online university in Australia. MUSC is one of the responses embedded in the Student Personalised Academic Road to Success (SPARS) program at USQ, described as a case study in this chapter.

We realise that the student-peer learning communities can be established at every transition phase, but we consider that such a response makes more impact for students due to the psychosocial demands that they experience at this 'hang-in-there' stage. Another reason is that in most universities, a large amount of attention and resources are already being placed in orientation programs for commencing students and using student-peer-assisted learning during the first year experience. But not many universities would consider responses for moving-through students. Again, it is best if such student-peer learning communities are integrated into the non-curricular activities and also at the curricular program level. Such student-peer support will only further facilitate the micro-environments where the student development and engagement are already churning. Of course in an agile PBL ecology for learning, peer learning is integrated in forms of authentic faculty-student and student-student interactions through authentic problems and assessments, collaborative and group-based learning, integrative iterative teaching and learning processes, which include peer feedback and reflections on learning and development.

Moving-Out Practices

Moving out is a process associated with the passing or exiting from a familiar university or higher education environment (towards graduation) and beginning a move into some new settings postgraduation such as starting postgraduate studies or a new job. An agile PBL university must recognise and respect that students during this phase might still experience feelings of grief and might be fearful of the unknowns because they are leaving behind familiar surroundings, people and structures that they have grown accustomed to, even if this transition is significantly reduced in an agile PBL context, as the transition process is continuously being managed and is embedded in the curriculum – teaching, learning and assessment. Again, in an agile PBL ecology for learning, the boundaries between transitions and systems are significantly blurred, thereby reducing the potentially negative impacts of the transitions.

Nevertheless, the responses during the moving-out phase are more about recognition and celebration to ease students moving out into the future as seamlessly as possible. Ideally, this occurs in such a way that students themselves do not even know and feel that they are transiting into unfamiliar territories because they have been prepared from the outset. They are (or should be) change ready! The key here is to help these students frame their completing year or semesters in the context of easing them into unfamiliar but exciting future possibilities and environments that are in the macro-system. Of course, these should already be integrated in the curricular environments, as discussed in earlier chapters, through practices such as interconnecting employers in the authentic curriculum design, authentic problems or cases, assessments for learning and/or one of the information sources or experts that students can turn to for information. Where possible and relevant, it is important to interconnect and integrate future employers with students in authentic work experience such as service learning, work-integrated learning and internships, just to name a few. An agile PBL curriculum and pedagogy from the outset *is* the support for this transition phase, enabling and empowering students to move into the world beyond university, while all the while drawing from the world beyond university.

Strategic Institutional Conditions for Student Success

Kuh et al. (2005) shared six mattering institutional conditions that foster student engagement and persistence. These six conditions are drawn from a study of 20 diverse 4-year colleges and universities in the United States that have higher than predicted student success (graduation rates) and through the National Survey of Student Engagement (NSSE) have demonstrated to be using effective practices for fostering student success among students from diverse backgrounds, abilities and aspirations (Pascarella et al., 2010).

- A 'living' mission and 'lived' educational philosophy

  This is about having clearly articulated educational purposes and aspirations and having a coherent and well-understood philosophy that guides 'how we do things here' (Kuh et al., 2005, p. 25). The institution's focus on student success is consistent with institutional values, traditions and educational purposes and goes to great lengths in making its mission, values and aspirations transparent and understandable to all stakeholders and has a steadfast focus on students and their success.

- An unshakeable focus on student learning

Effective institutions' learning environments are characterised by four common themes: valuing student learning, experimenting with engaging pedagogies, demonstrating a cool passion for talent development and making time for students (Kuh et al., 2005, p. 65). Student learning and personal development are a priority; faculty and professional staff who are committed to student learning are recruited and retained; faculty and professional staff make time for students; active and collaborative learning approaches are employed; students are challenged to raise their aspirations; timely and apt feedback are provided; and they work with the students they have, ignoring the adage to recruit the best and brightest. The important message with this condition is that powerful learning environments and significant outcomes can be achieved no matter what the institution's resources or students' preparation. That is, both institution and students can succeed despite the odds.

- Environments adapted for educational enrichment

Effective institutions are those that have created a 'sense of place' (Kuh et al., 2005, p. 93) for students. This condition demands that resources and people are linked to address issues that affect the quality of life on and off the campus and to alter and shape the environment to create spaces and settings where teaching and learning can flourish. This is similar to our interconnection principle. Effective institutions connect to the surrounding communities situated outside the institutions' environment and adapt the physical structures to a 'human scale' sending messages to students' feelings of well-being, belonging and identity. This is a crucial characteristic of an agile PBL ecology for learning.

- Clear pathways to student success

This condition recognises that many students who enter universities often come without clear direction; they are unlikely to know what they want, nor do they necessarily have the strategies to succeed in universities. This is particularly true for students who are first in their families to attend higher education. Recognising that students need coherence in learning towards student success, effective educational practices are those that have created pathways clearly marked to show them what to expect and what success looks and feels like. That is, institutions create structures and practices that help students bring meaning to their university experiences. For example, they create guideposts such as first year seminars, advising sessions and celebrations such as graduations, while institutional publications accurately describe what students say they experience and intentionally tell students about the resources and services available to help them succeed.

- Improvement-oriented ethos

Educationally effective institutions are in a 'perpetual learning mode – monitoring where they are, what they are doing, where they want to go, and how to maintain momentum toward positive change' (Kuh et al., 2005, p.133). There is a 'can-do' ethic that permeates these institutions, mirroring the learning organisations. The issue of sustainability and continuous improvements will be discussed in Chap. 8. Educationally effective institutions are confident in questioning whether their performance matches what they are and their potential, are inclined towards innovation and systematically collect information about various aspects of student performance and use this to inform policy and decision-making. Most importantly, efforts to improve and innovate are geared towards a desire to be best at what they do with the students they have.

- Shared responsibility for educational quality and student success

   The message here is that no single unit or office can on its own enhance the overall quality of large numbers of students. Everyone is needed to make the students feel that they matter. Senior administrators and faculty staff of such institutions 'walk their talk' by modelling behaviour that speaks of a focus on students and illustrates learning-centred priorities.

A Case Study of Crossing Boundaries in a University Ecology for Learning: Student Personalised Academic Road to Success Initiative

As part of a larger university-wide project known as the Connected Student Learning Project at the University of Southern Queensland, a regional, online university in Australia, a mattering integrative student engagement framework known as the Student Personalised Academic Road to Success (SPARS) was conceptualised (shown in Fig. 6.1). Conceptualised in 2012, it integrated the academic learning

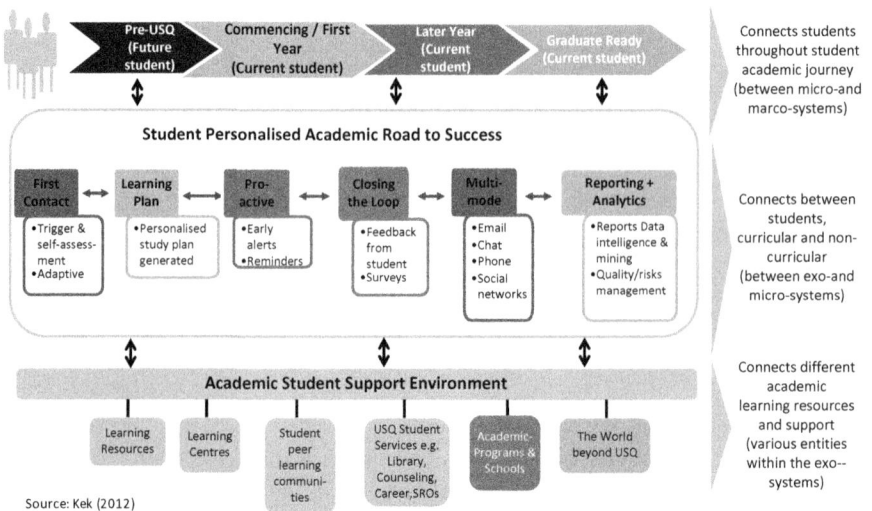

Fig. 6.1 Student Personalised Academic Road to Success (SPARS)

support, with the psychological, social, administrative and career domains of knowledge. It was an inter-institutional collaborative project involving academic staff, academic developers, librarians, student administration staff, psychological counsellors and career development advisors. The framework was conceptualised to signal to students that they matter because the concept of SPARS and the resultant online tool, Academic Success Planner (ASP), were a result of the university listening to their students' voices of wanting an integrated, seamless student learning experience. Right down to the name of the online tool, 'Academic Success Planner' was suggested by the students. The over-aching idea was to create a one-stop, online space for student learning and development.

SPARS (Kek, 2012) was conceptualised as a response to widening student participation in higher education with wide-ranging abilities and aspirations. It was underpinned by human development theories and concepts and conceptualised to enable the university to shape and create meaningful learning environments to better interconnect students to cross between curricular and non-curricular boundaries seamlessly and enable them to achieve student success, from when they move in and move through to when they move on from the university. In short, the framework was designed to fully engage across an agile ecology for learning.

The primary objective of SPARS was to create a comprehensive student learning support that enable students to be more fully engaged in their learning by fostering confidence, commitment and persistence among students and, secondarily, to achieve high institutional student success in the form of high retention rates. According to Kek (2012, p. 1), SPARS '… facilitates student academic success and experiences by *connecting and formalising* essential informal academic learning support, non-academic student support, administrative support and strategic quality enhancement processes into *a single support point* … to increase student retention/progression as well as to enhance students' experiences throughout their journey in the university'.

Student support programs based on the SPARS framework, when fully operational, would perform the following key functions:

- Providing an adaptive online system that triages students to the relevant support and resources, based on the students' self-identified learning needs, where and when they need it.
- Generating and immediately delivering to students a personalised plan or portfolio, targeting their self-identified needs, for their information or for them to take action. The plan or portfolio should comprise a suite of resources and support integrating relevant academic and nonacademic student support.
- Integrating proactive measures such as an early alert system to feedforward to academic/faculty and administrative staff.
- Integrating assessment to close the loop on student support.
- Integrating multichannel modes of communication to engage with students.

- Incorporating quality enhancement and improvement processes by leveraging data analytics collected from the person-environment interactions, for reporting purposes and to inform decision-making.

In the case of SPARS, the university entities (support, resources and persons) outside the students' immediate micro-system, supporting students in their respective siloed spaces, are now *interconnected* and *integrated* into the students' formal and informal micro-systems, in a seamless manner. They are those found in the exo-systems of the agile ecology for learning.

The persons in the university units (exo-systems) can be considered the legitimate peripheral participants (Lave & Wenger, 1991) who support and facilitate student learning and development, through the creation and sustainment of their confidence, commitment and persistence, from entry to graduation, and are interconnected to the students' micro-system to create formal and informal learning opportunities. They were staff from student services, counselling, career development, library and learning and teaching services. SPARS also interconnects these persons and university units with the academic staff who teaches into the students' micro-system and their general work environments at the exo-level where they perform non-teaching tasks, such as monitoring their students' overall academic development. As such, not only the persons are interconnected, the systems or tools used in these contexts are also being integrated – the university's core customer relationship management system that incorporates assessment and quality improvement processes used by teachers and administrative staff and the learning management systems used by students and teachers for learning, teaching and assessing.

In summary, SPARS is an adaptive, personalised, online academic student support system that generates personalised academic learning support to every undergraduate student at all stages of the transition cycle and is adaptive to their learning demands, when and where they need it. It is still very much in its infancy, and it is too early to say that the initiative has been impactful in promoting student success and retention. Only time will tell. However, in a Report of the Review of the Demand-Driven Funding System in Australia by Kemp and Norton (2014), the initiative is considered to be a promising, innovative response to improve the overall quality of the student experience. The report was a review of 'the extent to which the demand driven funding arrangements impacting the higher education sector in Australia are increasing participation, supporting students from low socio-economic status backgrounds and rural and regional communities and meeting the skills needed in the (current) economy' (Kemp & Norton, 2014, p. iii). What is important is this case study demonstrates how the different layers of an agile PBL ecology for learning cross boundaries are connected.

Conclusion

In an agile PBL ecology, it is not just the micro-environment, in which students invest considerable time, effort and emotions as part of their learning and development that is important. The macro- and exo-environments situated outside the classrooms are as important as the teaching staff in the courses and programs in enabling an agile PBL way-of-being and becoming. This is because these environments combined to form proximal and distal effects that influence students through their interactions with others, tools and systems in the different environments as they cross boundaries in the university and beyond. Furthermore, we must recognise that university students' learning journeys during their time at university are rather messy and include formation of their identities, a sense of being and becoming, inside and outside their immediate micro-environment. Therefore, the different environments in a university play an important role in students achieving success because of the amount of interactions and interchanges that students are engaged in, not just with their learning but with identity formation – personal and professional/academic disciplinary – when they move in, move through and move on from the university. This means that universities must be agile too – responsive and open to diverse and widening student participation, in shaping and creating mattering environments that authentically engage students cognitively, behaviourally and emotionally – and give them a sense that they genuinely matter.

References

Bar-On, R., & Parker, D. A. (2000). *Bar-On emotional quotient inventory: Youth version, technical manual.* North Tonawanda, NY: Multi-Health Systems.

Barron, P., & Corbin, L. (2011). Student engagement: Rhetoric and reality. *Higher Education Research and Development, 31*(6), 759–772. doi:10.1080/07294360.2012.655711.

Boyatzis, R. E., Stubbs, E. C., & Taylor, S. N. (2002). Learning cognitive and emotional intelligence competencies through graduate management education. *Academy of Management Journal on Learning and Education, 1*(2), 150–162.

Bronfenbrenner, U., & Morris, P. A. (2006). The bioecological model of human development. In W. Damon & R. M. Lerner (Eds.), *Handbook of child psychology* (6th ed., pp. 793–828). Hoboken, NJ: Wiley.

Brouwer, E., & Kruithof, M. (2010). Learning how to learn, teaching how to teach. In H. van Berkel, A. Scherpbier, H. Hillen, & C. van der Vleuten (Eds.), *Lessons from problem-based learning* (pp. 107–116). Oxford: Oxford University Press.

Chickering, A. W. (1969). *Education and identity.* San Francisco: Jossey-Bass.

Chickering, A. W. (2006). Every student can learn -if …. *About Campus, 11*(2), 9–15.

Chickering, A. W., & Kuh, G. D. (2005). *Promoting student success: Creating conditions so every student can learn* (Occasional Paper No. 3). Bloomington, IN: Indiana University Centre for Postsecondary Research.

Chickering, A. W., & Reisser, L. (1993). *Education and identity* (2nd ed.). San Francisco: Jossey-Bass.

Coates, H., & Ransom, L. (2011). *Dropout DNA and the genetics of effective support* (AUSSE Research Briefing, Vol. 11, pp. 1–17). Melbourne, Australia: Australian Council for Educational Research (ACER).

Evans, N. J., Forney, D. S., Guido, F. M., Patton, L. D., & Renn, K. A. (2010). *Student development in college: Theory, research and practice* (2nd ed.). San Francisco: Jossey-Bass.

Goodman, J., Schlossberg, N. K., & Anderson, M. L. (2006). *Counselling adults in transition: Linking practice with theory* (3rd ed.). New York: Springer.

Gross, J., & Thompson, R. (2006). *Emotion regulation: Conceptual foundations, Handbook of emotional regulation.* New York: Guilford Press.

Hager, P., & Hodkinson, P. (2009). Moving beyond the metaphor of transfer of learning. *British Educational Research Journal, 35*(4), 619–638.

Healey, M., Flint, A., & Harrington, K. (2014). *Engagement through partnership: Students as partners in learning and teaching in higher education* (pp. 1–76). York, UK: The Higher Education Academy.

Hinchliffe, G. W., & Jolly, A. (2011). Graduate identity and employability. *British Educational Research Journal, 37*(4), 563–584. doi:10.1080/01411926.2010.482200.

Holmes, L. (2013). Competing perspectives on graduate employability: Possession, position or process? *Studies in Higher Education, 38*(4), 538–552. doi:10.1080/03075079.2011.587140.

Hung, W., Harpole Bailey, J., & Jonassen, D. H. (2003). Exploring the tensions of problem-based learning: Insights from research. *New Directions for Teaching and Learning, 2003*(95), 13–23.

Kek, M. Y. C. A. (2012). *Integrated student learning journey initiative (ISLJI) Final Paper: The integrated student learning journey – Student Personalised Academic Road to Success (SPARS): A framework for the provision of adaptive and student-directed, on-line, on-demand, integrated study support to students*. Paper submitted to the Director, Learning and Teaching Support, Office of Pro-Vice Chancellor (Learning, Teaching and Quality), University of Southern Queensland.

Kek, M. Y. C. A., Darmawan, I. G. N., & Chen, Y. S. (2007). Inter-relationships of individual characteristics, family, learning environments, learning approaches, and student outcomes in a Malaysian private university. *International Education Journal, 8*(2), 318–338.

Kek, M., & Huijser, H. (2011). Exploring the combined relationships of student and teacher factors on learning approaches and self-directed learning readiness at a Malaysian university. *Studies in Higher Education, 36*(2), 185–208. doi:10.1080/03075070903519210.

Kemp, D., & Norton, A. (2014). *Review of the demand driven funding system*. http://www.education.gov.au/report-review-demand-driven-funding-system

Kimmins, L. R. (2014). Meet-up for success: The story of a peer led program's journey. *Journal of Peer Learning, 6*(1), 103–117.

Kuh, G. D. (2003). What are we learning about student engagement from NSSE. *Change, 35*, 24–32.

Kuh, G. D. (2004). *The National Survey of Student Engagement: Conceptual framework and overview of psychometric properties*. http://nsse.iub.edu/nsse_2001/pdf/framework-2001.pdf

Kuh, G. D. (2009). The national survey of student engagement: Conceptual and empirical foundations. *New Directions for Institutional Research, 2009*(141), 5–20.

Kuh, G. D., Kinzie, J., Schuh, J. H., Whitt, E. J., & Associates. (2005). *Student success in college*. San Francisco: Jossey-Bass/Wiley.

Lairio, M., Puukari, S., & Kouva, A. (2013). Studying at university as part of student life and identity construction. *Scandinavian Journal of Educational Research, 57*(2), 115–131. doi:10.1080/00313831.2011.621973.

Lave, J., & Wenger, E. (1991). *Situated learning: Legitimate peripheral participation*. Cambridge, UK: Cambridge University Press.

Meyer, J. H. F., & Land, R. (2005). Threshold concepts and troublesome knowledge (2): Epistemological considerations and a conceptual framework for teaching and learning. *Higher Education, 49*(3), 373–388.

Moust, J. H. C., Van Berkel, H. J. M., & Schmidt, H. G. (2005). Signs of erosion: Reflections on three decades of problem-based learning at Maastricht University. *Higher Education, 50*(4), 665–683.

Pascarella, E. T., Seifert, T. A., & Blaich, C. (2010). How effective are the NSSE benchmarks in predicting important educational outcomes? *Change, 42*, 16–22.

Pascarella, E. T., & Terenzini, P. T. (2005). *How college affects students: A third decade of research*. San Francisco: Jossey-Bass.

Savin-Baden, M. (2014). Using problem-based learning: New constellations for the 21st century. *Journal on Excellence in College Teaching, 25*(3&4), 197–219.

Schlossberg, N. K. (1981). A model for analyzing human adaptation to transition. *The Counseling Psychologist, 9*(2), 2–18.

Schlossberg, N. K. (1989). Marginality and mattering: Key issues in building community. *New Directions for Student Services, 48*, 5–15.

Schlossberg, N. K. (1997). A model of worklife transition. In R. Feller & G. Walz (Eds.), *Career transitions in turbulent times* (pp. 93–104). Greensbo, NC: ERIC Counselling and Student Services Clearinghouse.

Schlossberg, N. K. (2008). *Overwhelmed: Coping with life's ups and downs* (2nd ed.). Lanham, MD: M. Evans and Company.

Schlossberg, N. K., Lynch, A. Q., & Chickering, A. W. (1989). *Improving higher education environments for adults: Responsive programs and services from entry to departure*. San Francisco: Jossey-Bass.

Solomonides, I. (2012). A critique of the nexus between student engagement and lifelong learning. *International Journal of Continuing Education and Lifelong Learning, 5*(1), 65–81.

Timmermans, J. A. (2010). Changing our minds: The development potential of threshold concepts. In J. H. F. Meyer, R. Land, & C. Baillie (Eds.), *Threshold concepts and transformational learning* (pp. 3–19). Rotterdam, The Netherlands: Sense Publishers.

Trowler, V., & Trowler, P. (2010). *Student engagement evidence summary*. York, UK: The Higher Education Academy.

Uden, L., & Beaumont, C. (2006). *Technology and problem-based learning*. Hershey, PA: Information Science Pub.

Wimpenny, K., & Savin-Baden, M. (2013). Alienation, agency and authenticity: A synthesis of the literature on student engagement. *Teaching in Higher Education, 18*(3), 311–326.

Zepke, N. (2013). Student engagement: A complex business supporting the first year experience in tertiary experience. *The International Journal of the First Year in Higher Education, 4*(2), 1–14.

Chapter 7
Agile Staff Professional Learning for Learning

Introduction

A human resource crucial to the success of an agile PBL curriculum and pedagogy is the academic teaching staff who are also known in the PBL literature and field as PBL facilitators. Facilitating or teaching students in an agile PBL environment is hugely important, yet it is a role that is very challenging for many academic staff involved in PBL, regardless of the educational contexts. In this book, we prefer to term this important human resource 'the agile PBL teacher', as they are a central element in an agile PBL ecology for learning. Being a facilitator of learning is of utmost importance in any PBL context or curriculum, however, an agile PBL teacher also performs a number of other academic tasks that are equally important, in that they prepare students and induct them into a particular way-of-being and becoming. In this chapter, we explore characteristics deemed important for an agile PBL teacher with a focus on activating (facilitating) student learning and developing. We also discuss academic or faculty development and issues involved in preparing agile PBL teachers. We echo Shulman's (1987) concern that with much knowledge available on effective teaching, the question is 'how the extensive knowledge of teaching can be learned at all during the brief period allocated to teacher preparation?' (p. 7).

An Agile PBL Teacher Is an Activator for Learning

The PBL teacher has always been considered a critical and essential element to the success of PBL curriculum (all PBL models) and its educational goals (Barrows, 2002; Savery, 2006; Schmidt & Moust, 1995). However, teaching might be more challenging in an online or technology-enhanced PBL environment (Jonassen, 2007). The PBL teacher might be a critical element to the success of a PBL curriculum, but their conceptions of what they think their role as a PBL tutor entails or their

© Springer Science+Business Media Singapore 2017
M.Y.C.A. Kek, H. Huijser, *Problem-based Learning into the Future*,
DOI 10.1007/978-981-10-2454-2_7

beliefs (Hendry, 2009; Moore & Kain, 2011), as well as their teaching behaviours, actions or approaches undertaken (or not!) in their individual PBL classrooms, usually occur behind closed doors (Barrett & Moore, 2011; Hendry, 2009; Kek & Huijser, 2011b; Martyn, Terwijn, Kek, & Huijser, 2014). However, it is what they do or do not do that really matters! That is, what they do behind those closed doors has a significant impact on whether learning is activated. Have they stimulated students in engaging in active collaborative and communicative interactions with one another? Have they enabled collaborative knowledge building, not just sharing or exchanging information? Have they questioned if students' self-directed learning and overall learning are meaningful? Were they present in the student group learning process at all? Have they established a positive enabling climate and relationship with the students in the group learning environment? Have they approached the learning process by scaffolding and modelling for students, to support them, and then fade their control to ease students' dependence on them? These are good teaching practices, particularly for group learning in any PBL contexts where students not only acquire knowledge, skills, competencies and values but also their sense of identities and sense of being and becoming. A key additional question in an agile PBL ecology for learning is whether they have drawn on the different systems in the ecology, thereby drawing on students' prior knowledge base and situate their learning in authentic learning environments.

But how can we develop or train agile PBL teachers, when more often than not, they are placed in the curriculum – to design, to teach and to assess future learning, soon after they are selected or recruited? This can be detrimental, particularly in an agile PBL curriculum. Agile PBL teachers must themselves understand and engage in a PBL way-of-being – cognitive, behavioural and affective – as experienced by their students, so they themselves embody the kind of person needed for the position of an agile PBL teacher (Dawson, Britnell, & Hitchcock, 2010; Shulman, 2005).

Parallel to the paradigm shift in learning, from a traditional way of learning to learning from students' perspectives, the role of an agile PBL teacher has also undergone a paradigm shift. As the creator of his/her teaching environment, the agile PBL teacher's role has significantly shifted from a traditional academic role. In terms of supporting student learning in an agile PBL context, the agile PBL teacher must activate collaborative knowledge building and productive discourse (Hmelo-Silver & Barrows, 2008; Scardamalia, 2002). This is similar to Barrett and Moore's (2011, p. 115) concept of 'dialogic knowing …where this kind of knowledge is generated when people create and re-create knowledge together'. Barrett and Moore posit that 'dialogic knowing is what underpins good learning and is at the heart of problem-based learning, and should be maximised by both students and teachers by talking and listening to each other, by sharing ideas, by confronting divergent views, and by approaching problems in interactive, collaborative, communicative ways' (p. 115). The agile PBL teacher guides the students, usually in groups, through non-directive ways by questioning students at the metacognitive level (Barrows, 2002), rather than simply communicating-transmitting-conveying knowledge or materials to the students (Jonassen, 2012) as in the traditional teaching context. We argue that for students to learn a way-of-being and to become adaptive experts, agile PBL teachers *must* enable collaborative knowledge building, not just sharing of information, through dialogues with students, functioning all the time on a metacognitive level and challenging and encouraging self-directed learning, inquiry, reflection and critical reasoning, by modelling dialogue, providing scaffolds and then fading, and by using silences when appropriate to let students be independent from the teachers. Agile PBL teachers must activate these forms of learning themselves to consequently influence their students. Furthermore, they need to be collaborative themselves and reach out beyond the university walls to involve others from different systems in the agile PBL ecology for learning, for example, employers.

We prefer to think of an agile PBL teacher as an activator for student learning through the model-scaffold-fade approach more so than a facilitator of learning. We concur with Mayo and Donnelly (1995) that the term, facilitate, does not really capture the dynamics of what a PBL teacher really does and must do in the student learning process. An agile PBL teacher must be actively involved and seen by students to be engaged in the group's learning process by activating discussions and stimulating elaboration, refinement and transformation of knowledge. The agile PBL teacher also must know when to pull back, keep silent and fade in the process. In short, it is about striking the right balance between challenging students and leaving them be, at different points in the learning process. There are no hard and fast rules around this, and it depends to an important extent on exercising professional judgement.

Silen (2006) terms a PBL teacher as someone who has a keen sense of being attentive and aware to students, the learning process, and to what is occurring in the group as a whole, a PBL teacher who is 'present' (p. 380) in body and mind. In an agile PBL curriculum, the agile PBL teacher teaches with the model-scaffold-fade approach to generate dialogic knowing, and the teacher must then be *present* (body and mind) while engaging with the students. It is important to note that in an agile PBL ecology for learning, 'the teacher' refers to the teacher role, rather than a specific teacher, as the teacher role can be occupied by the actual teacher as well as by various employers at different stages in the learning process. Only by having the agile PBL teacher 'present', whether in online and face-to-face teaching environments, by being keenly attuned to the students' learning process in the group, would they recognise the opportunities for dialogue generated and would they be able to respond in a timely and appropriate manner to the students' learning needs, to ensure that knowledge building or re/creation occurs productively. The agile PBL teacher's presence can diminish as students become more experienced and confident in their learning process, and this is in many ways up to the discretion of the teacher, but fading should definitely be on an uphill trajectory over time. However, this does draw attention to the importance of agile PBL teachers recognising the right time to 'fade out', which is something that is counterintuitive for many teachers and jars to some extent with their professional identity.

In fact, *not* 'fading out' is an instinctive part of many teachers' (PBL and not PBL) sense of teacher identity and therefore not an easy 'habit' to break. Fading out does further support Barrow's original modelling, 'scaffolding with fading'-based facilitation or teaching strategy, where an agile PBL teacher's interventions diminish as students progressively take on more responsibility for their own learning. This approach to teaching is important to note for it is easy to mistake agile PBL as another form of inquiry or discovery learning without, or at least with minimal, teacher intervention or guidance (Kischner, Sweller, & Clark, 2006). It is because of this misconception that some PBL teachers think it is a waste of their time to be in PBL learning spaces – virtual and face to face – when in their mind being a PBL teacher means not providing students with answers or not giving lectures or even information. Some PBL teachers believe they should not be there (some would attend the initial stage, i.e. the problem analysis stage, but would keep silent throughout the PBL session and be largely absent for the synthesis stage). In fairness, this is probably a minority, but it is based on a common misconception that should be carefully managed.

The role of an agile PBL activator for learning, that is, to activate the student learning process in a group setting, might appear to be simple enough, but the tasks required are really very different from those of a communicator or transmitter, even if it does require good communication. The change in the role is different to such an extent that Savin-Baden (2003, p. 27) describes the role of PBL tutors as follows: '… facilitation is not about procedures or rules, but about creating different possibilities for learning'. The fact remains that teachers find it challenging to teach in a PBL environment or program. They would find it even more challenging to teach in an agile PBL ecology for learning, particularly those new to PBL, and many would not necessarily know what creating different possibilities for learning might mean in practice in such an environment. The agility required would be quite a departure from the tightly controlled (and controllable) spaces of a more traditional, bounded, territorial, university environment, and we imagine that an agile PBL teacher would negotiate multiple boundaries inside and outside the university on a continuous basis. And this does not just involve the physical but crosses into others' territories in the domains of knowledges, skills, attitudes and dispositions because agile PBL is interdisciplinary.

In summary, an agile PBL teacher's role is indeed different from the traditional academic's role and even from a regular PBL teacher's role. For an agile PBL teacher to be creating different possibilities for learning, he/she must unlearn old ways of teaching to be able to do the following:

• Position students in the centre of the curriculum to develop a way-of-being and becoming by designing a curriculum in which one's discipline or professional declarative knowledge is interconnected with others' knowledges, skills, competencies and values for future learning.
• Reorientate their roles from a teacher who communicates or transmits discipline-based content to a PBL activator for learning, who is present in group-based learning and functioning at a metacognitive level, so as to generate dialogic knowledge, enabling collaborative knowledge building and re-/creation of knowledge, through a modelling-scaffolding-fading approach to teaching.
• Support self-directed learning as opposed to encouraging teacher dependency.

- Make curricular and pedagogical connections with other contexts and systems inside and outside the university as opposed to just connecting within disciplinary and academic contexts in the micro-system.
- Activate deep learning as opposed to surface learning.
- Embrace ubiquitous technologies, resources, information and learning as opposed to resisting them.
- Design and use assessments for learning and partnering with persons in the four systems as opposed to maintaining assessment of learning.
- Share control with students and partners outside the macro-system as opposed to students and external partners as mere receivers of university education.
- Cross boundaries to interconnect and integrate student development and engagement with relevant parts inside and outside the university ecology, as opposed to fragmented and disconnected student development and engagement within curricular boundaries.

Qualities of an Agile PBL Teacher

Content Expertise or Non-content Expertise

Within the PBL research on tutors or tutoring in general, many quantitative studies in the early years focused on the qualities or characteristics of an effective or ideal tutor, and the debate was around whether the PBL tutor needs to be a content or subject matter expert or not. Mayo and Donnelly (1995) stated that an ideal tutor is one who knows the PBL learning process within a small group setting very well and who is able to foster the metacognitive and reasoning process in students. However, there was often no mention of content expertise. Schmidt and Moust's study (1995) on the other hand, using structural equation modelling, showed that an effective tutor is one who is an expert in the domain subject matter and is armed with high social congruence, that is, a commitment to students' learning. This would enable the tutor to perform well in terms of cognitive congruence, that is, the ability to express oneself in a language understood by students. Yet, a 2011 study by Chng, Yew and Schmidt (2011) showed that the tutor's ability to communicate with the students, or social congruence, is more important than subject matter expertise. Moreover, Groves, Rego and O'Rourke (2005) reported that both subject matter knowledge and facilitation skills are equally important characteristics of effective tutors.

A comprehensive meta-analysis of 94 quantitative studies, for 223 outcomes, covering studies from 1976 to 2007, conducted by Leary, Walker, Shelton and Fitt (2013), reported that there is no relationship between tutor content expertise and the student learning process, implying that student or peer tutors perform as well as staff tutors in PBL curricula. Interestingly, they also noted that student learning decreases as tutor experience increases. Though the evidence was inconclusive, they did note that a drawback of meta-analyses was that the review excluded qualitative studies that could have provided a richer insight into the qualities of an effective tutor on student learning.

In short, what these studies imply is that the ability to facilitate well, and in our case to activate learning in an agile PBL environment, is more important than having subject matter expertise alone.

Skilled Facilitation and Group Functioning Skills

So what can be gleaned from qualitative studies in PBL research? Many of the qualitative studies focus on facilitation strategies or actions of experienced or expert PBL tutors or what good facilitation must achieve in group learning. For example, they engage with the notion that tutors must be 'present' – body and mind – in the learning process so that they know what the students are learning (Connolly & Silen, 2011; Silen, 2006); they learn the importance of reflective practice and of promoting self-directed learning in PBL tutorials (Silen & Uhlin, 2008), generating dialogic knowledge in a PBL group by ensuring all students participate in constructing and elaborating knowledge and adopting shared control principles (Barrett & Moore, 2011), while also learning what the productive and disruptive facilitation strategies are to generate productive discourse (Hmelo-Silver & Barrows, 2006, 2008; Zhang, Lundeberg, & Eberhardt, 2011); and finally the importance of active listening, using silences (Barrett & Moore, 2011; Zhang et al., 2011) and having a positive relationship with, and providing timely responses to, students (Goh, 2013).

A case study of two secondary school teachers by Pecore and Bohan (2011) confirmed Hmelo-Silver's (2004) proposition that PBL facilitation comprises four components – motivation, facilitation, collaboration and reflection. They reported that for teachers to be successful in facilitation, they must:

- Motivate students by selecting problems that engender student ownership.
- Foster a positive student-teacher relationship.
- Facilitate to ensure student activities are structured and carefully monitored through PBL stages.
- Create a collaborative culture where students are provided with the opportunities to develop and practise collaboration skills, and productive collaboration among students requires the support of the teachers.
- Provide opportunities for students to reflect on both content and process.

Conceptions of PBL and Teaching

Hendry's (2009) study used a phenomenographic methodology to study PBL tutors' conceptions of their role and how they develop as tutors in a hybrid PBL medical program. Four qualitatively different conceptions of PBL of increasing complexity were reported. Interestingly, when these different conceptions of PBL were considered in total, they corresponded more to the directive view, where a PBL tutor is viewed as a resource, instead of the supportive view, where a PBL tutor focuses on group process and functioning. In terms of how they developed as PBL tutors, all emphasised the element of improving their performance as tutors. The most sophisticated conception of developing as a tutor included using student feedback, particularly face-to-face feedback, and engaging in discussions with colleagues as ways to help improve tutor performance. The least sophisticated conception emphasised building content knowledge of students and made no mention of using student feedback to improve tutor performance.

Another qualitative study by Moore and Kain (2011) also showed that beginning tutors' (or 'student tutors' in their words) understanding and beliefs about the purpose and values of PBL influence how they manage their roles or behave in their PBL tutorial sessions. Beginning tutors with conceptions of PBL as being about learning content primarily, and who view the tutor's role as one that focuses on appropriate content, had a directive, content-focused and lenient style. That is, they were least persistent about students learning the problem-solving process, using scaffolding tools and roles and giving constructive feedback. This simple conception of PBL relates to tutor behaviours that tend to support dependence of their students on the tutor and maintenance of the status quo. On the other hand, beginning tutors with conceptions of PBL as being about individual growth and development of skills needed for the future viewed their tutor roles as helping students learn the process and guiding students initially by asking probing questions to provoke deeper thoughts and then fading away. Thus, they had more empowering, process-focused and persistent styles. That is, these tutors were firmer and more persistent about using problem-solving processes, scaffolding tools and giving constructive feedback to students.

These findings are congruent with studies and findings from the student approaches to learning (SAL) and approaches to teaching fields. Entwistle, Mccune and Walker (2001) stated, for example, that regardless of the number of categories of conceptions of teaching, these approaches can be described as consisting of one category that is teacher focused and content oriented, with an emphasis on the reproduction of correct information, and another category that is student focused and learning oriented, with an emphasis on conceptual change and development of students.

What these qualitative studies on conceptions of PBL imply is that PBL teachers' actions or behaviours are influenced by their conceptions of PBL or their approaches to teaching.

Approaches to Teaching in PBL Curricula

Conceptions of teaching are related to approaches to teaching (Trigwell & Prosser, 1996). Broadly, a teacher's approach to teaching can be described as student focused or teacher focused (Prosser & Trigwell, 1999). Trigwell, Prosser and Ginns (2005) describe teacher-focused approaches to teaching as being characterised by teachers who conceive of learning as information accumulation, and they focus on teacher-focused strategies aimed at transmitting information to students well. By contrast, student-focused teachers are those who conceive of teaching as helping students to develop and change their conceptions, and they employ more sophisticated student-focused strategies that focus on conceptual changes in students.

Recent quantitative studies from the teaching and learning fields carried out in PBL environments show that the approach to teaching that a PBL teacher employs in their PBL sessions does impact on the quality of student learning (Kek & Huijser, 2011a; Martyn et al., 2014). A quantitative study by Kek and Huijser (2011a), guided by a two-level integrated ecological framework, was designed to examine the student and teacher factors and their influences on student learning and outcomes, of a PBL medical curriculum. Data was drawn from 392 students and 32 teachers situated in 44 PBL classrooms. Using hierarchical linear modelling (HLM), the analyses revealed that at the teacher ecological level (which corresponds to a combination of the micro- and exo-systems in an agile PBL ecology for learning), PBL teachers who employed a student-focused teaching approach influenced students to adopt deep approaches to learning, and those PBL teachers who employed student-focused approaches to teaching and shared control in the classroom with the students helped students to be more self-directed in their learning. Another quantitative study by Martyn et al. (2014) using hierarchical multiple regression analysis on a single first year PBL nursing foundation course revealed that a PBL approach to teaching, characterised by facilitation skills that guided students to inquire freely by generating, evaluating and synthesising ideas and that used real-world problems, was a statistically significant factor in positively predicting the development of students' critical thinking skills.

Importance of Professional Learning

When all the above studies and findings from multiple perspectives are put together, teaching in any PBL-based environment is challenging and multifaceted. One message is clear though, which is that staff training or professional learning is critical in preparing teachers to teach in a PBL environment, particularly in an agile PBL ecology for learning where agile PBL teachers need to model an agile PBL way-of-being themselves. They must function at the metacognitive level, challenging and encouraging self-directed learning, inquiry, reflection and critical reasoning. Similarly, they must be able to function in teams themselves, collaborating with different stakeholders and actors across different systems of the agile PBL ecology for learning, as and when appropriate. Moust (2010) reminds us that the tasks of a PBL teacher are not simple and rather demanding, but because many PBL teachers, including agile PBL teachers, have difficulty attending to all the roles simultaneously, professional or faculty development is important to help academic staff optimise their PBL teacher roles. This echoes Barrows' (2002) passionate reminder to us as to why he considered training and continuous professional learning of a PBL teacher to be vital. In his view, the success or failure of a PBL initiative and its goals, including agile PBL, is instrumentally dependent on having skilled PBL teachers activating student learning and development. Crossing boundaries and linking the four different systems in an agile PBL ecology for learning only add more complexity to this equation. However, we reiterate Barnett's passionate plea to imagine 'feasible utopias' (2013) here, which is precisely what we are giving voice to here.

Professional Learning in PBL

Professional learning for a PBL program usually consists of planned activities to increase the professional competence of the PBL teachers and staff involved in the planning, designing, teaching and assessing PBL. The professional learning ranges from a focus on individual teachers to groups of teachers, with more and more professional learning programs integrating professional learning activities into their workplace and throughout their staff's teaching careers, instead of planning for isolated or separate activities at specific times in the calendar that are usually only attended by those teachers who are already committed anyway. This is because professional learning can be rather divorced and separated from the realities of the roles and journeys of PBL teachers, and this is even more pronounced in an agile PBL ecology for learning where the interconnections between educating and beyond should be much clearer and the boundaries much more blurred.

We argue that professional learning for agile PBL curricula should be designed with the agile PBL philosophy and principles in mind, and it should be delivered with the same learning process that students go through, especially in terms of how to teach PBL sessions. In other words, it should model the learning and teaching practices that are expected in an agile PBL ecology for learning. The typical, isolated, one-off and generic workshops should either go or be limited to the extent to which it is a part of the students' learning experience.

We strongly argue that to prepare agile PBL teachers to be skilled activators for learning, these teachers *must* experience the PBL learning process as *students* themselves first, before experiencing it as PBL activators for learning. Through this approach, the teachers get to experience what and how their students learn – think, feel and do. If this makes them uncomfortable, because it takes them out of their comfort zone, then that is exactly the point. It should mirror the PBL cycle and should be conducted on a regular basis. Time for reflection and discussion must be offered to these PBL teachers before they get to experience facilitation. Similarly, these sessions should be agile in the sense that they should never follow the exact same pattern, as agile PBL teachers, like agile PBL students, should become comfortable with discomfort and in particular with the affective effect of such discomfort. In this way, agile PBL teachers will be able to understand, both on an affective and cognitive level, why the learning process is designed and sequenced the way it is and why the approach to teaching follows a model-scaffold-fade pattern, and thus they will in general be able to understand the underlying theories and principles of agile PBL. Ultimately, they would have undergone a certain kind of formation or transformation – philosophically, epistemologically and emotionally – to become the kind of agile PBL teachers who activate learning as a way-of-being and becoming in students (Dawson et al., 2010; Shulman, 2005).

The crux of an agile PBL ecology for learning is preparing student for *future* learning, where the future is increasingly complex and learning is ubiquitous and where the boundaries between education and beyond are increasingly blurred. Agile PBL teachers must also have knowledges, skills, competencies, values and attributes that are expected of their students! Therefore, professional learning in an agile PBL context must include learning, mentoring, coaching, reflecting and discussing and collaborating with peers, colleagues and partners outside the university. Professional learning also includes learning on site, taking time out from teaching, to immerse themselves in the industry-based workplaces beyond the university walls. Agile PBL teachers would learn how to facilitate authentic PBL projects in the workplace and how to negotiate different elements of the curriculum with employers and mentors, for example, assessment and working in interdisciplinary teams. In this way, agile PBL teachers would be in a better position to enable, engage and empower students for future learning.

In short, the professional learning program of an agile PBL ecology for learning should be modelled on an agile PBL philosophy and its associated values or as the adage goes: 'teach what you preach!'

Knowledge Base of an Agile PBL Teacher

An agile PBL teacher is still a teacher, whether the learning environment and curriculum is traditional or agile PBL, albeit with the understanding and knowledge of the underlying differences in philosophy. Hence, to consider the domains of knowledge that an effective student-focused teacher, which an agile PBL teacher is, must attain, we first consider Shulman's (1986, 1987) seminal worldview about teacher education for a new paradigm of education, which focuses on student learning. In many teacher education programs, the emphasis has long focused on one or the other domain of knowledge, that is, either on knowledge of content or knowledge of pedagogy. It was Shulman (1986) who reconceptualised teacher education by advancing another type of domain knowledge known as pedagogical content, which is an amalgam of content and pedagogy knowledge. Shulman (1986, p. 8) described it as 'the blending of content and pedagogy into an understanding of how particular topics, problems, or issues are organised, represented, and adapted to the diverse interests and abilities of learners, and presented for instruction'.

According to Shulman (1987, p. 8), at the minimum, teacher training or preparation programs would include:

- Content knowledge – subject matter content per se.
- General pedagogical knowledge – broad principles and strategies of classroom management and organisation.
- Curriculum knowledge – (1) have a good grasp of the curriculum materials of the course that he/she is teaching, but also (2) be familiar with the curriculum materials under study by his/her students in other courses they are studying at the same time, referred to as lateral curriculum knowledge, and (3) be familiar with the curriculum materials that have been and will be taught in the same subject area during the preceding and subsequent years of the program or what Shulman calls vertical curriculum knowledge (Shulman, 1986, p. 10).
- Pedagogical content knowledge – this is knowledge that goes beyond subject matter knowledge per se. It is the integration of content or subject matter expertise and pedagogy for teaching, providing teachers with the ability to transform what they understood or know of the subject matter and elicit understanding among students or search for that understanding themselves.
- Knowledge of learners and their characteristics.
- Knowledge of the educational contexts.
- Knowledge of the educational outcomes, purposes, goals and values and their philosophical and historical grounds.

Similar to Shulman's (1986, 1987) categories of a knowledge base for general teacher training, Moust (2010) has adapted these categories with two other types of knowledge for a PBL-type environment and curriculum. These are the types of knowledge that a PBL teacher would need to be able to carry out his/her responsibilities and tasks effectively and efficiently.

Moust's (2010, p. 47–50) knowledge base for a PBL teacher includes:

- Content knowledge – subject matter knowledge per se.
- General pedagogical knowledge – the purpose of this knowledge is to help PBL teachers understand the main teaching and learning processes promoted in a PBL environment. The general pedagogical knowledge includes knowledge about educational subjects with relevance to higher education, basic knowledge and skills with respect to the principles and theories of learning and teaching of adults and knowledge about curriculum and problem design, assessment and PBL educational concepts such as constructive, contextual, collaborative learning, the learning process underpinning PBL, questioning and elaboration.
- Pedagogical content knowledge – the purpose of this knowledge is that the content knowledge can be organised and represented in such a manner that students can understand. This unique knowledge is developed through repetitive teaching experiences and becomes the PBL teachers' mental and personal toolbox of strat-

egies and procedures that he/she can use to advance the content and ideas seamlessly at various stages of the learning process so as to achieve the PBL goals.

- Group dynamics – the purpose of this knowledge is that a collaborative learning climate where students can work together in an open, safe and trusting manner can be fostered. The knowledge about group dynamics includes knowing how to get a group started, how groups develop over time, what groups should do to function effectively, how to handle conflicts between group members and how to provide constructive feedback on group behaviours.
- Process instruction – the purpose of this knowledge is to ensure self-directed learning skills are being developed and fostered by PBL teachers. Even though process instruction is part of general pedagogical knowledge, it is given attention as a separate knowledge base that a PBL teacher must have because self-directed learning skills are too important a goal and aspect of PBL to leave to chance or incidental teaching. PBL teachers must acquire specific skills in this area of pedagogical knowledge.

In addition to Moust's (2010) five knowledge bases for a professional learning program, we suggest extending an element of what we know about conceptions of teaching into the pedagogical content. PBL, as well as agile PBL, as we already know is a different philosophy and approach from the more traditional ways of thinking about learning and teaching. Therefore, for any change in a teacher's behaviours to occur, i.e. actions in a formal teaching and learning space, agile PBL teachers need to explore their own views about the nature of teaching and learning and knowledge in general. A teacher's approach to teaching is influenced by the holder's conceptions of what agile PBL is and how one is meant to teach in an agile PBL ecology for learning. This is so much so that Trigwell and Prosser (Prosser & Trigwell, 1999; Trigwell & Prosser, 1996) deem a change in teaching conceptions to be a *prerequisite* in preparing teachers to teach. Helping teachers to explore their conceptions of themselves as agile PBL teachers should therefore be part of preparing or training teachers in the knowledge, skills and various techniques or strategies that are part of an agile PBL ecology for learning, which can then be meaningful and productive to students and student learning.

Importance of Integrating Technology into the Knowledge Base

We propose that in addition to the content and pedagogical knowledge bases espoused by Shulman (1987) and Moust (2010), who adapted it for PBL, agile PBL teachers should also be competent in technology knowledge, as well as adaptive users (read: lifelong learners) of technology. With the emergence and rapidly increasing use of information and communication technologies in society, it is a given that a university, and especially an agile PBL curriculum, must embrace and embed rich, interconnected information and communication technologies into agile PBL contexts of learning, teaching and assessing. Examples of applications are the use of virtual patients, digital objects, virtual reality and gaming to support learning of knowledge and skills; virtual learning environments and the use of web 2.0 tools such as web conferences, wikis and podcasts to support communication and collaborative group work; and e-portfolios, computerised testing and workplace testing to support assessment (Donkers, Verstegen, De Leng, & De Jong, 2010). With the powers of the web advancing to web 3.0, adaptive and personalised learning is the next revolution in education, as well as in the other systems of the agile PBL ecology for learning.

However, it is a development that raises numerous implementation issues that we believe are still being discovered, implemented and adapted. Jonassen (2007) has proposed, as research questions, some of the tricky implementation issues that PBL researchers should and are investigating, such as (1) how faithfully can PBL methodologies be applied online, (2) how can groups collaborate effectively to negotiate meaning and build knowledge, (3) how can PBL teachers effectively activate and guide learning online and (4) how can self-directed learning be supported online. To these questions we would like to add: (5) how can self-directed learning be supported in a web 3.0 context without reverting back to the traditional mode of online distance learning, whereby online instructors upload course materials and readings online and students do self-study or study these materials independently, and (6) what compromises, if any, are required to engage students in an online PBL environment?

In addition to the implementation issues noted by Jonassen (2007), we are also cognisant that students and teachers alike are not necessarily technologically competent in the learning and teaching context. They might be frequent users of social media and technologies in their personal or private lives, but that does not necessarily translate to learning and teaching (Kennedy, Judd, Churchward, Gray, & Krause, 2008). Both students and teachers need to be trained or prepared in information and communication technology knowledge and use to maximise affordance of technology use in their learning and teaching environments. However, in an agile PBL context, new technologies and the need to adapt them for appropriate use in learning, teaching and assessing, professional work functions, as well as in the world outside the university, are an integral part of the process and should therefore be incorporated by osmosis into the design of PBL problems, teaching, assessing and general professional work. For agile PBL teachers, as for their students, this may be rather daunting because in addition to the content and pedagogy knowledge bases they need to arm themselves with, they also need to be technologically competent and skilled, which requires continuous upgrading (read: lifelong learning). However, this is the reality of life in the twenty-first century and therefore also in an agile PBL ecology for learning.

Technological Pedagogical Content Knowledge (TPACK)
Framework

An effective professional learning model for integrating technology in teaching that we consider useful and philosophically aligned with agile PBL is the technological pedagogical content knowledge or TPACK framework (Mishra & Koehler, 2006). In addition to content and pedagogical knowledge, TPACK also explicitly considers the role that knowledge about, as well as in the use of technology, plays in effective teaching.

There are three major knowledge components that form the foundation of TPACK, resulting in four intersected knowledge relationships (Mishra & Koehler, 2006). The three major knowledge components are (1) content (C), (2) pedagogy (P) and (3) technology (T). The subsequent intersected relationships are (1) pedagogical content knowledge (PCK), which is the intersection between C and P; (2) technological content knowledge (TCK), which is the intersection between technology and content; (3) technological pedagogical content knowledge (TPK), which is the intersection between technology and pedagogy; and lastly (4) the overlap of these three intersections forming the technological pedagogical content knowledge or TPACK in short.

It is the introduction of the interconnectedness or the integration of technology into content and pedagogy knowledge, forming an emergent knowledge that goes beyond just content, pedagogy and technology individually, that is the appealing part for faculty development, particularly when it comes to teaching in an integrated teaching and learning environment such as an agile PBL ecology for learning. TPACK does not exist in a vacuum but rather is grounded and situated in specific contexts surrounding the content, pedagogy and technology knowledge, and it is the dynamic transactional relationship between these three knowledge components that distinguishes it from many other similar frameworks developed to understand and explain teachers' use of technology such as ICT-related PCK, knowledge of educational technology, technological content knowledge, electronic pedagogical content knowledge (ePCK) and technological pedagogical content knowledge-web (TPCK-W) (Koehler, Mishra, Kristen, Shin, & Graham, 2014).

The implication of the TPACK model for professional learning program design is that agile PBL teachers must engage fully in all three knowledge bases in an integrated manner. This is very similar to an agile PBL approach where knowledge, skills, competencies and emotions are tightly interwoven and enmeshed and not easily separated. If the professional learning activities only emphasise the development of knowledge and skills, pedagogy and technology separately or in isolation (such as in a more traditional paradigm of learning and teaching), such teacher education and professional development programs are 'doomed to fail' (Koehler et al., 2014, p. 109).

Challenges in Preparing PBL Teachers

The tasks of an agile PBL teacher might be daunting to a teacher, novice and expert, but the task of preparing teachers in the university, performed by professional or academic developers, is even more intimidating and challenging. Even though the common threshold concept held by professional or academic developers is about facilitating a systemic change process in individuals and in groups (Timmermans, 2014), it is found that many of them are involved in research and scholarship of learning and teaching, as well as facilitate change process (Kek & Hammer, 2015). On the one hand, they enact their role in a range of different ways while occupying a unique organisational position between academic staff and senior administrators and managers in higher education (Bovill & Martensson, 2014). On the other hand, many academic developers work in murky, liminal spaces as unwanted migrants from other disciplines than the teachers they work with (Land, 2004; Manathunga, 2006). However, this does of course give them the ideal preparation as 'natural boundary crossers' in an agile PBL ecology for learning.

Another tension is that PBL teachers are commonly recruited for their subject matter expertise and research and are already experts in their own disciplines and fields. Changing what they might have been familiar and comfortable with in terms of how they have always taught, and how they have always thought about teaching and learning and curriculum design, and convincing them of the need for a trans-formed role as an agile PBL teacher may be a huge and difficult shift for them. There are those who will be enthusiastic and keen to try and later persevere and sustain the new (agile PBL) practices, and there are also those who will work hard in the beginning but towards the end become disillusioned and revert back to their former practices. We liken these agile PBL teacher behaviours to Harden's (2007) PBL teacher behaviour patterns. They include the *ostriches*, teachers who think agile PBL is a passing fad and there is no benefit in preparing or training for it; the *peacocks*, teachers who seem to talk the talk but in reality do not walk the walk when they are in their own walled gardens of their own agile PBL classrooms (in other words, there is very little agility about it); and the *beavers*, teachers who are eager to work hard to implement agile PBL, but they can become disillusioned, giv-ing up 'the walk' to become peacocks.

In explaining these different behaviours, Savin-Baden and Major (2004) used Moore's (1999, cited in Savin-Baden & Major, 2004) work related to the develop-ment and implementation of technological innovation in companies. They used this to illuminate how different PBL teacher behaviours can be managed when imple-menting a faculty development program or activities in PBL programs. Moore (1999, cited in Savin-Baden & Major, 2004) argued that there are chasms between two distinct marketplaces. The first chasm is in the early market that tends to be dominated by those keen to experiment (early adopters), along with insiders who see the benefits of the new development. The second chasm refers to people who ultimately want the benefits of the new innovation but are slower to take up the innovation and are cynical about its possibilities (laggards). What Moore argued is that there are gaps or chasms between distinct groups of people in the marketplace – innovators, early adopters, early majority, later majority and laggards – following Rogers (2003) adoption and diffusion of innovation model. That is, there is a disjoint between innovators and early adopters, a disjoint between early adopters and early majority and so on. The chasms have created difficulty for any group to accept the innovation if it is presented to them in the same way as the group preceding it. Therefore, Savin-Baden & Major, 2004 argued that to implement an effective faculty development, these chasms in the adoption and diffusion of innovation must be recognised and closed before most PBL teachers can accept and work with PBL. Of course in an agile PBL ecology for learning, there is an additional layer of complexity, which relates to the inherent boundary crossing in the ecology. This means that the adoption and diffusion do apply not only within an individual university (i.e. contained within micro- and meso-systems) but also across different universities (incorporating macro-systems). Again, this requires us to imagine 'feasible utopias' (Barnett, 2013).

Strategies for Crossing Chasms in Professional Development

Savin-Baden and Major (2004, p. 112–113) proposed eight strategies for crossing and managing the chasm:

- Use different types of faculty development approaches for each group.
- Demonstrate to early adopters how PBL has worked effectively in other disciplines and universities.
- Once the early majority have become familiar with PBL, find ways of making it easier for the late majority to adopt. For example, provide opportunities for them to watch it in action and/or provide a buddy system for new PBL teachers; in an agile PBL ecology for learning, this means it becomes crucial to document and communicate early success stories from the beginning, so they can serve as exemplars of good practice in action.
- Accept that the late majority will take time to adjust and that many will need both considerable time and research evidence. Give them time to learn and reflect.
- Do not take criticisms personally; see all criticism as part of the process of progress.
- Do not force the laggards to become involved, but instead negotiate with them as to what they are prepared to do without feeling compromised.
- Be realistic about what is possible within your department or institution and ensure you have allowed enough time for preparation. Many people try to implement PBL too quickly and so face resistance from the early majority, which is the quickest ways to fail at the onset; again, in an agile PBL ecology for learning, this includes being very careful in the selection of 'external' participants and negotiating what is 'feasible' or what may be considered to be too 'utopian'.

- Accept that laggards take time to get involved, but ultimately if they do not do so, they pose a threat to the long-term sustainability of the PBL program.

Practices in Creating Learning Possibilities

We offer here a selection of recent thinking on teaching in PBL-based curricula and teaching with technologies, drawn from a variety of literature (Barrett & Moore, 2011; Chuprina & Zaher, 2011; Connolly & Silen, 2011; Davis, 2008; Goh, 2013; Hmelo-Silver & Barrows, 2006, 2008; Juwah et al., 2004; Mishra & Koehler, 2009; Silen & Uhlin, 2008; Zhang et al., 2011) and our own practices:

- Position students in the centre of an agile PBL curriculum, ensuring every student participates and contributes to the construction, elaboration, refinement and transformation of knowledge.
- Create a safe and nonthreatening learning environment where there is a sense of shared ownership and control in the group.
- Be present – body and mind. Monitor group dynamics so as to balance interventions or direction with support or scaffolding for students because when students receive too much or no support, it adversely affects learning, which is why Barrow's scaffolding with fade strategy – model-scaffold-fade – is so important. An agile PBL teacher's interventions should diminish as students progressively take on responsibility for their learning.
- Encourage construction, elaboration, refinement and transformation of knowledge, rather than just encouraging the sharing of knowledge. Make the knowledge matter, in that it should be applicable in an authentic context, so that the stakes are as high as possible, while at the same time appropriately scaffolded. Apply a combination of facilitation strategies:

  - Revoicing – restating what students say by repeating, paraphrasing, clarifying or reconceptualising their ideas. This is one of two major facilitation strategies to promote productive collaborative knowledge building, discourse and participation. For example, 'So, are you all saying that xxx is to be considered?' 'What I am hearing this group saying is that …'. *However*:

    Revoicing that is too quick, frequent and affirmative is not productive as it tends to cut off discussion, leaving no room for reinterpretation and meaning negotiation and loose opportunities for deep exploration of ideas; only when used selectively and in a negotiatory manner are students able to reinterpret and elaborate their ideas.

  - Questioning – asking questions is the other major facilitation strategy to promote productive collaborative knowledge building, discourse and participation, *but*:

Ask questions at the metacognitive level rather than providing explanations. In other words, agile PBL teachers must be diagnostic in their minds on what and why students do and say what they say. Ask students why. For example, 'Why do you think xxx occurs?'

Ask questions to stimulate critical appraisal of ideas or hypotheses generated by students; don't just accept them as they are. For example, 'What is the relationship of the idea xxx to the problem?' 'What are your thoughts on the ideas proposed?' Of course 'external' facilitators and clients play an important role in this too, and various levels of negotiation may need to be involved in this process.

Ask questions to stimulate critical appraisal of the various information resources that students are going to use and have used during their self-directed learning session, that is, before and after the self-directed learning stage. Before the self-directed learning stage, e.g. 'Why use this information resource?' 'How will this information help you to manage the problem?' After self-directed learning, e.g. 'What was the publication date of that book?' 'How do you know that the information is reliable?' 'How does the information support or not support the ideas?'

Asking open-ended questions is not effective in producing productive discourse if they are not built on students' ideas or when the discussion topics are changed frequently. Only when teachers selectively focus on the important questions or topics arising from the students' discussion and persist by pushing students for ideas will the discussion be productive.

- Model the kinds of questions that students need to be asking themselves.
- Make student thinking (reasoning, problem-solving) visible to all students; for example, use the FILA schema – facts, ideas/hypothesis, learning Issues and action – for all students to 'visualise' reasoning or thinking or problem-solving of the problem.
- Apply active listening or attentive silence so as to be present with the group and offer opportunities or room for students to reinterpret, elaborate and make meaning or provide information when needed.

• Provide feedback and feedforward to students. It is not good enough to say 'That is good', 'Well done' or 'This is not good enough!'. Again, external partners outside the university are also important in this process, as they lend a crucial level of authenticity to it.

• Provide opportunities for students to reflect on their acquisition and integration of knowledge, group functioning, reasoning and self-directed learning skills, through peer assessment and self-assessment.

• Conduct reflections of one's facilitation skills as an agile PBL teacher, either through a self-assessment activity with the students within a PBL group or outside the PBL student group process, e.g. through personal professional practitioner reflections through a personal teaching journal or e-portfolio. Include the process of collaborating with multiple stakeholders across institutional boundaries in this activity.

- Continuing support through engagement with peers. Establish community of practice or learning communities and mentor programs where novice and experienced agile PBL teachers can exchange teaching perspectives and ideas, to build their own knowledge base and/or use it to adapt them to their own situations. However, such peer communities must be guided by skilled facilitators (Mcdonald, 2014). This principle also echoes the importance of developing skilled agile PBL teachers in activating student learning and building knowledge! Only continuing support through peer engagement that is supported by skilled facilitators would make such learning communities serve as instrumental and generative vehicles to diffuse technologies and pedagogical content knowledge and in the process transform teaching conceptions. In addition, it would stimulate conceptual, technological and pedagogical transformation of knowledge and learning (renewal), among and within teachers, courses, programs, departments and organisations as a whole, ultimately impacting student learning, development and success. The latter would ultimately be witnessed in the form of assessment of students engaging with innovative authentic assessments, creative use of technologies and/or creative adaptations or repurposing of technologies for teaching and learning, problems and student groups, exchanges with industry partners or employers and also sharing of self-directed learning plans for professional growth.
- Engagement and conversations/dialogues with peers also include students, employers and other constituents of the institution and beyond.
- Embrace peer teaching review or evaluations of each other, including reflections on conceptions of agile PBL and the teaching and learning process so that agile PBL teachers can visualise their professional growth and identity development as agile PBL teachers, e.g. through a personal teaching journal or e-portfolio, and improve their teaching skills.
- Interconnect and collaborate with colleagues from across institutions, e.g. orientation committees, student advising units, learning centres and career development, to integrate student development and engagement with students' academic learning environment and to support *every* student transition, from entry to graduation and beyond. In an agile PBL ecology for learning, this means of course that the boundaries between such transitions are increasingly blurred and therefore ideally much smoother than in a more traditional higher education environment. For student success is everybody's business, not just that of the academic teachers.

Conclusion

Teaching is multifaceted and to enable teachers to become better or competent teachers is a courageous act. Provision of professional learning towards the development of any PBL program, not just agile PBL, is challenging and requires hard work but is achievable as student success is everyone's business. It is not just the teachers themselves who are responsible for educating students, but every constituent in the institution is equally responsible in creating and sustaining a mattering learning environment, leading to student success for student, teachers and administrators of the institution and ultimately benefiting the workplace, communities and society at large. In an agile PBL ecology for learning, this responsibility crosses boundaries within the university and also beyond the university.

Teacher development in an agile PBL context is best conducted with a long-term, integrated and continuous development and support approach. Single, one-off and generic topical workshops are largely ineffective (Hendry, 2009; Lyberg-Ahlander, Lundskog, & Hansson, 2014; Savin-Baden & Major, 2004; Zhang et al., 2011). PBL teachers require and have commented that continuous (and agile!) support throughout development time is needed (Lyberg-Ahlander et al., 2014) because they have to experience and *be* what agile PBL teachers should be (Dawson et al., 2010; Shulman, 2005). Having teachers in a professional learning program and having activities where social interactions and dialogue with peers and relevant stakeholders such as academic developers, employers and students would make agile PBL teachers traverse from being legitimate peripheral participants to becoming fully engaged participants (Lave & Wenger, 1991) in an agile PBL ecology for learning. This aids to generate the conversations and knowledges needed for agile PBL teachers to learn teaching practices, which have a long tradition of being conducted behind 'closed doors' – alone and in silos. Agile PBL teachers would only attend professional development activities if they are directly relevant to them and attend to their desire for self-improvement and connecting with colleagues and peers (Steinert et al., 2010). This may relate to narrowly defined professional learning as it relates to teaching practice, but it may also relate to professional learning as it relates to industry currency and upgrades, which in turn benefits collaboration beyond the university boundaries of the agile PBL ecology for learning.

Most of all, we argue that the staff responsible for designing and implementing a PBL professional learning program must talk the talk and walk the walk, that is, they must teach what they preach! However, this is a challenging proposition because many of them are perceived as migrants to agile PBL contexts (Manathunga, 2006). An integrated approach in the design and implementation of an agile PBL professional learning program based on an agile PBL philosophy and principles should be used. Bear in mind that in 'teaching' agile PBL teachers, covering a number of knowledge bases in isolation would not work, which is similar to agile PBL teaching, learning and assessing – it is simultaneously engaging students in knowledge, skills, values and attributes for future learning. Once again, we imagine a 'feasible utopia' for professional learning, but one that we believe is ultimately worth pursuing if we are serious about learning that suits a twenty-first-century context.

References

Barnett, R. (2013). *Imagining the university*. Oxon, UK: Routledge.

Barrett, T., & Moore, S. (2011). Students maximising the potential of the problem-based learning tutorial. In T. Barrett & S. Moore (Eds.), *New approaches to problem-based learning: Revitalising your practice in higher education* (pp. 115–129). Milton Park, UK: Routledge.

Barrows, H. S. (2002). An overview of authentic problem-based learning. In K. N. L. Wee & Y. C. M. A. Kek (Eds.), *Authentic problem-based learning: Rewriting business education* (pp. 1–9). Singapore, Singapore: Prentice Hall.

Bovill, C., & Martensson, K. (2014). The challenge of sustaining academic development work. *International Journal for Academic Development, 19*(4), 263–267. doi:10.1080/13601 44X.2014.969981.

Chng, E., Yew, E. H. J., & Schmidt, H. G. (2011). Effects of tutor-related behaviours on the process of problem-based learning. *Advances in Health Sciences Education, 16*(4), 491–503.

Chuprina, L., & Zaher, L. (2011). Successful learning and teaching approaches: Self-reflection as a bridge to self-directed and lifelong learning. In K. D. Kirstein, J. M. Hinrichs, & S. G. Olswang (Eds.), *Authentic instruction and online delivery: Proven practices in higher education* (pp. 53–68). Lexington, KY: CreateSpace.

Connolly, D., & Silen, C. (2011). Empowering tutors. In T. Barrett & S. Moore (Eds.), *New approaches to problem-based learning: Revitalising your practice in higher education*. Milton Park, UK: Routledge.

Davis, N. (2008). How may teacher learning be promoted for educational renewal with IT? In J. Voogt & G. Knezek (Eds.), *International handbook of information technology in primary and secondary education* (pp. 507–519). New York: Springer Science+Busines Media, LLC. Vol. 20, Part One.

Dawson, D., Britnell, J., & Hitchcock, A. (2010). Developing competency models of faculty developers: Using world cafe to foster dialogue. In L. B. Nilson & J. E. Miller (Eds.), *To improve the academy: Resources for faculty, instructional, and organizational development* (Vol. 28, pp. 3–24). San Francisco: Jossey-Bass.

Donkers, J., Verstegen, D., De Leng, B., & De Jong, N. (2010). E-learning in problem-based learning. In H. van Berkel, A. Scherpbier, H. Hillen, & C. Van der Vleuten (Eds.), *Lessons from problem-based learning* (pp. 117–128). Oxford, UK: Oxford University Press.

Entwistle, N., Mccune, V., & Walker, P. (2001). Conceptions, styles and approaches within higher education: Analytic abstractions and everyday experience. In R. J. Sternberg & L. F. Zhang (Eds.), *Perspective on thinking, learning, and cognitive styles* (pp. 103–130). Mahwah, NJ: Lawrence Erlbaum Associates Inc.

Goh, K. (2013, September 9–11). *What good teachers do to promote effective student learning in a problem-based learning environment*. Paper presented at the joint 7th Biennial international conference & ERAS conference, Nanyang Girls' High School, Singapore.

Groves, M., Rego, P., & O'rourke, P. (2005). Tutoring in problem-based learning medical curricula: The influence of tutor background and style on effectiveness. *BMC Medical Education, 5*(20). doi:10.1186/1472-6920-5-20.

Harden, R. M. (2007). Outcome-based education – The ostrich, the peacock and the beaver. *Medical Teacher, 29*(7), 666–671.

Hendry, G. D. (2009). Problem-based learning tutors' conceptions of their development as tutors. *Medical Teacher, 31*(2), 145–150. doi:10.1080/01421590802146026.

Hmelo-Silver, C. E. (2004). Problem-based learning: What and how do students learn? *Educational Psychology Review, 16*, 235–266.

Hmelo-Silver, C. E., & Barrows, H. S. (2006). Goals and strategies of a problem-based learning facilitator. *The Interdisciplinary Journal of Problem-Based Learning, 1*(1), 21–39.

Hmelo-Silver, C. E., & Barrows, H. S. (2008). Facilitating collaborative knowledge building. *Cognition and Instruction, 26*, 48–94.

Jonassen, D. (2007). Issues in implementing problem-based learning online. In O.-S. Tan (Ed.), *Problem-based learning in elearning breakthroughs* (pp. 207–226). Singapore, Singapore: Thomson Learning.

Jonassen, D. (2012). Preface. In D. Jonassen & S. Land (Eds.), *Theoretical foundations of learning environments* (Vol. 2, pp. vii–x). New York: Routledge.

Juwah, C., Macfarlan-Dick, D., Matthew, B., Nicol, D., Ross, D., & Smith, B. (2004). *Enhancing student learning through effective formative feedback.* York: York Science Park/The Higher Education Academy (Generic Centre).

Kek, M. Y. C. A., & Hammer, S. (2015). Theorising academic development as an academic discipline? Exploring academic developers' ways of knowing, theorising and use of methods. In J. Huisman & M. Tight (Eds.), *Theory and method in higher education research* (Vol. 1, pp. 235–255). Bingley, UK: Emerald Group Publishing.

Kek, M., & Huijser, H. (2011a). Exploring the combined relationships of student and teacher factors on learning approaches and self-directed learning readiness at a Malaysian university. *Studies in Higher Education, 36*(2), 185–208. doi:10.1080/03075070903519210.

Kek, M. Y. C. A., & Huijser, H. (2011b). The power of problem-based learning in developing critical thinking skills: Preparing students for tomorrow's digital futures in today's classrooms. *Higher Education Research and Development, 30*(3), 317–329.

Kennedy, G. E., Judd, T. S., Churchward, A., Gray, K., & Krause, K. (2008). First year students' experiences with technology: Are they really digital natives? *Australasian Journal of Educational Technology, 24*(1), 108–122.

Kischner, P. A., Sweller, J., & Clark, R. E. (2006). Why minimal guidance during instruction does not work: An analysis of the failure of constructivist, discovery, problem-based, experiential, and inquiry-based teaching. *Educational Psychologist, 41*(2), 75–86.

Koehler, M. J., Mishra, P., Kristen, K., Shin, T. S., & Graham, C. R. (2014). The technological pedagogical content knowledge framework. In J. M. Spector, M. D. Merrill, J. Elen, & M. J. Bishop (Eds.), *Handbook of research on educational communications and technology* (4th ed., pp. 101–111). New York: Springer. doi:10.1007/978-1-4614-3185-5_9.

Land, R. (2004). *Educational development: Discourse, identity and practice.* Maidenhead, UK: Open University/Society for Research into Higher Education.

Lave, J., & Wenger, E. (1991). *Situated learning: Legitimate peripheral participation.* Cambridge, UK: Cambridge University Press.

Leary, H., Walker, A., Shelton, B., & Fitt, M. H. (2013). Exploring the relationships between tutor background, tutor training, and student learning: A problem-based learning meta-analysis. *Interdisciplinary Journal of Problem-Based Learning, 7*(1), 44–66. doi:10.771/1541.5015.1331.

Lyberg-Ahlander, V., Lundskog, M., & Hansson, K. (2014). Experiencing the role of PBL tutor. *Clinical Linguistics and Phonetics, 28*(1–2), 36–46. doi:10.3109/02699206.2013.816371.

Manathunga, C. (2006). Doing educational development ambivalently: Applying post-colonial metaphors to educational development? *International Journal for Academic Development, 11*(1), 19–29.

Martyn, J., Terwijn, R., Kek, M. Y. C. A., & Huijser, H. (2014). Exploring the relationships between teaching, approaches to learning and critical thinking in a problem-based learning foundation nursing course. *Nurse Education Today, 34*(5), 829–835. doi:10.1016/j.nedt.2013.04.023.

Mayo, W. P., & Donnelly, M. B. (1995). The characteristics of the ideal problem-based learning tutor in clinical medical. *Evaluation and The Health Professions, 18*(2), 124–136.

Mcdonald, J. (2014). *Community, domain, practice: Facilitator catch cry for revitalising learning and teaching through communities of practice (ALTC Teaching Fellowship Final Report).* Sydney: Office of Learning and Teaching, Department of Education, Australia. Retrieved from http://www.olt.gov.au/resource-community-domain-practice.

Mishra, P., & Koehler, M. (2009). Too cool for schools? No way! Using TPACK framework: You can have your hot tools and teach with them, too. *Learning &Leading with Technology, 36*(7), 14–18.

Mishra, P., & Koehler, M. J. (2006). Technological pedagogical content knowledge: A framework for teacher knowledge. *Teachers College Record, 108*(6), 1017–1054.

Moore, T., & Kain, D. L. (2011). Student tutors for problem-based learning in dental hygiene: A study of tutor actions. *Journal of Dental Education, 75*(6), 805–816.

Moust, J. (2010). The role of the tutor. In H. van Berkel, A. Scherpbier, H. Hillen, & C. Van der Vleuten (Eds.), *Lessons from problem-based learning* (pp. 47–56). Oxford: Oxford University Press.

Pecore, J. L., & Bohan, C. H. (2011). Problem-based learning: Teachers who flourish and flounder. *Curriculum and Teaching Dialogue, 14*(1–2), 125–138.

Prosser, M., & Trigwell, K. (1999). *Understanding learning and teaching: The experience in higher education.* Buckingham, UK: Open University Press.

Rogers, E. M. (2003). *Diffusion of innovation* (5th ed.). New York: Free Press.

Savery, J. R. (2006). Overview of problem-based learning: Definitions and distinctions. *Interdisciplinary Journal of Problem-Based Learning, 1*(1), 9–20.

Savin-Baden, M. (2003). *Facilitating problem-based learning: Illuminating perspectives.* Maidenhead, UK: Society for Research into Higher Education & Open University Press.

Savin-Baden, M., & Major, C. H. (2004). *Foundations of problem-based learning.* Maidenhead, UK: Society for Research into Higher Education & Open University Press.

Scardamalia, M. (2002). Collective cognitive responsibility for the advancement of knowledge. In C. Bereiter & B. Smith (Eds.), *Liberal education in a knowledge society* (pp. 67–98). Chicago: Open Court.

Schmidt, H. G., & Moust, J. H. C. (1995). What makes a tutor effective? A structural-equations modeling approach to learning in problem-based curricula. *Academic Medicine, 70*(8), 708–714.

Shulman, L. S. (1986). Those who understand: Knowledge growth in teaching. *Educational Researcher, 15*(4), 4–14.

Shulman, L. S. (1987). Knowledge and teaching: Foundations of the new reform. *Harvard Educational Review, 57*(1), 1–22.

Shulman, L. (2005, February 6–8). *The signature pedagogies of the professions of law, medicine, engineering, and the clergy: Potential lessons for the education of teachers.* Paper presented at the Math Science Partnerships (MSP) Workshop: Teacher education for effective teaching and learning, The National Research Council's Center for Higher Education, Irvine, California, USA.

Silen, C. (2006). The tutor's approach in base group (PBL). *Higher Education, 51*(3), 373–385.

Silen, C., & Uhlin, L. (2008). Self-directed learning – A learning issues for students and faculty! *Teaching in Higher Education, 13*(4), 461–475.

Steinert, Y., Macdonald, M. E., Boillat, M., Elizov, M., Meterissian, S., Razack, S., et al. (2010). Faculty development: If you build it, they will come. *Medical Education, 44*(9), 900–907.

Timmermans, J. A. (2014). Identifying threshold concepts in the careers of educational developers. *International Journal for Academic Development, 19*(4), 305–317. doi:10.1080/13601 44X.2014.895731.

Trigwell, K., & Prosser, M. (1996). Congruence between intention and strategy in university science teachers' approaches to teaching. *Higher Education, 32*, 77–87.

Trigwell, K., Prosser, M., & Ginns, P. (2005). Phenomenographic pedagogy and a revised approaches to teaching inventory. *Higher Education Research and Development, 24*(4), 349–360.

Zhang, M., Lundeberg, M., & Eberhardt, J. (2011). Strategic facilitation of problem-based discussion for teacher professional development. *Journal of Learning Sciences, 20*(3), 342–394. doi:10.1080/10508406.2011.553258.

Chapter 8
Agile Curriculum Sustainability: Continuous Improvement

Introduction

When it comes to implementing a curriculum that aligns with an agile PBL ecology for learning, there are a myriad of elements and factors to consider, and they all impact to some extent on the ultimate success: graduates who can demonstrate the desired learning outcomes and are empowered with agile twenty-first-century skills that allow them to contribute to society with agency. The development, implementation and teaching of an agile PBL curriculum are ideally at the very least a whole-of-institution endeavour, which involves the micro- and exo-systems, but the goal from the beginning should always be to consciously involve all systems in the ecology. Excluding, for example, the macro-system from curriculum and pedagogy exposes the curriculum to the risk of not achieving the desired learning outcomes identified and required for a twenty-first-century supercomplex world. However, we do realise that a fully functioning curriculum in alignment with an agile PBL ecology for learning is an ideal situation, whereby the whole institution is on the same page and 'every duck is lined up'. This whole-institution implementation represents one end of a continuum, whereas agile PBL implemented in single courses taught by individual enthusiastic lecturers is considered at the other end of the continuum. The latter is primarily based within the micro-system, while the former involves interplays and interconnections in the entire ecology. The case we outline in this chapter leans towards the former, and the idea is that readers treat this as the ideal scenario, as something to work towards, but we do recognise that in many universities, implementing PBL in the way we are imagining here would constitute a radical change and would require a radical overhaul in all aspects of the way the institution functions. This may not be possible or feasible in many universities, at least not in the short term, so the idea is to concentrate on what would be an institutional 'feasible utopia' (Barnett, 2013). However, it is worth considering Paul's (2010) warning in this respect:

© Springer Science+Business Media Singapore 2017   151
M.Y.C.A. Kek, H. Huijser, *Problem-based Learning into the Future*,
DOI 10.1007/978-981-10-2454-2_8

One of the biggest mistakes that can be made in the implementation process of a PBL curriculum is to create a mixture of a traditional and a PBL curriculum. Although this may
seem an attractive compromise after controversial discussions within a faculty, this 'PBL
light' option (integrating components of both PBL and non-PBL-based methods) is more
expensive, confusing, divisive, and cumbersome to implement than an all-out transition to
a PBL approach. When in doubt or unable to implement a complete changeover, one would
be wiser to stick with the conventional curriculum as a whole. (p. 149)

There are a number of examples of institutions that have designed their whole
institution around a PBL curriculum right from the beginning, such as the University
of Maastricht in the Netherlands and Republic Polytechnic in Singapore. There are
others that have tried (or are still trying), such as Bahrain Polytechnic in the Arabian
Gulf, while there are still others that have implemented PBL in isolated pockets in
specific faculties, such as the Faculty of Engineering at the University of Southern
Queensland in Australia (Brodie & Gibbings, 2007) and particularly in medical
schools, for example, in the University of Limerick in Ireland, the International
Medical University and the Universiti Malaya in Malaysia. While Paul's (2010)
warning is important to consider, we should also recognise that there is no universal
agreement on this. Harvard Medical School, for example, has created and implemented a hybrid version of PBL (rather than a complete PBL curriculum). 'By
creating a hybrid curriculum that promotes active learning and self-direction in concert with a variety of other teaching modes, we have tapped large numbers of faculty
as tutors, lecturers, lab leaders and clinical clerkship instructors' (Armstrong, 2008,
pp. 148–149). This points to the importance of achieving staff buy-in and engagement, and in this case, the engagement would arguably not have been achieved if
there had been a complete and radical overhaul of the curriculum, rather than a
hybrid version. To reiterate, there is a continuum of PBL implementation, and what
we are suggesting is an ideal version that sits at the far end of this continuum, which
can then be used as a potential model to be adapted to suit individual contexts.

In addition, it is important to consider the meaning of 'agile' in an agile PBL
ecology for learning. The examples above refer to relatively rigidly defined (and
therefore not particularly agile) versions of PBL, including more traditional versions. While the fundamental principles of PBL may still be very much part of such
approaches to implementing PBL (Barrows, 1998), it is the agility that is potentially
missing. This is what Savin-Baden (2014) has recognised with her new constellations of PBL for the twenty-first century. In other words, there are different degrees
and applications, and sticking to one in a rigid way may not be agile enough to
respond to ever-changing circumstances and ever-changing career and job contexts
(Lyons, Schweitzer, & Ng, 2015) in the twenty-first century. The concept of an agile
PBL ecology for learning that we have been developing in this book allows for
imagining different combinations of the PBL constellations, and it forces the consideration of how different systems in the ecology interact and intersect, for example, partnering students from the micro-system, their families and friends from the
meso-system, non-curricular persons from the exo-systems and the external partners such as employers from the macro-system. The goal in agile PBL ecology for
learning is to support people inside and outside the university as empowered contributors and not just mere receivers of a university education.

In this chapter, we discuss some of the factors that are involved in an overhaul of the curriculum towards an agile PBL. This is then followed by an outline of how to make this practice sustainable and how to create a culture of continuous improvement, so that the agile PBL curriculum and pedagogy stay agile in the long term. This is crucial when embarking on this challenging journey in the first place. Again, the ultimate prize is a continuous stream of graduates who are empowered to function – think, feel and do – successfully in twenty-first-century supercomplex contexts.

Imagining a Sustainable Version of Agile PBL

In this chapter, we address a number of different aspects of what would make an agile PBL curriculum sustainable, and continuous improvement is a key factor in that process. However, the seed of sustainability of an agile PBL curriculum is sown during the implementation or transition phase, for it is here that the foundations are put in place that will sustain practice in the long run. In Chap. 6, we discussed one of Kuh, Kinzie, Schuh, Whitt and associates' (2005) six institutional conditions for student success as having an improvement-oriented ethos deeply infused in the institution, so they are in a 'perpetual learning mode' (p. 133), otherwise known as a lifelong learning disposition (Head, Van Hoeck, & Garson, 2015). This not only relates to curriculum and pedagogy design and development itself but actually relates to the way the whole university is organised, as all departments and functions (particularly on the micro and exo-levels) are parts of a holistic approach to an agile PBL implementation. For example, the budget has to be aligned with agile PBL requirements; the human resource department needs to understand the skills and attitudes of agile PBL teachers, rather than traditional teaching expectations of academic staff during the recruitment phase; professional development needs to be tailored to agile PBL needs; and the budget needs to be adjusted to support that. The list goes on and is rather long. This is not to scare anyone away from imagining and implementing agile PBL, but it is rather to draw attention to the fact that it needs careful planning, and it is not something that can be done as a fad or an individual's 'project'. Overall then, this chapter addresses three key areas around sustainable agile PBL curriculum and pedagogy development:

- Implementation and transition
- Sustainability and renewal
- Evaluation and continuous improvement

Underlying all of this, from a theoretical perspective, is the idea of 'the learning organisation' (Senge, 1990; Thomas & Allen, 2006), which applies in particular to sustainability and continuous improvement phases, as well as 'diffusion of innovations' theory (Rogers, 2003; Xiong, Payne, & Kinsella, 2015) which applies more directly to the implementation and transition phase. The latter starts from the assumption that the university is not developed from scratch, but rather has often been operational for a considerable time and most likely with a traditional – fixed, bounded – worldview and setup. If we think of agile PBL as an innovation, then we would need to allow for the diffusion process to take place and build this into the planning.

Implementation and Transition

Rogers' (2003) diffusion of innovations theory has a focus on technological innovations and their uptake in organisations or across different societies (Degerlia, Aytekinb, & Degerlic, 2015). However, we would argue that the categories and phases that he uses can be applied to other innovations, for example, curriculum innovations such as agile PBL. First, Rogers identifies four main elements in the diffusion of innovations:

1. Innovation

   'An innovation is an idea, practice, or project that is perceived as new by an individual or other unit of adoption' (Rogers, 2003, p. 12), such as a faculty or department. In this case of an agile PBL ecology for learning, it crosses many boundaries and territories, so it is not confined to the micro level alone. Importantly, innovations have perceived consequences that can be desirable or undesirable (functional or dysfunctional), direct versus indirect (immediate result or longer-term result), and anticipated versus unanticipated (recognised and intended or not) (Sahin, 2006). In general, people resist change, so communicating about these consequences in a way that changes perceptions is important. Especially when you intend to embark on a major overhaul, people need to be convinced of desirable consequences. In our case, every staff member needs to be convinced that an agile PBL will lead to desired learning outcomes and that the more conventional approaches will not.

2. Communication channels

   As noted above, persuasion of desirable consequences is a key element of diffusion, and communication channels play a central part in this. According to Rogers (2003, p. 19), 'diffusion is a very social process that involves interpersonal communication relationships'. Of course there are other organisational and social communication channels, such as mediated ones (email, newsletters, Facebook pages, website, etc.), but during the persuasion stage, interpersonal relationships are crucial. Consequently, this needs to be factored in, and time and space need to be created to allow for this type of communication to occur. In short, people need to feel a sense of ownership over the process, rather than a sense that radical changes are simply imposed. Recall that in Chap. 6 we discussed how mattering universities make their students feel they matter, which leads students to be more engaged. The same principle applies to staff. In implementing an innovation like agile PBL, mattering institutions use communications strategically to make their staff feel that they matter too, fostering and promoting staff buy-in. Furthermore, there needs to be a sense that genuine concerns and feedback are taken on board and have the potential to change the implementation journey. Again, within an agile PBL ecology for learning, this process is not confined to the institution, but importantly includes other stakeholders from the meso- and macro-systems. This makes a whole university implementation more complex, but it also reinforces the importance of agility, with the ultimate reward being an inclusive conception of an agile learning organisation that is liquid and comfortable at adapting to rapidly changing contexts.

3. Time

Time is crucial and needs to be allocated within reason. This is a delicate balance. Moving too fast can lead to the whole university implementation process to collapse, while moving too slow can lead to a lack of faith in the implementation ever coming to fruition. In other words, while there needs to be enough time to address concerns and explain consequences, there is also a need to build momentum and keep that momentum going.

4. Social system

Rogers (2003, p. 23) defines the social system as 'a set of interrelated units engaged in joint problem solving to accomplish a common goal'. This works differently in different social systems (Baecker, 2014; Barker, 2004), but in the university, this equates to faculties and departments or units engaged with common destiny and objectives. This is especially important in our case because of the interdisciplinary and cross-organisational nature of an agile PBL curriculum and pedagogy (see Chap. 4). We referred to it earlier in this chapter as getting the 'ducks lined up, and their beaks pointing in the same direction'. Agile PBL requires teachers, students, administrators, curriculum designers and support staff, as well as employers and other external partners outside the university, to work towards these common goals and outcomes. This is a process of negotiation, but it has to start from a common place of understanding for it to be successful.

These four elements feed into the innovation-decision process, which Rogers (2003, p. 172) describes as 'an information-seeking and information-processing activity, where an individual is motivated to reduce uncertainty about the advantages and disadvantages of an innovation'. In short, and in our case, this is to ensure that people in the university actually care enough to engage with the innovation in a serious way.

Rogers' innovation-decision process has five steps (2003, as cited in Sahin, 2006):

1. The knowledge stage

As noted in Chap. 3, this stage is about the what, how and why of the innovation. In other words, it is about awareness of agile PBL and of the benefits and expected outcomes of agile PBL, followed by how you would actually apply it in your own context. This stage is also about why you would go through all the trouble of changing your practice. In other words, 'what's in it for me and my students'? This is an important stage and relies on good organisational communication, but it is not enough in itself. As Sahin (2006, para 14) notes, 'an individual may have all the necessary knowledge, but this does not mean that the individual will adopt the innovation because the individual's attitudes also shape the adoption or rejection of the innovation'. In other words, the default position for most people is let's keep the status quo.

2. The persuasion stage

According to Rogers (2003), while the knowledge stage is cognitive centred, the persuasion stage is affective centred. It is the difference in TV advertising between explaining the science behind a washing powder and appealing to motherly instincts about the outcomes (happy babies) of a washing powder. In our case, it is at this stage people have to feel that agile PBL works or at the very least some of its constellations (Savin-Baden, 2014), by both seeing and feeling the results. This can only be effectively achieved by getting people involved in *doing* agile PBL, rather than just talking about it. Time becomes a factor in this stage, because it is not easy to organise overnight for all staff, but it is worth the investment. As all teachers know, there is nothing more powerful than the moment when 'the light comes on' in a student. In most cases, it's not just that the light comes on at a cognitive level, but that the light is felt on an affective level (Afzal & Robinson, 2010). It is at this level that the highest potential for change in attitudes occurs, and it is often accompanied by comments like 'I thought this would be much harder'.

3. The decision stage

At this stage a decision is made about whether to adopt or reject the innovation. At an organisational level, this means of course that some people won't actually have a choice if the university makes a decision to implement an agile PBL curriculum. However, the ideal is that you bring as many people in the organisation along as possible, and giving people the opportunity to trial and sample agile PBL, and thus to feel its benefits, is a useful strategy here. Rogers (2003) identifies two types of rejection: active and passive. When an innovation is actively rejected, it means that rejection follows a trial, while passive rejection means that it is rejected out of hand, without a trial. We could add a third type of rejection, which is a situation where people might say they have adopted an agile version of PBL, but in actual fact teach in much the same way as they always have, either through not understanding what agile PBL is about or by actively undermining the agile PBL process, usually because they feel it is being imposed. Again, it is crucial that enough time and space are created to ensure that as many people as possible in the organisation are on board.

4. The implementation stage

Once a decision to adopt is made, implementation begins, but this stage is still characterised by uncertainty, because the outcomes are not yet fully known. In the case of agile PBL, this is precisely the point, as the outcomes may never be fully known, as they are forever subject to change, hence the need for agility. The adaption that happens during this stage is also referred to as 'reinvention', which Rogers (2003) considers a positive thing, and indeed, 'the more reinvention takes place, the more rapidly an innovation is adopted and becomes institutionalised' (Sahin, para 18). Again, in the context of agile PBL, there is an added complication in that reinvention is an integral part of the process and is expected to occur on a continuous basis.

5. The confirmation stage

At this stage, the decision to implement the innovation has already been made, but individuals still look for support for the decision they made about it at an individual level. In other words, this is the stage where most people are ideally on board, even if they are still feeling their way through the new model, but there are a number of detractors who may try to get support for their desire to return to 'the old ways'. At an organisational level, it is important to carefully monitor this, as it has the potential to cause significant damage.

It is worth keeping in mind Sahin's (2006, para 16) warning that 'rejection [of the innovation] is possible in every stage of the innovation-decision process'. Naturally, some innovations are more likely to be adopted quickly than others, even if it ultimately always involves a level of unpredictability.

Nevertheless, Rogers (2003) identifies five attributes of innovations that more or less influence this process:

1. Relative advantage

'The degree to which an innovation is perceived as being better than the idea it supersedes' (Rogers, 2003, p. 229). This is important especially in terms of winning over the late majority and the laggards (see also Chap. 7). But it is also a crucial part of developing the initial case about the desirability of radical changes to the curriculum, which in turn will have a ripple effect in an agile PBL ecology for learning. Most of what we have been doing so far in this book works at this level and is trying to persuade readers that agile PBL is better than more traditional approaches to teaching and even better than other PBL-based approaches.

2. Compatibility

'The degree to which an innovation is perceived as consistent with the existing values, past experiences, and needs of potential adopters' (Rogers, 2003, p. 15). This attribute creates a potential risk in our case that needs to be carefully managed, as agile PBL has the potential for some teachers to profoundly disturb their own sense of their teacher identity (Ballantyne & Grootenboer, 2012; Pennington & Richards, 2016), as mentioned in Chap. 7. Similarly, for some students, for example, those who grew up with highly teacher-centred schooling systems, an agile PBL curriculum can be profoundly unsettling until they 'feel' its benefits. Again, this foregrounds the importance of good communication and adequate time to manage potential incompatibilities.

3. Complexity

'The degree to which an innovation is perceived as relatively difficult to understand and use' (Rogers, 2003, p. 15). PBL in general is a little deceptive in this respect, because many people tend to quickly understand it at a superficial level. A curriculum based on problem-solving does not sound like rocket science, and everyone knows what a problem is. However, 'teaching' in an agile PBL mode, designing an appropriately targeted and relevant (or authentic) problem and aligning this successfully with its place and time in the overall curriculum or program are actually rather complex (as discussed in detail in Chaps. 4 and 5). The challenge then from our point of view is to avoid people from turning away once they realise it is much more complex than what they initially thought. An additional challenge in an agile PBL ecology for learning is ensuring that the appropriate people from the macro-context are involved at the right times and that they have a good enough understanding of the aims, objectives and learning outcomes of the overall model.

4. Trialability

'The degree to which an innovation may be experimented with on a limited basis' (Rogers, 2003, p. 16). This is particularly important for early adopters as they reinvent the innovation while adapting it (Sadler, 2015). Again, adequate time and space to let this process run its course is the key here and needs to be considered in professional learning for staff and preparing students (as discussed in Chaps. 6 and 7).

5. Observability

'The degree to which the results of an innovation are visible to others' (Rogers, 2003, p. 16). Observability is quite closely linked to trialability, in that the early adopters need to be able to function as models that the early majority can follow. In other words, the early majority, and later the late majority, need to have opportunities to 'feel' the advantages and successful outcomes of an agile PBL. This is crucial if the objective is to 'line up the ducks'. This is particularly important in preparing staff and students as seen in Chaps. 6 and 7.

'Lining up the ducks' on an institutional level is a complex process that involves all levels of the university (the micro-, meso- and exo-systems). It gets more tricky when the university engages with external partners such as employers outside the university. According to Paul (2010, p. 147), 'the implementation of a PBL curriculum demands an open, transparent, and constructive process, based on rational arguments and not on emotion, and is aimed at persuading stakeholders rather than imposing change'. We have outlined above what such a process of persuading stakeholders involves. 'In effect it demands the integration and coordination of 'top-down' and 'bottom-up' processes' (Paul, 2010, p. 147). The top-down processes are there to support the bottom-up processes, and this involves, for example, the creation of time and space to work through the various stages of implementation. More specifically, it involves creating space and time in teachers' workloads to be able to learn and design new curricula and a new way of doing things; paying lip service to this is not enough and in fact runs the risk of having the opposite effect. Traversing system boundaries in an agile PBL ecology for learning will add further time demands on the process, as it involves liaising and communicating with external partners outside the university (the macro-system). Furthermore, this is not a 'front-loaded' task, but rather an ongoing one, as agile PBL demands continuous change and adaptation and thus ever-changing partners and stakeholders.

With regard to a whole-of-university approach, Paul (2010) identifies a set of key features that should be considered when implementing a PBL-based curriculum:

- Legal issues

    In most countries, various disciplines are regulated by legal frameworks and bodies that prescribe certain predefined standards and/or inclusions. This applies, for example, to medical education, but also to nursing, business, engineering and science (Hordern, 2015). When planning a major overhaul of the curriculum, it is important to carefully consider and incorporate these legal requirements from the very beginning and if needed to explain and convince regulatory bodies of the desirability of the changes.

- Best practice

    This is potentially the most problematic from our point of view or at least in the way Paul (2010, p. 147) imagines this: 'The implementation should be based on best practice and evidence from other model projects and established PBL curricula'. On the face of it, this seems like an excellent idea and hard to argue with. However, if this becomes a dogmatic rule, it can also get in the way of innovation and experimentation, which is an integral and continuous element of an agile PBL. So it is crucial to find the right balance here between evidence-based practice, based on model cases, and innovative practice that may at times be 'unproven' – again, this very much mirrors twenty-first-century world. An agile form of PBL, combining various constellations (Savin-Baden, 2014) at different times, is what we imagine to be most appropriate here.

- Governance

    As noted, the aim is to get all the ducks lined up, and governance is key to that. Everyone with a stake in the curriculum should be on board with the suggested changes or at least engaging with them. As agile PBL requires cross-disciplinary decisions that need to be signed off on a regular basis at the highest faculty levels, governance of the implementation relies on broad-based support all the way up the leadership hierarchy and beyond (at senior leadership levels in the macro-system).

- Transparency and communication

    Another key element of the 'ducks lining up argument' is good, regular and transparent communication, based on an atmosphere of trust. Continuous innovation sometimes requires the courage to go boldly where no one has gone before; in fact, this is a central characteristic of an entrepreneurial attitude and should thus be modelled by the university itself (Macmahon & Huijser, 2015). However, this has a tendency to scare the wits out of some people. It is only when those people feel they mattered in the process, rather than having decisions about curricular changes imposed on them, that they will stay engaged (if not necessarily happy). This requires honest and transparent communication, rather than secrecy and backroom dealings.

- Financial matters

    There is a strong perception that PBL-based approaches are more expensive than traditional curricula (Paul, 2010) as it requires more resources, but this is not necessarily the case, and it depends on how the curriculum is designed. However, to counter some of this common criticism, it is a good idea to have a well-developed budget to start off with. This should include the flexibility involved in the interdisciplinary nature of the problem design in agile PBL, which has potential implications for traditionally siloed faculty budgets. Furthermore, the involvement of employers in the design of problems, their provision of physical sites of learning and their involvement in the assessment of student learning and outcomes and creation of products/artefacts have budgetary and financial implications that need to be carefully addressed and shared in some cases. In other words, this is not just a case of relying on employers' goodwill and donated time for their involvement in the learning process, but rather it requires a shift in attitude whereby employers take partial responsibility for playing their part in the overall agile PBL ecology for learning, which includes taking financial responsibility. The case study of transforming a marketing communications program into agile authentic PBL mode in Chap. 4 shows how future employers are clients in the learning and teaching process of agile PBL, but they could also contribute a nominal sum towards student costs in the creation of learning-related products and/or artefacts.

- Assessment (and evaluation) and quality control

   In an interdisciplinary context especially and in cooperative arrangements with employers, quality control can pose serious challenges. This applies in particular when the arrangements potentially change each time a new problem is designed. However, while this seems like a daunting prospect, it is definitely possible as long as clear and agreed-upon quality guidelines are established and systematically applied (Tam, 2001).

- Educational competence

   An agile PBL does not allow for teachers to rest on their laurels and teach the same course in the same way for years. Quite the opposite, agile PBL requires teachers to be lifelong learners and continuously on top of their profession and disciplinary fields of expertise. It is therefore crucial that teachers can clearly see the rewards for engaging in this process. Simply saying that it is exciting will win no one over. Teachers need to see a bang for their buck, and this means incorporating reward structures (in the form of actual rewards such as time allocations, opportunities for continuous professional learning, research and scholarship outcomes (see Chap. 9) related to their practice). In the end, good teaching is good teaching, but collegial support and teamwork, as well as professional learning opportunities and rewards, go a long way towards developing a culture of continuous improvement or, indeed, a learning organisation (Senge, 1990), and indeed where a mattering organisation 'walks the talk', staff feel they matter, enabling them to be more engaged in actively producing breakthrough actions and solutions to problems faced in the organisation (Marquardt & Yeo, 2012).

- Recruitment strategies

   Recruitment is a key element of the long-term sustainability of an agile PBL. As Paul (2010, p. 148) notes, 'having an open mind about education, modern ideas about teaching concepts, and an open ear to students' interests should be a basic quality in each appointee'. Thus, the recruitment process should be designed to assess these qualities in potential appointees. As noted above, teachers (as well as employers) in an agile PBL context need to be lifelong learners, as they need to be able to model what the projected outcomes for students will be. (See also Chaps. 6 and 7 on preparing both students and teachers in an agile PBL ecology for learning).

• Career development

   An additional advantage of agile PBL is that nothing happens in the same way twice; as in an agile PBL curriculum, problems are continuously designed, updated, adapted and redesigned. This also means that there is a lot of scope for research and scholarship to become an integral part of the process. As with other elements of this approach, boundaries potentially blur as the dividing line between teacher, students and researchers (and between the four systems in the agile PBL ecology for learning) will become increasingly porous as the curriculum enters the final years and as continuous improvement and evaluation are enshrined into the program. As Paul (2010, p. 149) notes, 'nothing is deadlier for educational programs than the notion that teaching is for those whose research performance is below par'. It is crucial that research and scholarship are part and parcel of the curriculum and of curriculum evaluation on a continuous basis. However, this should be made explicit in a career policy (Wolfhagen & Scherpbier, 2010).

This list can easily come across as rather intimidating and very daunting to even consider. However, this is to illustrate on the one hand the enormity of the task, but at the same time the excitement of what could be achieved if everyone was on the same page or what would be a 'feasible utopia' (Barnett, 2013). Our argument here (with Paul, 2010) is that to really get the projected benefits from an agile PBL, a whole-of-institution approach is required, as agile PBL involves everyone in the university, as well as many stakeholders beyond the university. And since agile PBL is about continuous improvement and adaptation to changing circumstances and indeed is about engaging with and influencing those circumstances, it requires every employee to be a lifelong learner and to be forever alert to potential improvement and not be complacent to the dynamic twenty-first-century world.

Sustainability and Renewal

It becomes clear that implementation is never fully achieved in an agile PBL ecology! What we have established is that you can create and control the circumstances under which an agile PBL can thrive (taking into account all systems in an agile PBL ecology for learning), but to ensure ongoing sustainability requires a shared and unshakeable commitment to continuous renewal and improvement. Doing PBL according to a rigid formula is anathema to that idea. This is not the same as arguing that there are no rules to agile PBL, but rather that there are many 'constellations'

(Savin-Baden, 2014) within an agile PBL ecology for learning – persons, tools, systems, approaches and frameworks – that are perfectly appropriate for particular contexts (Moust & Roebertsen, 2010) and, more importantly, are most likely to lead to the desired learning outcomes, which, as we have argued in Chap. 2, are the educational bottom line of an agile PBL.

Overall, sustainability and continuous renewal and improvement are about a whole-of-institution approach, and the concept of the 'learning organisation' (Ortenblad, 2013; Senge, 1990) is useful here, as it is focused on continuous improvement at all levels of organisations. There are numerous definitions of the learning organisation concept. Dixon (1999, as cited in Thomas & Allen, 2006, p. 123), for example, defines the organisational learning as 'the intentional use of learning processes to continuously transform the organisation'. Thomas and Allen (p. 126) themselves see the learning organisation as being 'about building learning and knowledge creating capacity in individuals and enabling the effective dissemination of this knowledge through the organisation'. In both definitions, there is an emphasis on making learning an intentional and explicit part of organisational practice, which in turn builds capacity for lifelong learning in all people associated with the organisation.

Senge (1990, p. 3) defines the learning organisation as 'one in which people continually expand their capacity to create the results they truly desire, where new and expansive patterns of thinking are nurtured, where collective aspirations are set free, and where people are continually learning how to learn together'. The key here is that not only is this about continuous improvement but also about continuous innovation, which is very relevant to an agile PBL ecology. Indeed, as Ng (2004, p. 94) points out, 'most companies are built for continuous improvement, rather than discontinuous innovation. They know how to get better at what they have always been doing, but they do not know how to be different'. Daring to be different, and becoming comfortable with difference and with thinking beyond 'what is' to 'what could be' (i.e. imagining a feasible utopia), is what suits an agile PBL ecology and is intimately linked to twenty-first-century skills (Davies, Fidler, & Gorbis, 2011).

According to Higgins (1995, as cited in Ng, 2004, p. 94), an innovative organisation has a generic set of characteristics which include the following:

- A stated and working strategy of innovation
- Forming teams
- Rewarding creativity and innovation
- Allowing mistakes
- Training in creativity
- Managing the organisational culture
- Creating new opportunities proactively

Again, what we see here is an emphasis on establishing proactive and explicit measures to create an environment in which learning and innovation can thrive. There are a number of available models that outline the necessary elements that underlie the learning organisation (e.g. Thomas & Allen, 2006), but we will discuss two that appear to be the most appropriate for our purposes here. The first is Ng's (2004) interpretation of Senge's (1990) five disciplines, and the second is Phillips (2003) ten-pillar ideal learning organisation model.

Senge (1990) identified what he called five 'disciplines' that underpin the learning organisation, and he claimed that the five disciplines, when used in concert, facilitate organisational learning (Retna, 2006). Ng (2004) adds that these five disciplines are critical to the development of an innovative organisation:

1. Personal mastery

   'The discipline of continually clarifying and deepening one's personal vision, of focusing one's energy, of developing patience and seeing reality objectively' (Ng, 2004, p. 95). The argument here is that at an individual level, we need to cultivate the ability and attitude required for innovation. Ng's (p. 95) description of this is worth quoting because it is closely aligned with an agile PBL process: 'He [sic] must focus his energy on walking the less trodden path, where there are no clear rules to follow. He must develop patience, for in seeking the unconventional, he needs to drive himself forward despite the pressure to conform or the stings of failure'. In other words, resilience is a key component of this personal mastery for staff and students, as is becoming comfortable with the discomfort that the unknown presents (see also Chap. 4). As Ng (p. 95) rightly notes, 'effective innovation requires a discipline to deviate from the norm in a constructive manner'. Agile PBL ecology for learning opens up possibilities where resilience can be nurtured, while the overall university, supported by employers and society in general, creates an organisational context in which it can thrive.

2. Mental models

   'Mental models are the deeply ingrained assumptions, generalisations and images that influence how an individual understands the world and how he takes action' (Ng, 2004, p. 95). In short, this is about developing the ability to think outside of the box, which requires challenging mental models, which in turn is the basis of transformative learning (Mezirow, 2008; Sipos, Battisti, & Grimm, 2013; Taylor, 2008). 'Transformational [sic] learning is a process of deep reflection and discovery that leads to profound shifts of direction, behaviours, values, beliefs and operating assumptions' (Ng, 2004, p. 96). An innovative learning organisation is one where thinking outside the box to come to new understandings and practice is valued and encouraged. Of course this is crucial to the sustainability of agile PBL, as the expectation is that it will continuously undergo reinventions in its continuous process of renewal.

3. Shared vision

   'With a genuine vision, people are galvanised to action, not because they have to, but because they want to' (Ng, 2004, p. 96). As noted above, implementing whole-of-institution agile PBL involves everyone in the university, and it is therefore vital that everyone understands and believes in the shared vision of empowering students who can confidently and successfully function in a future supercomplex twenty-first-century context or at least that they can comfortably and courageously engage with the ideas (see also Chap. 6 on the six institutional conditions for student success). We have been arguing (imagining) throughout this book that this shared vision goes beyond the university and instead involves all four systems in an agile PBL ecology for learning. But within the university, as Ng (p. 97) argues, 'innovation should not be the exclusive domain of the research and development arm. When innovation is compartmentalised in this manner, others in the university assume that innovation is not their job', which would be detrimental in a supercomplex, interdisciplinary world.

4. Team learning

    'Team learning is vital because teams, not individuals, are the fundamental units in modern organisations' (Ng, 2004, p. 97). Of course, team learning is also central to an agile PBL ecology for learning, so it is important that team learning is being modelled by everyone in the university, especially curricular/academic and non-curricular/professional and support staff. As noted in Chap. 5, team learning is especially important in an interdisciplinary context, and 'it is difficult to build capacities for thinking collectively about new ways of doing business if the members of the team do not understand how one another think or work' (Ng, 2004, p. 97).

5. Systems thinking

    'The essence of systems thinking lies in a shift of the mind to see interrelationships rather than linear cause-effect chains and see processes of change rather than snapshots' (Ng, 2004, p. 98). When we say the implementation of an agile PBL requires a whole-of-institution approach, we think 'interacting systems' as detailed in Chap. 2, an agile PBL ecology for learning as the framework for future learning where students are situated at the centre of the university. In other words, the implementation process is seen as affecting all parts of the university, not just teachers and students, but staff inside and partners outside the university. It is seen as requiring staff to move beyond disciplinary and institutional boundaries and work together in teams and to learn continuously. Systems thinking then is about laying the foundations and preparing the ground for the learning organisation to open up and be opened to possibilities.

These five broad 'disciplines' show considerable overlap with Phillips' (2003, pp. 99–100) ten-pillar ideal learning organisation model, but the latter breaks it into smaller components:

1. Will

    The whole institution maintains a passionate commitment to continuous improvement and innovation through continuous learning.

2. Leadership

    Leadership is facilitative and supportive of personal development; it has an active concern for all staff, values their contribution and is prepared to listen; it thinks systemically and is keenly aware of current reality.

3. Strategic thinking and vision

    Strategic leadership maintains clarity and acceptance of the strategic direction. In our case, this means keeping a focus on agile PBL and its projected graduate outcomes, even if there is initial resistance.

4. Communication

Open dialogue at all levels encourages the sharing of ideas, knowledge and insights. An atmosphere of trust prevails. This is crucial, especially if there is major curriculum change required, as this process of change creates considerable anxiety among staff who have not changed their practice for a long time. Seriously engaging with relevant persons inside (meso- and exo-systems) and external to the university (those in the macro-system) may cause even more potential anxiety.

5. Learning and development

This relates to fostering whole-of-institution lifelong learning within an overall agile PBL ecology for learning. The acquisition of innovative ideas and knowledge is facilitated, feedback loops evaluate its usefulness and new technology is embraced to foster learning and development.

6. Innovation and decision-making

Initiative and experimentation are encouraged in a safe environment; accountable mistakes are seen as an opportunity to learn and as a by-product of the search for continuous improvement.

7. Change management

The core knowledge base is continually questioned and evaluated, and challenge and change are regarded without suspicion and normalised in everyday practice.

8. Intellectual capacity and knowledge management

All staff are encouraged to share responsibility for the development of intellectual capital and, in our case, contribute to the whole gamut of creating and sustaining agile PBL, such as listening to students, designing and planning the curriculum, development of authentic problems and innovative authentic assessments, teaching, evaluating, researching and scholarship of teaching and learning. Tacit knowledge is willingly and readily transferred.

9. Measurement and assessment

Measurement and assessment are accepted as necessary indicators of changes in attitude, behaviour, performance and commitment to continuous improvement, rather than approached with suspicion. New tools for evaluation are continuously sought and incorporated, for example, increased use of big data and data analytics for better information on learning and teaching and for better institutional decision-making and actions (Johnson, Adams Becker, Estrada, & Freeman, 2014; Leavy & Rheinschmidt, 2010; Siemens, 2012; West et al., 2015).

10. Reward and recognition

Incentives improve performance, strengthen motivation, encourage personal learning and advancement and foster job satisfaction. In our case, reward and recognition need to be explicitly built into the process of implementation, because staff need to see and be convinced about what is in it for them and for their students before they embark on a big process of changing their practice. The same applies to employers who are engaged in the agile PBL process.

In effect, Phillips' (2003, p. 105) model can function as a checklist for establishing the extent of implementation at any time. Moreover, because agile PBL is fundamentally about continuous improvement, currency and innovation, this checklist can also function as a barometer of sustainability at any one time in the continuous improvement process. In other words, it can provide a map of where in the process momentum is being lost and where staleness threatens to occur. This will in turn ensure that the appropriate response can be applied and that the agility of the PBL process in the overall ecology for learning is maintained.

Evaluation and Continuous Improvement

Evaluation is a key element of implementing and sustaining agile PBL. One needs to continuously evaluate whether you are on track and whether you are reaching the outcomes that you set out to achieve (Secolsky, Denison, & Stake, 2012). This is even more urgent in a curriculum that is *never* exactly the same twice and is subject to continuous renewal. In that context, how do you ensure quality? Bowden and Marton (2000) have defined quality assurance as the planned and systematic activities put in place to ensure that quality requirements for a product or service are fulfilled. Stalmeijer, Dolmans, van Berkel and Wolfhagen (2010, p. 157) apply this definition to a university context and note that this 'implies that quality assurance can focus on the quality of teaching staff, faculty development, and quality of assessment, but also on managerial processes; input, throughput, and output of students; and human resource management'. This is important in our case, as it recognises that each of these elements relates to each other and should not be evaluated in isolation, particularly if the approach is fundamentally a whole-of-institution approach and beyond. Again, we imagine an agile PBL ecology for learning to be potentially very powerful, if all the clogs in the machine are in motion, but the ecology is at the same time fragile as each element is dependent on the other.

Stalmeijer et al. (2010) identify two different streams in quality: accounting for quality and improving quality. Accounting for quality is about measurement against predefined standards: assurance, accountability, audit and assessment. This is usually performed by external agencies. By contrast, improving quality is about enhancement, empowerment, enthusiasm and excellence. Improving quality is thus about what you do with the outcomes of continuous evaluation and how you respond to it. This is ideally a cyclical process for an agile PBL ecology for learning, comprising three elements (Stalmeijer et al., 2010, p. 157):

1. Defining and measuring quality
2. Judging quality against predefined standards to determine strengths and weaknesses
3. Making improvements based upon the information collected

The most difficult part in our case is to pin down the 'predefined standards'. In other words, when your program and curriculum are subject to constant changes and shifts in focus, the standards you are measuring against need to be flexible enough (or indeed agile enough) to take into account the bigger picture of what agile PBL sets out to achieve. However, challenging as this may seem, it is not impossible, but it does need to be carefully managed and systemically implemented. This applies in particular at the level of problem design, assessment design and teaching in agile PBL and how those three core components are meeting the learning outcomes and more broadly the long-term or future learning outcomes. Again, this type of evaluation and quality assurance cannot be left up to a centralised 'quality unit', but instead needs to be integrated and normalised as part of everyday practice among every staff in the university.

Especially the improvement part 'requires rich data, usually collected through more diagnostic-type questionnaires (open-ended questions), interviews, focus groups, observations, and document analysis' (Stalmeijer et al., 2010, p. 158). Increasingly, there are now digital tools available to acquire vast amounts of data, including rich data. Data analytics can potentially provide rich data to aid and enrich cycles of continuous evaluation, as they collect a steady stream of data (West et al., 2015). The EduTech Wiki (2013) points out that analytics in various forms have been used widely for many years (e.g. analysis of grades and test scores, student and teacher evaluation surveys). However, the scope of data analytics or big data has expanded to include the use by educational institutions for various stakeholders, and as such the way analytics is defined and implemented may vary, including the following:

- For individual learners to reflect on their achievements and patterns of behaviour in relation to others
- As predictors of students requiring extra support and attention
- To help teachers and support staff plan supporting interventions with individuals and groups
- For functional groups such as course teams seeking to improve current courses or develop new curriculum offerings
- For institutional administrators taking decisions on matters such as marketing and recruitment or efficiency and effectiveness measures
- For comparisons between systems (state, regional, national and international)

Many of the uses of analytics here can be seen in the SPARS case study in Chap. 6. Again, if we apply this to a whole-of-institution approach, in an agile PBL ecology for learning, there is a lot of scope to improve the process of continuous evaluation and improvement. However, the process needs to be truly systemic and cyclical, without any shortcuts. As Dolmans et al. (2003, as cited in Stalmeijer et al., 2010, p. 160) stress, 'in order to ensure that quality assurance is a true cyclic process that results in continuous improvement, quality assurance should be integrated within regular organisational working patterns'. Only when it becomes part of normalised practice does it have the effect of genuine improvement, rather than staff going through the motions of compliance to 'please' external agents or internal units.

In practice, the most important requirement is to implement a systemic approach to continuous improvement and innovation and to normalise this approach into everyday practice. As noted, a whole-of-institution approach does not always end at the faculty boundary, especially not in an interdisciplinary approach to agile PBL. What is needed then is systemic approach to the establishment of working parties that have a core membership, but are fluid enough to absorb new temporary members as and when needed, including team members from different systems in the agile PBL ecology for learning. These working parties include members from the faculty and course teams, non-curricular staff as well as partners outside the university and students where possible.

We are suggesting that these working groups be modelled on communities of practices (Hara, 2009; Wenger, 2009) and/or action learning practices (Marquardt & Yeo, 2012) and will be multiplied across the university, without exceptions. In other words, every staff inside the university would be a member of at least one core community of practice or action learning group but would also contribute to others as and when needed. This would include senior management. Importantly, the systemic bit includes the creation of space and time in staff workloads to allow them to engage in communities of practice and/or action learning groups in a meaningful way. However, building communities of practice and/or action learning groups would be a waste of time and effort if the approaches and processes undertaken in these communities are ineffective in producing innovative and fresh solutions to the problems at hand. We are imagining that these communities of practice and/or action learning groups would use an agile PBL approach to managing the problems. In learning organisations, this agile PBL orientation at work is more widely known as action learning groups. This is especially important in the context of agile PBL, in which curriculum renewal and innovation are central elements. In this context, every staff inside the university need time and spaces to think and to engage with their peers inside and outside the university, to enable 'out of the box' thinking for breakthrough solutions ((Marquardt & Yeo, 2012) and to ultimately work towards a 'feasible utopia' (Barnett, 2013).

Building Communities of Practice and Action Learning Communities

Community of Practice

Wenger (2009) defines communities of practice as 'groups of people who share a concern or a passion for something they do and learn how to do it better as they interact regularly'. The learning how to do it better is about renewal and innovation, while the regular interaction is about sustainability. Many communities of practice have three key elements in their setup: the knowledge domain, the community and the practice. Together, these three provide the reasons and impetus to meet regularly, and together they provide a structure for such meetings, so that it does not become a loose arrangement where people merely have chat and a cup of tea. Serious work needs to take place if the outcomes of continuous improvement and innovation are to be achieved and if trust is to be developed. For Wenger, communities of practice engage in the following activities:

- Problem-solving
- Requests for information
- Seeking experience
- Reusing assets
- Coordination and synergy
- Discussing developments
- Documentation projects
- Visits
- Mapping knowledge and identifying gaps

To this we can add the elements related to an agile PBL ecology for learning: problem design; assessment design; mapping learning outcomes; evaluating the program; identifying suitable workplaces and engaging students and suitable partners outside the university, e.g. employers; organising the logistics of 'problems on location'; professional learning for staff; and student support. As a way of modelling and normalising practice, each of these topics can be presented as a problem for the relevant community of practice. For example, a problem might be the design of a problem for a first year course with a particular set of learning outcomes. Another problem might be to design assessment for the same course and to map and constructively align this with the learning outcomes of the overall program. Obviously, this will then also entail communication with other communities of practice, especially in an interdisciplinary context, so they would either meet together as groups or they would invite a spokesperson from another community of practice, as and when appropriate. Another topic (and thus problem) could be how to design an appropriate evaluation for a particular course or set of courses. The list is endless, but what is attractive about this is that this system is not only fluid, agile and responsive to changing circumstances and contexts, but that it also creates space for future possibilities. Hence, this is far removed from the traditional reasons for meeting up with colleagues, which tend to be highly structured staff meetings which tend to be about administrative processes only and which tend to have very little time reserved for thinking about the curriculum and for peer engagement.

Action Learning Working Groups

As a possible alternative to communities of practice groups, we suggest forming action learning working parties. Organisations that have employed action learning communities have the capability to fully understand today's problems and team learning necessary to develop solutions that are powerful, sustainable and cost-effective (Marquardt & Yeo, 2012). For example, organisations such as Toyota, DuPont and Boeing are a few of the 31 case studies presented by Marquardt and Yeo

(p. 27) to illustrate how action learning was used to illuminate how 'common things were done uncommonly well' in these organisations, in an agile manner.

Action learning is a powerful problem-solving tool that provides a structured yet spontaneous way of examining complex issues and offering concrete and useful solutions (Dijksterhuis & Meurs, 2006, as cited in Marquardt & Yeo, 2012). The process is usually employed in a team, in our case, a community of practice solving an agile PBL problem, where they learn and take action together, in an iterative process of solving complex problems (Marquardt & Yeo, 2012). The elements of the group learning and taking action together enable 'breakthrough' moments to occur that 'help them to understand the importance of group dynamics in promoting creativity and generating opportunities for greater collaborative inquiry that involves conceptualisation, experimentation and evaluation' (Marquardt & Yeo, 2012, p. 30). We suggest that it is through these moments that the action working groups will be able to fulfil the ultimate goal of action learning which is 'an amazing, highly effective problem-solving process that capitalises on the power of human imagination and courage' (Marquardt & Yeo, 2012, p. 31).

Marquardt and Yeo (2012, pp. 201–223) have proposed ten critical strategies for breakthrough problem-solving with action learning which is similar to an agile PBL process:

- Select a problem that is urgent and complex.
- Use questions and reflection.
- Foster a receptive mindset and attitude among action learning team members.
- Use skilled coaching/facilitation of the action learning team.
- Integrate learning into action learning projects.
- Establish clear norms and enforce them.
- Formulate explicit timelines and expectations for the action learning team.
- Allocate power and responsibility to the action learning teams.
- Ensure membership diversity within action learning teams.
- Enlist the commitment and support of top leadership.

Conclusion

At this stage of the book, it may seem like an enormous task to implement the agile PBL model that we are imagining here, and we do not deny that it would be. However, if we consider the recent developments in higher education (Davies, 2012) and the increasing demoralisation of the higher education workforce (Hil, 2012), we argue that this is not only worth the trouble of change on an epic scale, but that in fact it is crucial if higher education is to continue to have a leading role in shaping societies. Agile PBL taking place in an agile PBL ecology for learning is what we imagine to be a mattering approach that enables continuous improvement and breakthrough innovation, as well as sustainability, because staff matters (as do students and employers). It values and engages staff in the changes required, rather than impose change in a top-down fashion. Most importantly, it enables the development of knowledges and skills in both staff and students that would put them in good stead of functioning successfully in a twenty-first-century context of supercomplexities.

References

Afzal, S., & Robinson, P. (2010). *Modelling affect in learning environments-motivation and methods* (pp. 438–442). Paper presented at the Advanced Learning in Technologies (ICALT), 2010 IEEE 10th International Conference.

Armstrong, E. (2008). A hybrid model of problem-based learning. In D. Boud & G. Felletti (Eds.), *The challenge of problem-based learning* (pp. 137–150). London: Routledge.

Baecker, D. (2014). *Complex system in social theory*. Retrieved March 18, 2016, from http://ssrn.com/abstract=2512647. doi:http://dx.doi.org/10.2139/ssrn.2512647.

Ballantyne, J., & Grootenboer, P. (2012). Exploring relationships between teacher identities and disciplinarity. *International Journal of Music Education, 30*(4), 368–381.

Barker, K. (2004). Diffusion of innovations: A world tour. *Journal of Health Communication, 9*(S1), 131–137.

Barnett, R. (2013). *Imagining the university*. Abingdon, UK: Routledge.

Barrows, H. S. (1998). Essentials of problem-based learning. *Journal of Dental Education, 62*(9), 630–633.

Bowden, J., & Marton, F. (2000). Quality and qualities. In J. Bowden & F. Marton (Eds.), *The university of learning*. London: Kogan Page.

Brodie, L., & Gibbings, P. (2007). *Developing problem-based learning communities in virtual space*. Paper presented at the Connected: 2007 International Conference on Design Education, University of New South Wales, Sydney, Australia.

Davies, M. (2012). Can universities survive the digital revolution? *Quadrant Online*. Retrieved March 8, 2013, from http://www.quadrant.org.au/magazine/issue/2012/12/can-universities-survive-the-digital-revolution

Davies, A., Fidler, D., & Gorbis, M. (2011). *Future work skills 2020* (pp. 1–14): Institute for the Future for the University of Phoenix Research Institute. Retrieved September 26, 2016, from http://cdn.theatlantic.com/static/front/docs/sponsored/phoenix/future_work_skills_2020.pdf

Degerlia, A., Aytekinb, C., & Degerlic, B. (2015). Analyzing information technology status and networked readiness index in context of diffusion of innovations theory. *Procedia – Social and Behavioral Sciences, 195*, 1553–1562.

Edutech Wiki. (2013). *Learning analytics*. from Accessed 18 May at http://edutechwiki.unige.ch/en/Learning_analytics-Introduction

Hara, N. (2009). *Communities of practice: Fostering peer-to-peer learning and informal knowledge sharing in the workplace*. Berlin/Heidelberg, Germany: Spinger-Verlag.

Head, A., Van Hoeck, M., & Garson, D. (2015). Lifelong learning in the digital age: A content analysis of recent research on participation. *First Monday, 20* (2). Retrieved March 17, 2016, from http://firstmonday.org/ojs/index.php/fm/article/view/5857/4210. doi:10.5210/fm.v20i2.5857

Hil, R. (2012). *Whackademia: An insider's account of the troubled university*. Sydney, Australia: UNSW Press.

Hordern, J. (2015). Higher apprenticeships and the shaping of vocational knowledge. *Research in Post-compulsory Education, 20*(1), 17–34.

Johnson, L., Adams Becker, S., Estrada, V., & Freeman, A. (2014). *NMC horizon report: 2014 higher education*. Austin, TX: The New Media Consortium.

Kuh, G. D., Kinzie, J., Schuh, J. H., Whitt, E. J., et al. (2005). *Student success in college*. San Francisco: Wiley.

Leavy, M., & Rheinschmidt, S. (2010). How the ICCOC uses analytics to increase student success. *Educause Review Online*. Accessed 18 May 2014 at http://www.educause.edu/ero/article/how-iccoc-uses-analytics-increase-student-success.

Lyons, S., Schweitzer, L., & Ng, E. (2015). How have careers changed? An investigation of changing career patterns across four generations. *Journal of Managerial Psychology, 30*(1), 8–21.

Macmahon, C., & Huijser, H. (2015). 'We don't need no education?' Moving towards the integration of tertiary education and entrepreneurialship. In M. Harmes, H. Huijser, & P. A. Danaher (Eds.), *Myths in education, learning and teaching: Policies, practices and principles* (pp. 97–113). New York: Palgrave.

Marquardt, M. J., & Yeo, R. K. (2012). *Breakthrough problem solving with action learning: Concepts and cases*. Stanford, CA: Stanford University Press.

Mezirow, J. (2008). An overview on transformative learning. In P. Sutherland & J. Crowther (Eds.), *Lifelong learning: Concepts and contexts* (pp. 24–38). London/New York: Routledge.

Moust, J., & Roebertsen, H. (2010). Alternative instructional problem-based learning formats. In H. van Berkel, A. Scherpbier, H. Hillen, & C. van der Vleuten (Eds.), *Lessons from problem-based learning* (pp. 129–141). Oxford, UK: Oxford University Press.

Ng, P. T. (2004). The learning organisation and the innovative organisation. *Human Systems Management, 23*(2), 93–100.

Ortenblad, A. (2013). On differences between organizational learning and learning organization. *The Learning Organization, 8*(3), 125–133.

Paul, M. (2010). How to organise the transition from a traditional curriculum to a PBL curriculum. In H. van Berkel, A. Scherpbier, H. Hillen, & C. van der Vleuten (Eds.), *Lessons from problem-based Learning*. Oxford, UK: Oxford University Press.

Pennington, M., & Richards, J. (2016). Teacher identity in language teaching: Integrating personal, contextual, and professional factors. *RELC Journal, 1*, 19. doi:10.1177/0033688216631219.

Phillips, B. T. (2003). A four-level learning organisation benchmark model. *The Learning Organization, 10*(2), 98–105.

Retna, K. S. (2006). The learning organisation: A comparative study of Singapore organisations. *International Journal of Learning, 13*(1), 95–101.

Rogers, E. M. (2003). *Diffusion of Innovation* (5th ed.). New York: Free Press.

Sadler, E. (2015). *Innovation adoption and collective experimentation*. Retrieved March 18, 2016, from http://econ.as.nyu.edu/docs/IO/35809/SSRN_id2497798.pdf

Sahin, I. (2006). Detailed review of Rogers' diffusion of innovations theory and educational technology-related studies based on Rogers' theory. *The Turkish Online Journal of Educational Technology, 5*(2), 14–23.

Savin-Baden, M. (2014). Using problem-based learning: New constellations for the twenty first century. *Journal on Excellence in College Teaching, 25*(3&4), 197–219.

Secolsky, C., Denison, D., & Stake, R. (Eds.). (2012). *Handbook on measurement, assessment, and evaluation in higher education*. New York: Routledge.

Senge, P. M. (1990). *The fifth discipline: The art and practice of the learning organisation*. New York: Doubleday.

Siemens, G. (2012, 29 April–2 May). *Learning analytics: Envisioning a research discipline and a domain of practice*. Paper presented at the proceedings of the 2nd International conference on learning analytics and knowledge, Vancouver, BC.

Sipos, Y., Battisti, B., & Grimm, K. (2013). Achieving transformative sustainability learning: Engaging heads, hands and heart. *International Journal of Sustainability in Higher Education, 9*(1), 68–86.

Stalmeijer, R., Dolmans, D., Van Berkel, H., & Wolfhagen, I. (2010). Quality assurance. In H. van Berkel, A. Scherpbier, H. Hillen, & C. Van Der Vleuten (Eds.), *Lessons from problem-based learning* (pp. 157–166). Oxford, UK: Oxford University Press.

Tam, M. (2001). Measuring quality and performance in higher education. *Quality in Higher Education, 7*(1), 47–54.

Taylor, E. W. (2008). Transformative learning theory. *New Directions for Adult and Continuing Education, 119,* 5–15.

Thomas, K., & Allen, S. (2006). The learning organisation: A meta-analysis of themes in literature. *The Learning Organization, 13*(2), 123–139.

Wenger, E. (2009). *Communities of practice: A brief introduction.* Accessed 18 May 2014 at http://www.ewenger.com/theory/

West, D., Huijser, H., Heath, D., Lizzio, A., Toohey, D., & Miles, C. (2015). Higher education teachers' experiences with learning analytics in relation to student retention. In T. Reiners, B. R. von Konsky, D. Gibson, V. Chang, L. Irving & K. Clarke (Eds.), *Globally connected, digitally enabled: Proceedings of the ascilite 2015 Conference* (pp. 296–307). Perth, 29 November–2 December.

Wolfhagen, I., & Scherpbier, A. (2010). Curriculum governance. In H. van Berkel, A. Scherpbier, H. Hillen, & C. Van Der Vleuten (Eds.), *Lessons from problem-based learning* (pp. 151–156). Oxford, UK: Oxford University Press.

Xiong, H., Payne, D., & Kinsella, S. (2015). Peer effects in the diffusion of innovations: Theory and simulation. *Social Science Research Network.* Retrieved March 18, 2016, from http://ssrn.com/abstract=2606726. doi:10.2139/ssrn.2606726

Chapter 9
Agile PBL Research: Developing a Sustainable Research and Scholarship Agenda

Introduction

Traditionally, there has been, and continues to be, a huge dichotomy in the university between research on the one hand and teaching on the other. Barnett (2016) calls this dialectic of function, one of seven forms of dialectic that a university faces. Universities have seen themselves primarily as research institutions, and teaching has always played second fiddle. This is partly due to the status awarded to research in comparison to teaching. Furthermore, and related to this, funding has always been intimately tied to research output. The result of all this is that research is a much more profitable pursuit for those in search of career advancement and promotion than teaching, despite considerable efforts to change this. Even within research, educational research has had a struggle to gain recognition as a legitimate field of research, especially when it comes to applied educational research. This is exemplified at Maastricht University where 'after a prolonged and heated debate with opponents who viewed education as nothing more than a service, academic status was [finally] granted to the Department of Educational Development and Research in 1977' (Van Der Vleuten, Domans, & van Merrienboer, 2010, p. 219). However, that status is never guaranteed and needs to be reasserted at regular intervals.

The research versus teaching dichotomy has significant implications for the implementation of an agile PBL and therefore needs to be taken into account and addressed in a systemic way. A key characteristic of an agile PBL as we have outlined in this book is that the curriculum is continuously renewed and updated and thus never finalised. In this context, evaluation and data gathering about the efficacy of agile PBL becomes vital, and this needs to be engaged in by everyone who is involved in it, including teachers, industry representatives and, especially, the students (Healey, Flint, & Harrington, 2014). In other words, the lines between teacher and researcher, as well as between teacher and student and even between employer and employee, are increasingly (and deliberately) being blurred within an agile PBL ecology for learning. This impacts on people's professional identities, which means

© Springer Science+Business Media Singapore 2017
M.Y.C.A. Kek, H. Huijser, *Problem-based Learning into the Future*,
DOI 10.1007/978-981-10-2454-2_9

that in most cases it will require a significant change management process. However, integrating research and scholarship into the teaching, learning and evaluation cycle will create significant 'carrots' in the form of a growth in individual research output and therefore individual career advancement (see also Chap. 6). The broad field called the scholarship of teaching and learning has been concerned with raising the status of teaching by linking it to a research and scholarship agenda for more than two decades now (Boyer, 1990; Hutchings, Huber, & Ciccone, 2011; Prosser, 2008; Shulman, 1987), with considerable success. In this chapter we will therefore draw extensively on the literature and models proposed within this field.

Importantly though, within an agile PBL ecology for learning, we are not content to focus purely on the scholarship of learning and teaching. Instead, we are concerned with extending the research and scholarship agenda to explicitly include educational innovation. Furthermore, technological advances are increasingly changing the higher education context (Bradwell, 2009; Davies, 2012; Huijser, 2008) and indeed the conceptualisation of knowledge itself, which in turn has an impact on the ways in which research and teaching are defined. As Benson and Brack (2009) note:

> Current advances in learning technologies offer unprecedented opportunities for collaborative engagement, access to information, interaction with content, and individual empowerment which have potential to raise questions about the nature of scholarship that may challenge existing beliefs and values, and assumptions about knowledge. (p. 74)

In other words, the nature of knowledge itself is changing: the way it is accessed, digested, consumed, engaged with and disseminated. This in turn has an inevitable impact on teaching and learning, and it has created the possibility, and indeed the practice, of ubiquitous learning (Cope & Kalantzis, 2009). As we have argued throughout this book, it is important that we engage with this seismic shift and that we develop a curriculum and pedagogy that is agile and adaptive enough to stay relevant and is continuously evaluated and improved. As always, the focus is on the outcomes of developing knowledges, skills, dispositions and attributes that are needed to function successfully, and with sufficient agency, in the twenty-first century. The research and scholarship agenda that we outline in this chapter is a collaborative pursuit and involves all stakeholders, including teachers, employers and students, in other words, all systems of an agile PBL ecology for learning. In the twenty-first century, research is a fundamental part of everything we do, which is why research and scholarship are fully integrated in an agile PBL curriculum.

Revisiting the Scholarship of Teaching and Learning (SoTL)

Boyer's SoTL

In his seminal work on the scholarship of teaching and learning, Boyer (1990) argued that the activity of universities should be reconceptualised. He identified four distinct but interdependent and interrelated forms of scholarship (cited in Laksov, Mcgrath, & Silen, 2010, p. 4):

1. Discovery – Can be equated with research, where we strive to discover new knowledge. This is what is sometimes called 'pure' or 'fundamental' research (Van Der Vleuten et al., 2010) and is separated from application-oriented research (or scholarship). We can see the jostling for position that is inherent in the terminology around this and the implied hierarchy of importance (Brew, 2006).

2. Integration – Involves relating new discovery to what we already know in practice. Of course this becomes more complex in an agile PBL context, as the disciplinary and university boundaries become increasingly blurred.

3. Engagement – This was initially called 'application', but was changed by Boyer into engagement, because it involves something more than just application; it involves both the application and use of new knowledge, 'so that a propulsive movement of the search for new discoveries and new fields of application is created' (Laksov et al., 2010, p. 4). This is interesting from our point of view, as it has an explicit 'future thinking' element to it. Moreover, it can be neatly aligned with the outcome of entrepreneurial skills and attitudes, which are key elements of an agile PBL. In other words, 'engagement' refers to both current and future applications of new knowledge and indeed potential future research agendas.

4. Teaching – This refers to the act of teaching, and the engagement part ensures an informed and conscious practice as an agile PBL teacher and an agile PBL student or, in an agile PBL ecology for learning, a combination of evidence-based and reflective practices.

Boyer thus made an attempt to elevate the status of teaching in proportion to research, which, as noted above, has historically been on an unequal footing. The important shift here is from one in which teaching is seen as an isolated phenomenon, whereby the teacher is solely responsible for planning, conducting and evaluating teaching, to a situation that includes communication and dialogue between teachers and teachers, between teachers and students, between teachers and management and between teachers and support staff (Laksov et al., 2010). We can add partners such as employers outside the university to that mix as well, and of course we have already discussed the desirability of team teaching and assessing to address interdisciplinary problems.

Others have built on Boyer's work (e.g. Kreber, 2001; Trigwell, Martin, Benjamin, & Prosser, 2000). For Shulman (2000), there are three broad rationales for advocating a serious investment in the scholarship of teaching and learning: professionalism, pragmatism and policy (the three Ps of SoTL).

Professionalism

With regard to professionalism, Shulman (2000) argues that each of us is a member of at least two professions – that of our discipline and that of our profession as an educator:

> In both of these intersecting domains, we bear the responsibilities of scholars – to discover, to connect, to apply and to teach. As scholars, we take on the obligation to add to the core of understanding, scepticism, method and critique that defines our fields and their ever-changing borders. (p. 49)

Of course in an agile PBL ecology for learning, again, the fields and borders become even more blurred than what Shulman imagined here. But the important point is that he is talking about two interconnected activities: (1) scholarly teaching and (2) the scholarship of teaching.

Scholarly teaching is 'teaching that is well grounded in the sources and resources appropriate to the field. It reflects a thoughtful selection and integration of ideas and examples, and well-designed strategies of course design, development, transmission, interaction, and assessment' (Shulman, 2000, p. 50). There is an emphasis here on the scholarship of a particular discipline, how that particular discipline should be taught and what the appropriate resources would be. Again, this becomes more complex in a radically interdisciplinary context. Essentially however, this is about professional currency and keeping up to date with what's happening in your field or discipline (Considine, 2010). In a twenty-first-century context, this may be more effectively achieved by teams (rather than individuals), and if such teams are interdisciplinary, they will need to consider applications across disciplines, which would be a value add because it would work towards the development of an important twenty-first-century skill.

Shulman's (2000, p. 50) second activity is the scholarship of teaching. 'We develop a scholarship of teaching when our work as teachers becomes public, peer-reviewed and critiqued, and exchanged with other members of our professional communities so they, in turn, can build on our work'. This is beginning to sound a lot like *research* in the traditional sense, but there are different degrees to it. In this case, it also includes reflective practice, if such practice means that you collect evidence and data about your teaching and that you subsequently use that data to publish articles about your practice in scholarly journals or academic books. Interestingly, some researchers and research administrators, particularly in the 'hard' sciences, dismiss this type of scholarship as 'show and tell' or 'soft' research, rather than 'pure' or 'fundamental' research, which again reinforces the strength of the dichotomy between 'research' and 'teaching'. More recently, some learning and teaching journals have begun to recognise the importance of this type of scholarship by creating space in their journal for 'practice reports' (Mcintyre, Todd, Huijser, & Tehan, 2010), which are scholarly papers, based on reflective practice. They are often characterised by writing teams, and mentoring in a scholarly and professional community is an important part of such practice. This would suit an agile PBL ecology perfectly, as students could be involved in the process and mentored into developing output for public scrutiny (Gibbs, 2014; Laksov et al., 2010, p. 4). Furthermore, it would not need to be restricted to written output, but could include various forms of digital media where appropriate, sometimes referred to as alternative dissemination (O'Sullivan, 2009).

Pragmatism

Shulman's (2000) second rationale is pragmatism, because he is concerned that scholarship has a practical application and should not be purely focused on research output, as 'pure' research tends to be:

> By engaging in purposive reflection, documentation, assessment and analysis of teaching and learning, and doing so in a more public and accessible manner, we not only support the improvement of our own teaching. We raise the likelihood that our work is transparent to our colleagues who design and instruct many of the same students in the same or related programs. (p. 50)

Certainly this would gain even more currency in an agile PBL context, where interdisciplinary team teaching is an integral part of the process (Martyn, Terwijn, Kek, & Huijser, 2014). Team teaching itself already increases the likelihood of increased transparency between different teachers, but systematically implementing engagement in purposive reflection as a team, and documented assessment and evaluation of practice will align nicely with a continuous improvement and innovation agenda. Indeed, as we have noted throughout this book, while programs may have an integrity that is constant, the courses or units within are fluid and subject to perpetual change, as they seek to remain relevant in fast-changing contexts. Furthermore, the problems that students address 'on location' in various workplaces create many more variables than in the average classroom and should thus be rigorously and continuously evaluated. A 'pragmatic' scholarship agenda can serve a key role in this pursuit of developing a sustainable research and scholarship of teaching and learning agenda.

Policy

With regard to policy, Shulman's third P, the need to be accountable to external auditors and accrediting agencies has created an increasing need for the university to show 'measurable' outcomes (or at least outputs). To put it simply, engaging in this process is a matter of survival for the university, rather than a choice. The best engagement strategy is therefore to take some control over the process itself, and in particular taking charge of what is being measured and how it is being measured. Shulman (2000, p. 52) warns in this respect against metrics being employed 'because of convenience or economy of use, rather than because they serve as authentic proxies for the learning and development we seek to foster'. More recently, debates around applications of learning analytics are also beginning to address these concerns (Gasevic, Dawson, & Siemens, 2015; West et al., 2015). Applying learning analytics *for* learning is a particular problem when it comes to agile PBL, because it is subject to continuous change and adaptation. In addition, 'economy of use' does not take account of the 'messiness' involved in agile PBL, for example, the many intangible factors that have a major impact but cannot be easily measured. As Shulman suggests, one way of taking some control over the process is to demand an input into what indicators should be used to measure outcomes:

> They [indicators to measure the outcomes of higher education] should be the result of carefully conceptualised, designed and deployed studies of teaching and learning in each of our fields, conducted by scholars qualified to pursue them. This kind of work cries out for a vigorous scholarship of teaching and learning engaged by discipline and field-specific scholars of teaching (p. 52)

or, in our case, engaged by interdisciplinary (and cross-organisational) teams of agile PBL teachers, internal staff, partners outside the university and potentially students. More recently, and in response to the scholarship and research opportunities that data (and/or learning) analytics provide, Laurillard (2014, para 16) has made a similar point about teachers taking control of the agenda:

> Big data could improve teaching, but not without educators taking control of this extraordinary methodological gift. At present the field is being driven almost entirely by technology professionals who are not educators and have never taught online. Instead, we could be recruiting all lecturers everywhere to collaborate and generate their own large-scale data collection and analysis. Then big data could really make a difference.

Like Shulman however, Laurillard's argument suggests a functional concern for dealing with administrative impositions and a need to take control over the measures and indicators of teaching and learning outcomes, in terms of how the data is collected, what data is collected, how the data is being interpreted and what that data is being used for as a measurement (Knight, Buckingham Shum, & Littleton, 2014; West et al., 2015).

Trigwell and Shale's Model of Scholarship of Teaching

Rather than providing a rationale for the scholarship of teaching and learning however, as Shulman does, Trigwell and Shale (2004, p. 524) come from a different angle and outline three core aims:

- It should be a means through which the status of teaching may be raised.
- It should be a means through which teachers may come to teach more knowledgeably.
- It should provide a means through which the quality of teaching may be assessed.

This underlies a key overriding point, which is about students' experiences of university learning. 'Ultimately, it is that experience that a good conception of scholarship of teaching must serve to enhance' (Trigwell & Shale, 2004, p. 524). The point here is that different aims and objectives are often presented when it comes to the scholarship of teaching and learning. Shulman's approach, as outlined above, is functional and pragmatic and as a result focused to a large extent on universities' administrative requirements and academics' career development. These are important considerations, but Trigwell and Shale (p. 527) firmly shift the focus to students and their learning experiences and therefore by extension to learning outcomes: 'excellence in teaching discourse and excellence in the teaching that enables students to learn are two different things. If all that the scholarship of teaching achieved was greater sophistication in the ways we talk about teaching, it would have failed in its fundamental aims'. So the question then becomes: do we conduct scholarship of teaching and learning to improve the teaching and the learning outcomes of our students? Or do we conduct scholarship of teaching and learning to improve our professional standing and thereby advance our careers, in a similar way that 'pure' research does? Or can there be a productive combination of the two?

To answer those questions, we need to first take a step back and consider some conceptualisations of the scholarship of teaching and learning. Trigwell and Shale (2004, p. 525) draw on Kreber's (2001) work who identifies four differing conceptualisations:

- The process by which teachers conduct and publish research
- Scholarship of teaching as teaching excellence
- Scholarly processes in which teachers make use of the literature of teaching and learning to inform their own practice
- A combination of the first three, but explicitly includes one or more essential new scholarly elements, such as reflection or communication

In terms of the questions posed above and like Shulman (2000), Trigwell and Shale (2004) make an important distinction between 'scholarly' activity and 'scholarship' as a product. The latter refers to the first conceptualisation and is expressed in artefacts such as journal publications, while the former refers to conceptualisations two and three and is about a type of teaching practice that draws upon educational publications and is thus evidence based. The fourth conceptualisation provides a potential answer to the question about whether 'scholarly' activity and 'scholarship' as a product can be combined. In other words, it is possible to engage in both, at the same time, but only if the right balance is struck. If it is not, then there is a lot of scope to revert back to the unproductive research versus teaching binary referred to above, in which scholarship outcomes (artefacts) become the key focus, rather than teaching excellence.

With regard to striking the right balance, Trigwell and Shale (2004, p. 529) use the term 'pedagogic resonance', which they define as 'the bridge between teacher knowledge and student learning'. This is the key point for them and one which is very interesting from an agile PBL perspective. Their rationale is as follows:

> If we are interested in making knowledge in teaching [rather than knowledge about teaching] the substance of the scholarship of teaching (that is, defining as scholarship, the public demonstration of the knowledgeable activity that leads to learning), then our students and their experiences of our teaching constitute a crucial part of the critical scrutiny that such scholarship requires. If the knowledgeable activity of teaching were to be what we take to be the basis of our scholarship, the disciplinary community would include not only other teachers but also our students – not just as objects but as connoisseurs, and even 'legitimate peripheral participants'. (Trigwell & Shale, 2004, p. 528)

This is attractive from our point of view, because it blurs the lines between teachers and students, and indeed allows us to see such roles as being positioned on a continuum, whereby the ultimate objective is to move students into positions of independence and towards adopting the roles of peers and collaborators. Indeed, we would take this even a step further and suggest that students should be legitimate participants (rather than peripheral ones) in an authentic scholarship agenda as soon as possible and of course as long as it is appropriate. Importantly, this should not be mistaken as devaluing the role of the teacher, as the whole enterprise actually relies on the sound, evidence-based and skilled judgement of the teacher. In other words, the extent to which students are involved in authentic scholarship should not be a dogmatic decision, but a carefully evaluated one, and one based on scholarship and team discussion about the agile PBL ecology for learning (see Chap. 2), designing for the next generations of learners (see Chap. 3), interdisciplinarity and authentic problem design (see Chap. 4), authentic assessment (see Chap. 5) and mattering environments to support students and staff (see Chaps. 6 and 7). In this way, reflective practice can be fully integrated from an agile PBL perspective and thereby becomes an integral part of every student's way-of-being, which in turn will lead to students with strong critical (self-)reflection and adaptive skills, while they learn at the same time to be subjected to peer review and critique. Both are important twenty-first-century skills and dispositions.

Trigwell and Shale's (2004, p. 530) scholarship of teaching model has three main components that overlap to some extent:

1. Knowledge – which includes knowledge of discipline, knowledge of teaching/learning, conceptions of teaching/learning and knowledge of context
2. Practice – which includes teaching, evaluation/investigation, reflection, communication and learning
3. Outcome – which includes student learning, documentation, teacher learning and teacher satisfaction

For our purposes here, there are two very attractive elements within this model. Firstly, there is an explicit recognition of 'collaborative engagement together, through the act of teaching, [which is] the act of academic engagement in deliberate, collaborative meaning making with students' (Trigwell & Shale, 2004, p. 530). This is contained in the Practice part of the model, and the actions contained in that part of the model are thus not meant to be applied to individual teachers working in isolation, but rather to interdisciplinary teaching teams in collaboration with students and employers and, to add to the complexity of an agile PBL ecology for learning, other wider university teams (teachers and professional staff) that share responsibility in creating a mattering environment for students (Kuh, Kinzie, Schuh, Whitt, & Associates, 2005; Museus & Jayakumar, 2012).

The second attractive element relates to the Outcome part and includes the outcomes and artefacts of collaboration, 'including both students' and teachers' learning, the documentation that constitutes artefacts of the teaching act, such as course outlines, evaluation results, investigation results, etc., and teacher satisfaction. All contribute to what might be made available for public scrutiny' (Trigwell & Shale, 2004, p. 530). Trigwell and Shale do not explicitly include academic publications in the 'outcome' section of their model, but of course they could be part of the outcomes, and they could also be collaborative efforts between teachers and students and professional staff inside the university such as academic advisors in learning centres; educational developers, marketing professionals and student services staff; and partners outside the university such as employers and parents of students. Within an agile PBL ecology for learning, artefacts can of course (and ideally *should* as much as possible) include authentic products created such as engineering prototypes, reports and technical and non-technical solutions.

Furthermore, the 'etc.' part of their outcomes is also increasingly likely to include different types of media (e.g. videos shared on YouTube or Vimeo), as well as social media channels like Facebook groups or Twitter feeds, which have a more immediate and perpetual character, but which nevertheless produce data that can be used for evaluative purposes. To reiterate Benson and Brack's (2009, p. 78) important point:

> Recent developments in e-learning and teaching which place emphasis on aspects of social engagement and learner control, and appear to go beyond current understandings of democracy in the classroom, challenge assumptions about the role and control of teachers, and of the control of knowledge. They also challenge a range of other assumptions which include: the way scholarly work becomes public, peer-reviewed, critiqued and exchanged; the ownership of the work; and the criteria used to judge its quality.

We are only at the very beginning of this process of change, but the changes are nevertheless rapid and relentless. In many ways the traditional model of published peer-reviewed output is being superseded by a different and much more immediate form of peer review in a plethora of online, and increasingly mobile, spaces (Thelwall & Kousha, 2014, 2015). It is important that we engage with these changes in an agile PBL ecology, without losing the value of a more sustained and focused peer review process, which traditionally constitutes an important element of the scholarship and quality agenda. Again, this is not an either/or dilemma, but rather a fluid movement that ensures currency at all times but at the same time incorporates and preserves valuable elements of traditional academic practice, which is still prevalent in much of the higher education sector.

Trigwell and Shale's (2004) model of the scholarship of teaching is based on a realisation that the line between teachers and students has hitherto been too firmly drawn. 'Students do not appear as partners in learning. They do not appear as neophyte scholars in the community. They do not appear as critics or connoisseurs of teaching. When they do appear it is as objects of concern, objects of analysis, or presumptively passive consumers' (Trigwell & Shale, 2004, p. 534). In other words, they see teaching as an activity 'that emerges in collaboration with students as *partners* in learning' (p. 534, original emphasis). Thus, this serves an agile PBL research and scholarship agenda perfectly, and indeed agile PBL provides clear opportunities for collaborative partnerships between teachers and students, but also between teachers and employers, between teachers and professional staff and between teachers, professional staff, employers and students, in whatever combination is appropriate at the time. These need to be relationships based on trust and respect for the prior knowledge that each brings to the table. As noted, this can be imagined as a 'feasible utopia' (Barnett, 2013) as an agile PBL ecology for learning, but the 'ducks need to be aligned' as every ecology is potentially fragile.

Laksov, McGrath and Silen's Model of Teaching and Learning

Laksov et al. (2010) provide us with another scholarship of teaching and learning model that they have adapted from D'Andrea and Gosling (2005). Their model is much more stripped down than Trigwell and Shale's (2004) and shows a continuum within a university context, which leads from teaching to educational development, to the scholarship of teaching and learning, to educational research and ultimately to research itself. It thus keeps the dichotomy between teaching and research in place to some extent, but it allows for considerable movement between the two, with the scholarship of teaching and learning wedged between educational development and educational research. However, the value for our purposes lies in their treatment of the model and how they describe the implications and practical application of it. They describe the scholarship of teaching and learning (SoTL) as including the following elements:

- Theoretical knowledge of teaching and learning
- Skill to teach including a variety of different methods
- Experience of teaching and learning at different levels
- A deliberate approach to learning and knowledge
- An interest in education
- Content knowledge, or knowledge of the subject that students should learn [otherwise referred to as discipline knowledge]
- Pedagogical content knowledge, i.e. knowledge of how students can best learn a particular topic (Laksov et al., 2010, p. 6)

This is still rather teacher centred, as it assumes that the teacher is responsible for all of it, and there is no mention of a collaborative partnership with students. However, Laksov et al. (2010, p. 7) do mention collaboration explicitly when they usefully outline the ways in which SoTL becomes visible:

- Teaching is performed consciously at different levels – teaching is not purely based on intuition, but is designed and performed based on existing evidence.
- Learning and teaching is examined at different levels – this refers both to the examination of existing research and scholarship on a conceptual level and to the evaluation of teacher's own practice.
- Changes are applied and teaching is developed at different levels – the outcomes of the above examinations are applied to the next cycle of course development and teaching practice.
- Experiences of teaching and learning are published – the data gathered during the evaluations are written up in publishable form and thereby subjected to public scrutiny and peer review.
- Collaborations are established between teachers, students and at a system level – this is where collaborations are mentioned, but they are not particularly explicit about how to achieve such collaborations or indeed what kind of collaborations they are referring to.

In relation to the last point, the system level element, even if they do not elaborate on it, is important, as it suggests that some of these practices have to be very consciously and systematically implemented if they are to lead to overall sustainable practice (Chap. 8). This may take the form of time and space being created to allow for SoTL and, for productive collaboration, for example, to create a mattering environment to support students in agile PBL programs and university life in general (see Chap. 6) as well as staff (see Chap. 7). It may also be systematically locked in the form of various 'carrots' such as teaching awards, but also scholarship awards, where examples of excellence in scholarship (which may either be witnessed in terms of learning outcomes or in terms of publication outcomes) are celebrated. There is no stronger incentive than seeing your peers being celebrated for a practice that you could be involved in as well. In terms of the scholarship awards, these should of course include collaborations, which means that students and employers as well as professional staff in the institution would be eligible for these as well in an agile PBL ecology for learning.

Educational Research

When it comes to the scholarship of teaching and learning, there is definitely a sense of immediacy and practical application about it. In other words, it is an important part of continuous improvement and evidence-based practice. We have already outlined the importance of such practice in an agile PBL ecology for learning. However, this focus on immediacy should not become a limiting factor in terms of the evidence base. This applies to the ways in which scholarship is applied to teaching, but also to research practice that is focused on the future. A wider (educational) research agenda should therefore be incorporated into, and blended with, the scholarship of teaching and learning agenda. Part of this agenda would be a focus on innovation and development, as well as research into entrepreneurial opportunities (Macmahon & Huijser, 2015). The latter would apply to both students and professional staff inside the university and partners outside the university or in some cases to all. An explicit research agenda not only allows for a focus on the future, but if this agenda is integrated into the curriculum, it also inculcates students with a 'researcherly' disposition (similar to a scholarly disposition).

At Maastricht University (a PBL institution), the Faculty of Health, Medicine and Life Sciences has established a systematic approach to embedding educational research into its everyday practice. Van der Vleuten et al. (2010) identify what they call two organisational conditions – academic status for educationalists and a recognised research program – as having been critical for education research in their institution. This reinforces our point above about the need for a systematic approach to research and scholarship, including a systematic approach to creating space and time for it, as well as recognising it as a valuable and therefore valued activity. The research program in Van der Vleuten et al.'s (p. 219) case study pursues the following goals:

- To investigate the nature of human learning and learning environments
- To collect scientific evidence for health professions education
- To drive educational innovation
- To educate staff in education research

From the first point, we can see that this is a broader research agenda than scholarship of teaching and learning agendas usually are, and there is a broader research focus that zooms in on the broader idea of human learning and learning environments, which coincides with agile PBL ecology for learning. The data collected in this way would inform the learning and teaching design, which would then be further evaluated and redesigned, based on the scholarship agenda, much like Laksov et al.'s (2010) continuum. To make this more concrete, the research agenda would result in evidence-based ideas about what makes for an effective learning environment in the twenty-first century and how this changes over time. This would then be used to inform appropriate agile PBL problems, assessments, teaching and continuous improvement initiatives. Again, we are using *agile* PBL in a broad and 'fluid' sense because it needs to be responsive to a changing evidence base and emerging data and issues that the research agenda provides over time. This is not simply a reactive process, but also very much a proactive and future-oriented one. For example, if we have identified (based on available research) that our graduates need 'particular' skills to function in the twenty-first century (Davies, Fidler, & Gorbis, 2011), then our institutional research agenda should, for example, focus on the best ways to stimulate these 'particular' skills. This would then in turn inform the design of problems in a PBL ecology for learning, as well as the circumstances under which such problems would be addressed, for example, in a classroom or in a workplace (Edwards, 2015), or a combination thereof.

The second goal refers to educational research that is specifically tailored to particular disciplines, in Van Der Vleuten et al.'s (2010) case, the health professions. We have already discussed the need to go beyond disciplinary silos in earlier chapters (e.g. Chap. 4), so in agile PBL, the research focus should not purely be on individual disciplines, but rather should have an inbuilt focus on interdisciplinarity and on problems that require interdisciplinary approaches in order to address them successfully. Much like the interdisciplinary teaching teams we have been advocating, the research agenda should also be characterised by interdisciplinary research teams. To reiterate and to allay fears of 'watering down' disciplinary strength, this does not mean that we advocate doing away with disciplines altogether. Far from it, we recognise the legacy and the continuing importance of discipline-based specialisations. However, evidence increasingly suggests that most problems in the twenty-first century require a multidisciplinary approach (Mulderig, Macan, Hendricks, & Noel, 2014) and therefore an ability to work across disciplines or at the very least an ability to work in interdisciplinary teams. Universities have long had a silo mentality when it comes to disciplinary research, and this attitude continues to reverberate across the sector despite rhetoric to the contrary. For example, in our case study here, those in the health professions increasingly need to work in teams that combine, for example, business, entrepreneurial, marketing and technological expertise, rather than being purely focused on health and medicine, while another 'silo' takes care of another bit, and never the twain shall meet. Working across those tasks with a team that is used to discussing each other's roles and mutually reinforcing each other's skills is much more effective, and it is thus part of the research agenda to explore how such skills are most likely to develop, without undermining the development of discipline-specific expertise.

The third goal, research that drives educational innovation, is central to a research agenda in an agile PBL ecology for learning. In other words, in an agile PBL curriculum, nothing is taught in the same way twice, which again does not mean that there are no disciplinary fundamentals that are not part of the curriculum. However, it means that the way they are taught differs with every iteration of a course, because the problem that students need to address (in interdisciplinary teams) is different every time. A research agenda that focuses on educational innovation is therefore crucial, because agile PBL is about continuous innovation. This works both on the level of the curriculum and the teaching agenda itself, but importantly, it also applies to the level of teaching for innovation. In other words, agile PBL is not content to simply teach what is and what should be; rather, it has a strong focus on instilling in students a focus on what could be or perhaps a focus on a 'feasible utopia' (Barnett, 2013). This involves skills and dispositions that include critical thinking, entrepreneurialism (Oosterbeek, Van Praag, & Ijsselstein, 2010), social entrepreneurialism and future thinking (among others). All of these therefore need to be an integral part of the research agenda, and they need to be present in the teaching and learning context, for example, integrated in an agile PBL problem. This goal therefore exemplifies the nexus between research, scholarship, teaching and learning, as well as the merging of roles between researchers, teachers, employers and students. This is what we are talking about when we refer to the need to recognise and value the fluidity of siloed disciplinary boundaries and the need for agility in an agile PBL ecology for learning.

The final goal, educating staff in educational research, is a crucial element in the research agenda, as it is part of the overall agenda of change that is required in an agile PBL ecology for learning. In the current university climate, there are voices that advocate a more rigid boundary between researchers and teachers (Matchett, 2012; Probert, 2014), but we argue strongly that research, scholarship, teaching and learning are all part of a shared teaching and learning context and should not be separated. Quite the opposite, we argue throughout this book that the boundaries between systems are porous and should allow for liquid knowledge to flow in, out and in between. And that means interdisciplinary teams require a combination of skills, which includes research skills and design based on scholarship. In our case here, this applies to an agile university context, but we would argue that it applies to any disciplinary context, as there are no disciplines that exist in isolation, and if there are, they would likely benefit from some interdisciplinary contact. To return to Van der Vleuten et al.'s (2010) final goal, educating staff in educational research is therefore a very important part of an agile PBL ecology for learning and should be structurally built into each academic's workload and career progression pathways.

In the students' case, structurally build research skills in the agile PBL curriculum and have students partner as coresearchers in research.

From Theory to Practice

If we consider Laksov et al.'s model and continuum of teaching through to research, with the scholarship of teaching and learning somewhere in the middle, then this raises an urgent question: who is going to do what, and when? In other words, in practice, many academics feel devalued, overworked and demoralised enough as it is (Hil, 2012). How are we going to make them engage with agile PBL that requires them to engage in a number of roles and tasks that are different from the traditional teaching paradigm, as discussed in Chap. 7, and on top of that require them to engage in the scholarship of teaching and learning and in the university's research agenda?

The answers (and they are multiple) are not simple, but they do relate to instilling a sense of excitement and a sense of involvement in something revolutionary (a 'feasible utopia') and in something that has the potential to have a huge impact on the way we approach the 'business of educating students'. The answers relate to a number of different factors:

- Change management in a way that provides a certain amount of control to staff and a feeling that they matter, leading to a sense of ownership among staff. This means that one cannot simply impose the radical changes required for agile PBL to work, without involving staff in the process from the very beginning.
- Related to the first point is the importance of creating space and time for staff to engage in continuous experimentation, assessment, evaluation and research, without feeling completely overwhelmed and going to ground as a result. We discussed the use of communities of practice and action learning groups in this respect in Chap. 8, and these communities of practice and action learning groups can be a similarly important part of a sustainable research and scholarship agenda.
- Build into the university's human resource policy and process to create spaces for staff (academic and nonacademic) to take 'time out' from the university to the macro-system as sabbaticals or industry/professional internships for an extended period of time. Engagement in these out-of-university spaces can only renew staff's thinking, feeling and doing and help the university to sustain research and scholarship agenda.
- As part of the research agenda, it is important to provide staff with choices in what research special interest groups to engage with, or indeed which special interest group they would want to establish. In principle, there should be no limits to what can be included here, as long as the groups themselves can convincingly justify their need of existence and contribute to a sustainable and innovative research process and outcomes.

- Apart from time and space (in terms of workload), these action learning groups and communities of practice need incentives to stimulate particular outcomes. It is therefore a good idea to structurally build in potential (and competitive) rewards based on performance and outcomes (rather than outputs). Rewards can, for example, take the form of actual staff awards for performance, but can also include performance-based travel stipends for research and scholarship purposes.
- Incentives can include the research and scholarship outputs themselves, in the form of journal articles, book chapters, video presentations and so on. If an action learning group or community of practice can convincingly argue that they will produce a big research or scholarship outcome and/or product, if given focused development time, an incentive can be a funded writing retreat for that group (obviously based on track record and merit) (Barrett & Moore, 2011).
- Rather than a traditional model of staff professional learning, staff's expertise is recognised and utilised by other communities of practice and action learning groups. This not only allows staff to further develop their own expertise, but it is also a way of valuing prior skills, knowledge and expertise, which can be a strong motivator.

These are just some ideas around a radically changed practice model. However, the strongest incentive by far is that teaching in an agile PBL ecology for learning becomes a motivating and exciting practice in itself, and research and scholarship are literally woven through the curriculum. Everyone is involved in research, scholarship, design, teaching and learning, and this has the potential to remove the traditional dichotomy between teaching and research and create a more productive space where these different areas flow into and interact with each more seamlessly.

Van der Vleuten et al. (2010, p. 222) identify the central success factor for their research program as being that 'all staff members involved in education research also participate in educational development and teaching activities. Actual problems encountered in educational practice are often starting points for research'. Again, we can add students to research action learning groups and communities of practice, as well as employers and professional staff from the related systems of the agile PBL ecology for learning, and this would only diversify the input, thereby potentially strengthening the outcomes. In addition to the practical suggestions here, action learning groups and communities of practice themselves should have input in what kind of incentives would have a stimulating effect on their own practice, as a sense of ownership, and a level of control over the agenda is vital if any of this is to come off the ground. If this model works as it is envisaged, new initiatives and innovations will be generated at the grassroots, and senior management will only need to provide the broad boundaries and strategic directions or in short operate as facilitator.

Conclusion

We began this chapter by identifying a strong and lingering dichotomy between research and teaching, and throughout this chapter, we have argued what we have argued throughout this book: that the strict disciplinary and activity boundaries that characterise university structures and practice are no longer in step with what is needed in the twenty-first century when they move out of the university. We have argued that graduates need different skills that we do not necessarily teach in traditional university classrooms (including more traditional PBL-based classrooms). We have also argued that the nature of knowledge itself, and therefore the nature of all knowledge-related activities, such as teaching and learning, as well as research and scholarship, is changing and requires different approaches from the ones that have been in place for hundreds of years. This does not mean that we no longer value rigour or disciplinary specialisations; quite the contrary, we probably need them more than ever. However, it does mean that the knowledge environment has changed radically and that we have to respond to those changes and continue to respond to them if we are to stay relevant and if we are to have an ongoing impact on the agenda for continuous change in the twenty-first century. Most importantly, we have to be proactive in our responses to these changes if we want our students to be in a powerful position to engage with and direct the agendas for the twenty-first century. To do so, they need to be research and scholarship literate and involved in an agile research and scholarship agenda, and the same applies to their teachers and partners outside the university. So while research and scholarship are situated in the exo-system in the agile PBL ecology for learning, it should flow in and out, through all other systems through its porous boundaries, thereby informing, and being informed by, all other parts of the ecology.

References

Barnett, R. (2013). *Imagining the university*. Abingdon, UK: Routledge.

Barnett, R. (2016). *Understanding the university: Institution, idea, and possibilities*. Abingdon, UK: Routledge.

Barrett, T., & Moore, S. (2011). Students maximising the potential of the problem-based learning tutorial. In T. Barrett & S. Moore (Eds.), *New approaches to problem-based learning: Revitalising your practice in higher education* (pp. 115–129). Milton Park, UK: Routledge.

Benson, R., & Brack, C. (2009). Developing the scholarship of teaching: What is the role of e-teaching and learning? *Teaching in Higher Education, 14*(1), 71–80.

Boyer, E. L. (1990). *Scholarship reconsidered: Priorities of the professoriate*. Princeton, NJ: Carniege Foundation for the Advancement of Teaching.

Bradwell, P. (2009). *The edgeless university: Why higher education must embrace technology*. London: Demos.

Brew, A. (2006). *Research and teaching: Beyond the divide*. Houndmills, UK: Palgrave Macmillan.

Considine, J. (2010). *The connected curriculum framework: A fresh approach to curriculum re-design*. Kettering, UK: The Training Space.

Cope, B., & Kalantzis, M. (2009). *Ubiquitous learning*. Champaign, IL: University of Illinois Press.

D'andrea, V., & Gosling, D. (2005). *Improving teaching and learning: A whole institution approach*. Los Angeles: Society for Research into Higher Education & Open University Press.

Davies, M. (2012). Can universities survive the digital revolution? *Quadrant Online*. Retrieved March 8, 2013, from http://www.quadrant.org.au/magazine/issue/2012/12/ can-universities-survive-the-digital-revolution.

Davies, A., Fidler, D., & Gorbis, M. (2011). *Future work skills 2020* (pp. 1–14): Institute for the Future for the University of Phoenix Research Institute.

Edwards, D. (2015). *Work integrated learning: A lesson in good WIL*. Retrieved March 21, 2016, from https://rd.acer.edu.au/article/work-integrated-learning-a-lesson-in-good-wil

Gasevic, D., Dawson, S., & Siemens, G. (2015). Let's not forget: Learning analytics are about learning. *TechTrends: Linking Research and Practice to Improve Learning, 59*(1), 64–71.

Gibbs, G. (2014). *Research can help student learning – 53 powerful ideas all teachers should know about (Idea Number 17)*. Retrieved December 22, 2015, from http://www.seda.ac.uk/resources/ files/Publications_164_17.Research can help student learning.pdf

Healey, M., Flint, A., & Harrington, K. (2014). *Engagement through partnership: Students as partners in learning and teaching in higher education* (pp. 1–76). York, UK: The Higher Education Academy, UK.

Hil, R. (2012). *Whackademia: An insider's account of the troubled university*. Sydney, Australia: UNSW Press.

Huijser, H. (2008). Straddling the continuum between three course meals and snacks: The changing flavour of knowledge creation and dissemination. *Journal of the World Universities Forum, 1*(2), 85–91.

Hutchings, P., Huber, M., & Ciccone, A. (2011). *The scholarship of teaching and learning reconsidered: Institutional integration and impact*. Hoboken, NJ: Wiley.

Knight, S., Buckingham Shum, S., & Littleton, K. (2014). Epistemology, assessment, pedagogy: Where learning meets analytics in the middle space. *Journal of Learning Analytics, 1*(2), 23–47.

Kreber, C. (Ed.). (2001). *Scholarship revisited: Perspectives on the scholarship of teaching*. San Francisco: Jossey-Bass.

Kuh, G. D., Kinzie, J., Schuh, J. H., Whitt, E. J., & Associates. (2005). *Student success in college*. San Francisco: Jossey-Bass, Wiley.

Laksov, K. B., Mcgrath, C., & Silen, C. (2010). *Scholarship of teaching and learning: The road to an academic perspective on teaching*. Stockholm, Sweden: Karolinska Insttutet.

Laurillard, D. (2014). Big data can transform learning – as long as lecturers take control. *The Guardian Beta*. Retrieved June 4, 2014, from http://www.theguardian.com/higher-educationnetwork/blog/2014/jun/03/big-data-transform-university-learning?CMP=twt_gu.

Macmahon, C., & Huijser, H. (2015). 'We don't need no education?' Moving towards the integration of tertiary education and entrepreneurialship. In M. Harmes, H. Huijser, & P. A. Danaher (Eds.), *Myths in education, learning and teaching: Policies, practices and principles* (pp. 97–113). New York: Palgrave.

Martyn, J., Terwijn, R., Kek, M. Y. C. A., & Huijser, H. (2014). Exploring the relationships between teaching, approaches to learning and critical thinking in a problem-based learning foundation nursing course. *Nurse Education Today, 34*(5), 829–835. http://dx.doi.org/10.1016/j. nedt.2013.04.023.

Matchett, S. (2012). The shape of deals to come: Teaching-only academics arrive. *The Australian*. Retrieved June 7, 2014 fromhttp://www.theaustralian.com.au/higher-education/the-shape-of-deals-to-come-teaching-only-academics-arrive/story-e6frgcjx-1226504101286

Mcintyre, J., Todd, N., Huijser, H., & Tehan, G. (2010). Building pathways to academic success: A practice report. *International Journal of the FIrst Year in Higher Education, 3*(1), 109–118.

Mulderig, T., Macan, T., Hendricks, M., & Noel, J. (2014). Multidisciplinary research: Thinking outside the (corporate) box. *Industrial and Organizational Psychology, 7*(2), 248–251.

Museus, S., & Jayakumar, U. (2012). *Creating campus cultures: Fostering success among racially diverse student populations*. London: Routledge.

O'Sullivan, S. (2009). Intermedia: Culturally appropriate dissemination tools for Indigenous postgraduate research training. *Journal of Australian Indigenous Issues, 12*(1–4), 155–161.

Oosterbeek, H., Van Praag, M., & Ijsselstein, A. (2010). The impact of entrepreneurship education on entrepreneurship skills and motivation. *European Economic Review, 54*, 442–452.

Probert, B. (2014). The rise of teaching-only academics: Belated recognition or a slippery slope? *The Conversation*. Retrieved June 7, 2014, from http://theconversation.com/the-rise-of-teaching-only-academics-belated-recognition-or-a-slippery-slope-20438.

Prosser, M. (2008). The scholarship of teaching and learning: What is it? A personal view. *The International Journal of the Scholarship of Teaching and Learning, 2*(2). Retrieved March 21, 2016, from http://digitalcommons.georgiasouthern.edu/ij-sotl/vol2/iss2/2

Shulman, L. S. (1987). Knowledge and teaching: Foundations of the new reform. *Harvard Educational Review, 57*(1), 1–22.

Shulman, L. S. (2000). From minsk to pinsk: Why a scholarship of teaching and learning? *The Journal of Scholarship of Teaching and Learning, 1*(1), 48–53.

Thelwall, M., & Kousha, K. (2014). Academia.edu: Social network or academic network? *Journal of the Association for Information Science and Technology, 65*(4), 721–731.

Thelwall, M., & Kousha, K. (2015). Research Gate: Disseminating, communicating, and measuring scholarship? *Journal of the Association for Information Science and Technology, 66*(5), 876–889.

Trigwell, K., Martin, E., Benjamin, J., & Prosser, M. (2000). Scholarship of teaching: A model. *Higher Education Research and Development, 19*(2), 155–168.

Trigwell, K., & Shale, S. (2004). Student learning and the scholarship of university teaching. *Studies in Higher Education, 29*(4), 523–536.

Van Der Vleuten, C., Domans, D., & Van Merrienboer, J. (2010). Research in education. In H. van Berkel, A. Scherpbier, H. Hillen, & C. Van Der Vleuten (Eds.), *Lessons from problem-based learning* (pp. 219–225). Oxford, UK: Oxford University Press.

West, D., Huijser, H., Heath, D., Lizzio, A., Toohey, D., & Miles, C. (2015). Higher education teachers' experiences with learning analytics in relation to student retention. In T. Reiners, B. R. von Konsky, D. Gibson, V. Chang, L. Irving & K. Clarke (Eds.), *Globally connected, digitally enabled: Proceedings of the ascilite 2015 Conference, Perth, 29 Nov–2 Dec* (pp. 296–307). Retrieved 26 September 2016 from http://research.moodle.net/77/1/West%20%282015%29%20Higher%20Education%20Teachers%E2%80%99%20Experiences%20with%20Learning%20Analytics%20in%20Relation%20to%20Student%20Retention.pdf

Chapter 10
Conclusion

The justification for a university is that it preserves the connection between knowledge and the zest of life, by uniting the young and the old in the imaginative consideration of learning. The university imparts information, but it imparts it imaginatively. At least, this is the function which it should perform for society. A university which fails in this respect has no reason for existence. This atmosphere of excitement, arising from imaginative consideration, transforms knowledge. A fact is no longer a bare fact: it is invested with all its possibilities. It is no longer a burden on the memory: it is energising as the poet of our dreams, and as the architect of our purposes. Youth is imaginative, and if imagination be strengthened by discipline this energy of imagination can in great measure be preserved through life. …Fools act on imagination without knowledge; pedants act on knowledge without imagination. The task of a university is to weld together imagination and experience. (Whitehead, 1967, p. 93, The Aims of Education, written in 1929)

Agile PBL, within an agile PBL ecology for learning, is about humanising higher education through imaginative approaches to student learning, to teaching, to curriculum, to assessment, to professional learning, to interdisciplinary approaches that go well beyond the institutional walls, to student development and support, to curriculum sustainability, to research and the scholarship of teaching and learning, and to administration and leadership. Throughout this book, agile PBL has taken the idea of a human ecology seriously. In other words, an agile PBL curriculum is not contained in a discipline or a course, but instead is influenced by and affects the wider society. This, in turn, means that it affects others in various environments of the university and therefore should be the concern of all parts and layers of the university and beyond. In other words, all four systems in the agile PBL ecology for learning we have presented here affect each other, and so they should. Agile PBL then is about reinvigorating university education and blurring rigid siloed boundaries. There is no one person, nor the teacher, who is responsible for educating students. Rather, it is everyone's responsibility, including the students, employers and wider social networks inside and outside the university. Agile PBL is about welding together imagination and experience in potentially every layer of society; it is thus

© Springer Science+Business Media Singapore 2017
M.Y.C.A. Kek, H. Huijser, *Problem-based Learning into the Future*,
DOI 10.1007/978-981-10-2454-2_10

about making connections, rather than erecting barriers. Again, ecosystems – people and environments – do not exist in isolation, but are rather interdependent, and they interact with each other. When all elements connect, 'magic' can happen, or what we have with Barnett (2013) referred to as a 'feasible utopia'. However, ecologies are potentially also fragile, especially if different systems within it are competing, rather than complementing each other. We have imagined here that students who move out of an agile PBL university or ecology for learning will have the ability to think, feel and act on the connections between the four systems in the ecology, and they will be able to move freely between them. In this way they may become Whitehead's (1967) 'poets of our dreams and the architects of our purposes', confident in their abilities to unlock and apply their imagination.

The recurring theme in Whitehead's statement above is imagination, and this is not coincidently also the underlying 'dreaming' about an agile PBL ecology for learning, or the imagining of this 'feasible utopia'. Imagination in teaching is not just about imparting content and knowledge, but also about unlocking the human qualities and potential of education. Agile PBL is about continuous renewal, rather than a one-off project, and this requires delving deep into our inherent human imagination. Sir Ken Robinson (2006) has convincingly argued that education kills our creativity and imagination, but this is not a foregone conclusion; we can change this. Agile PBL is about reinserting imagination into the universities. Imagination is about continuous renewal, experimentation, reinventions, exploration, adaptation, creation and all of this in contexts that are relevant to those engaged in the process. It is not about maintaining the status quo, but about continuously questioning and rethinking the status quo. It is about imagining what a better future would look like and then taking control over that future, through imagination, rigorous dedication and humility – a 'feasible utopia' (Barnett, 2013). None of this is easy to achieve, as many universities are characterised by structures and boundaries that have seemingly been in place for a long time. However, if we choose the alternative, then we will wake up one day and the bottom will have fallen out, and the whole enterprise will have become largely irrelevant.

University structures are often concerned with clarity and clear boundaries around who does what, which is epitomised in disciplinary thinking. In reality, however, a university's ecology is not quite as neatly organised and involves a number of interacting ecologies which are part of a student's learning. In other words, the micro-, meso-, exo- and macro-systems are messy and porous, and we see a continuous blurring of boundaries between personal and academic learning and lives – work and study, personal and professional relationships, family, community and society. All of these are always already connected and interrelated and therefore impact on each other. It's just that these relationships are neatly and artificially separated in many universities. Agile provision in the university has 'the potential to enhance student learning, widen opportunities for participation in higher education, and develop graduates who are well-equipped to contribute to a fast-changing world' (Barnett, 2014, p. 10). An agile PBL takes these connections seriously and therefore infuses them into the relevant contexts in its overall ecology for learning.

In this book we have repeatedly discussed the links between the university and society. Again, this is about Whitehead's (1967) challenge for universities to be 'welding together imagination and experience'. The human dimensions of an agile PBL ecology for learning never stand still, but rather adapt continuously to ever changing circumstances and contexts. Moreover, agile PBL has a future-oriented focus, in that it is forever concerned with continuous improvement, not just of the curriculum, but of society itself on a global level. On a student level, the expected outcomes of the process are clear: graduates who are not afraid to think about solutions to current or future problems; graduates who are comfortable with change and indeed thrive in dynamic environments; graduates who feel a sense of responsibility as global citizens, rather than a singular focus on their own wealth accumulation; and graduates who are not constrained by the boundaries of their current position, but who are always looking out for better ways of doing things. In the immortal words of John Lennon, you may say we are dreamers, but we would argue that agile PBL is about creating an educational environment where dreaming is encouraged (the utopia part), as long as it is followed up by tangible and evidence-based solutions (the feasible part). In short, it is about injecting rigour into imagination.

An agile PBL ecology for learning is about humanising higher education. It is about integration and interconnectedness; it is about reciprocity and shared responsibility; it is about respect and collaboration, rather than about individual achievement; it is about fluidity and flexibility, between systems and within systems, rather than about rigid and inflexible boundaries. It is the combination of knowledges, skills, confidence and humility in the ability to be unafraid of the complex and uncertain world, for students, staff and other significant people in the university, as well as for employers and other relevant persons beyond the university. In doing so, we hope our imagining of an agile PBL ecology for learning, inspired by Bronfenbrenner's human ecology development model, can in some way inch towards a new awakening for higher education in improving 'the course of human life at the levels of both individual and their social world' (Lerner, 2005, p. xix).

References

Barnett, R. (2013). *Imagining the university*. Abingdon, UK: Routledge.

Barnett, R. (2014). *Conditions of flexibility: Securing a more responsive higher education system*. York, UK: The Higher Education Academy.

Lerner, R. M. (2005). Foreword: Urie. Bronfenbrenner: Career contributions of the consummate developmental scientist. In U. Bronfenbrenner (Ed.), *Making human beings human: Bioecological perspectives on human development* (Vol. ix–xxvi). Thousand Oaks, CA: Sage.

Robinson, K. (2006). *How schools kill creativity*. Retrieved April 27, 2014, from http://www.ted.com/talks/ken_robinson_says_schools_kill_creativity

Whitehead, A. N. (1967). *The aims of education and other essays*. New York: Free Press (first published by Macmillan in 1929).

Printed by Printforce, the Netherlands